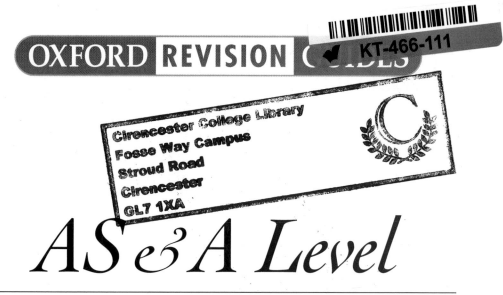

# AS & A Level

# ICT

## through diagrams

### Alan Gardner

Great Clarendon Street, Oxford OX2 6DP

Oxford University Press is a department of the University of Oxford.
It furthers the University's objective of excellence in research,
scholarship, and education by publishing worldwide in

Oxford  New York

Auckland  Bangkok  Buenos Aires  Cape Town  Chennai
Dar es Salaam  Delhi  Hong Kong  Istanbul  Karachi  Kolkata
Kuala Lumpur  Madrid  Melbourne  Mexico City  Mumbai  Nairobi
São Paulo  Shanghai  Taipei  Tokyo  Toronto

Oxford is a registered trade mark of Oxford University Press
in the UK and in certain other countries

British Library Cataloguing in Publication Data

Data available

ISBN 0 19 913435 9

10 9 8 7 6 5 4 3 2 1

Typeset by Fakenham Photosetting Limited, Fakenham, Norfolk

Printed in Great Britain

**Acknowledgements**

Many thanks to the staff and students at Greenshaw High School for their
help in the production of this book, and to Afshan and my family for their
support and encouragement.

Illustrations by Barking Dog Art.

# Contents

# Contents (cont.)

# Contents (cont.)

# Relation of contents to current examination specifications

This book has been designed primarily to cover the AQA specifications. All topics referred to in the AQA syllabus are covered by this book. There is also substantial coverage of the OCR specifications but they are not covered in their entirety. The Edexcel specifications have not been used as a primary reference point, although there are some areas of commonality.

The page and question references below are designed to help structure revision. The topic pages will, however, only make sense within a general framework of knowledge and understanding. In other words, the knowledge gained from the study of one topic will feed into the understanding of other topics. It is best to use this book as just one more resource to help you develop a broad and general understanding of Information and Communication Technology.

Finally, a note of caution: Information and Communication Technology is a field where accelerated change is the norm. By the time this book is published, new developments will have occurred. It is therefore necessary to ensure that you stay current with developments in this area if you are to be wholly successful in its study.

## AQA Syllabus
### AS Module 1 – Information: Nature, Role and Content

| Unit reference | Topic | See pages | Practice questions |
| --- | --- | --- | --- |
| 1.1 | Knowledge, information and data | 10, 17, 19 | 11, 18, 20, 22, 23 |
| 1.2 | Value and importance of information | 11, 132 | 12, 13 |
| 1.3 | Control of information | 130 | 139 |
| 1.4 | Capabilities and limitations of information and communication technology | 2, 3, 5 | 2–5 |
| 1.5 | The social impact of information and communication technology | 4, 6–9, 108 | 6–10 |
| 1.6 | Role of communication systems | 85–94 | 93, 94, 97–99 |
| 1.7 | Information and the professional | 105, 106 | 109, 110 |
| 1.8 | Information systems, malpractice and crime | 88, 114–117, 120, 121 | 120–122 |
| 1.9 | Software and data misuse | 128, 129 | 136–138 |
| 1.9 | Data protection and legislation | 130 | 139 |
| 1.10 | Health and safety | 110, 111 | 116–117 |

### AS Module 2 – Information: Management and Manipulation

| Unit reference | Topic | See pages | Practice questions |
| --- | --- | --- | --- |
| 2.1 | Data capture | 17, 18, 19 | 18, 19, 21, 22 |
| 2.2 | Verification and validation | 20, 21 | 22–27 |
| 2.3 | Organisation of data for effective retrieval | 54, 61, 55, 56 | 70, 73 |
| 2.4 | Software; nature, capabilities and limitations | 31, 35 | 41 |
| 2.4 | Nature and types of software | 40, 42–46, 49, 50 | 46, 51–63, 64–66 |
| 2.4 | Capabilities of software | 40 | 47 |
| 2.4 | Upgradability | 154, 155 | 164 |
| 2.4 | Reliability | 164 | 183 |
| 2.5 | Manipulation and/or processing | 143 | 29, 151 |
| 2.6 | Dissemination/distribution | 15, 16 | 16, 17 |
| 2.7 | Hardware; nature, capabilities and limitations | 32–38 | 38–45 |
| 2.8 | Security of data | 115, 120, 122 | 122, 131, 132 |
| 2.8 | Backup systems | 122, 123 | 133 |
| 2.9 | Network environments | 72 | 82, 84, 86 |
| 2.10 | Human/Computer interface | 99, 102 | 103, 106, 107 |

## A2 Module 4 – Information systems within organisations

| Unit reference | Topic | See pages | Practice questions |
|---|---|---|---|
| 4.1 | Organisational structure | 131 | 141 |
| 4.2 | Information systems and organisations | 141, 142, 147 | 142, 149, 150, 155 |
| 4.2 | Definition of a Management Information System | 141 | 149 |
| 4.2 | The development and life cycle of an information system | 157 | 166 |
| 4.2 | Success or failure of a Management Information System | 151 | 159 |
| 4.3 | Corporate information systems strategy | 136 | 145 |
| 4.3 | Information flow | 149 | 157 |
| 4.3 | Personnel | 144 | 154 |
| 4.4 | Information | 12, 13, 14, 140, 147 | 13–15 |
| 4.4 | Effective presentation | 15, 16 | 16, 17 |
| 4.4 | Data | 17, 18, 19 | 20–22 |
| 4.5 | The management of change | 152 | 160 |
| 4.6 | Legal aspects | 118, 119 | 125–127 |
| 4.6 | Audit requirements | 153 | 163 |
| 4.6 | Disaster recovery management | 124, 125 | 134, 135 |
| 4.6 | Legislation | 126–130 | 136–140 |
| 4.7 | User support | 167, 168 | 178–180 |
| 4.7 | Training | 165, 166 | 175, 176 |
| 4.8 | Project management and effective ICT teams | 169, 170 | 182 |
| 4.9 | Information and the professional | 107, 112, 113 | 118, 119 |
| 4.9 | Employee Code of Conduct | 107 | 111 |

## A2 Module 5 – Information: Policy, Strategy and Systems

| Unit reference | Topic | See pages | Practice questions |
|---|---|---|---|
| 5.1 | Policy and strategy issues | 133, 134, 135 | 143–145 |
| 5.1 | Methods of enhancing existing capabilities | 86, 154, 155 | 164–165 |
| 5.1 | Future proofing | 133 | 164 |
| 5.1 | Backup strategies | 122, 123 | 131–133 |
| 5.2 | Evaluation of software | 51 | 48, 49 |
| 5.2 | Evaluation criteria | 52 | 50 |
| 5.2 | Evaluation report | 51 | 49 |
| 5.3 | Database management concepts | 55, 62–69 | 68, 69, 74–79 |
| 5.4 | Communication and information systems | 72, 73, 90, 91 | 83, 96, 100 |
| 5.4 | Applications of communication and information systems | 75–81 | 83–87 |
| 5.4 | Distributed systems | 71 | 80 |
| 5.5 | Network security, audit and accounting | 75, 80, 81 | 88, 89 |
| 5.5 | Network environments | 75, 80 | 81 |
| 5.6 | Human/Computer interaction | 100 | 104 |
| 5.7 | Human/Computer interface | 101, 103 | 108 |
| 5.8 | Software development | 41 | 48, 50 |
| 5.9 | Software reliability | 163, 164 | 174, 183 |
| 5.10 | Protocols and standards | 27, 86, 97, 156 | 91, 102 |
| 5.10 | Communication standards | 83, 84 | 90 |
| 5.10 | Emergence of standards | 83 | 91 |

## OCR syllabus
### Module 2512: Information, Systems and Communications

| Unit reference | Topic | See pages | Practice questions |
|---|---|---|---|
| **5.1.1** | **Data, Information, Knowledge and Processing** | | |
| | Terminology | 10 | 11 |
| | Sources of data | 17 | 18, 21 |
| | Types of data | 57 | 71 |
| | Coding data | 19 | 22, 23 |
| | Test data | 164 | |
| | Quality of information | 12 | 21 |
| | Cost of information | 11 | 12 |
| | Knowledge and processing | 141, 144 | |
| | Input-process-output-feedback loop | 1, 5 | 1 |
| **5.1.2** | **Components of an Information System** | | |
| | Types of hardware | 32-39 | 38–45 |
| | Types of software | 40, 53 | 46, 64 |
| **5.1.3** | **Systems and User Interface Software** | | |
| | Operating systems | 53 | 65 |
| | User interfaces | 102 | 106 |
| | Utilities | 29, 53 | 66 |
| | Translators | | |
| **5.1.4** | **File and Database Concepts** | | |
| | Files, records, fields, key field, data types | 54, 57 | |
| | File organisation and access | 58 | 72 |
| | Entity, attributes, tables, relations | 65, 62 | 70 |
| | Comparison of flat file, hierarchical database and relational database | 55, 56 | 69, 70 |
| | Levels of access | 70 | 79 |
| **5.1.5** | **The Role of Communications and Networking** | | |
| | Protocols | 30, 83, 97 | 90, 102 |
| | Networking | 72–76, 95 | 81–93 |
| | Fax, e-mail, tele/video conferencing | 93, 109 | 98, 112–114 |
| **5.1.6** | **The Role and Impact of ICT: Legal, Moral and Social Issues** | | |
| | Capabilities and limitations of ICT | 2, 150 | 2–4 |
| | The role of communication systems | | |
| | The impact of ICT on individuals, society and organisations | 4, 6–9 | 5–10 |
| | Legal and moral implications resulting from the impact of ICT | 6, 8, 112 | 118, 119 |
| | Professional frameworks, codes of conduct and regulating bodies | 107, 113 | 111 |
| | Data protection | 128–130 | 139 |
| | Health and safety | 110, 111 | 116, 117 |

## Module 2514: Practical Applications of ICT using Standard/Generic Applications Software

| Unit reference | Topic | See pages | Practice questions |
|---|---|---|---|
| 5.3.1 | **Characteristics of Standard Applications Software and Application Areas** | | |
| | Common features of standard applications software | 40 | 47 |
| | Basic characteristics of applications found in business, commerce and education | 4–6 | |
| | Style sheets, templates and wizards | | |
| | Benefits and problems associated with tailoring applications software using forms, menus, buttons and macros | 103 | 108 |
| | Transfer of data between application areas | 27, 28 | 33–35 |
| 5.3.2 | **Applications Software used for Presentation and Communication of Data** | | |
| | Applications software used for presenting information | 42 | 51, 52 |
| | Standard documents | | |
| | Importing/exporting text and images | 25 | 30, 31 |
| | Clip art galleries and image libraries | 25 | 31 |
| | Mail merge techniques for fixed and variable fields | 43 | 52 |
| | Word processing and desktop publishing tools | 42, 46 | 51 |
| | Graphics tools and effects | 46 | 56–58 |
| | Multimedia and hypertext tools | 50, 96 | 63 |
| 5.3.3 | **Standard/Generic Applications Software for Modelling Data** | | |
| | Characteristics of modelling software | 44, 47 | 59, 60 |
| | Variables, formulae, functions and rules | 44 | |
| | Worksheets, workbooks, rows, columns, cells, ranges | 44 | |
| | Graphs and charts | 44 | |
| | Customising worksheets | 44 | |
| 5.3.4 | **Relational and Online Database Management Systems** | | |
| | Normalisation | 63–65 | 74 |
| | Entities, tables and relationships, records and fields | 54, 62 | 70, 74 |
| | Data dictionary | | |
| | Data-entry forms, reports | 54, 61 | |
| | Simple and complex queries | 59, 60 | 73 |
| | Static and dynamic data | | |
| | Filters, search engines | | |

## Module 2515: Communications Technology and its Application

| Unit reference | Topic | See pages | Practice questions |
|---|---|---|---|
| 5.4.1 | **Features of Networked Systems and the Systems Cycle** | | |
| | The development of networking | 72, 95, 97 | 1 |
| | Training and re-skilling | 165, 166 | 175–177 |
| | The importance of standards | 83, 84, 97 | 90, 91 |
| | Systems cycle | 157–162 | 166–174 |
| 5.4.2 | **Communications and Networked Systems** | | |
| | Benefits and drawbacks of network topologies | 76, 77 | 86, 87 |
| | Network components | 73–75 | 83, 84 |
| | Analogue and digital communication | 30, 82 | 37 |
| | Cable television networks | | |
| | Mobile communications | 82, 85 | 92, 93 |
| | Satellite communications | 48 | |
| | Optical communications | | |

# What is Information Technology?

Information Technology refers to a range of devices which assist in the work of Information Systems through the digital processing of data.

## What is a system?

A **system** is a collection of elements that combine in order to complete a specific task. Systems generally consist of a group of related **procedures**. These procedures are sets of rules and routines that must be followed if a task is to be accomplished. Typically in a system, these procedures are followed by **people** who use **resources** to assist them in the completion of the **task**. In any organisation there will be a number of interdependent systems in operation.

A school is an organisation. That is, it is a formal arrangement of human and non-human resources brought together to achieve a designated goal (i.e. the education of children). Schools contain a number of systems that have as their aim the accomplishment of a wide range of tasks, including:

- dealing with the intake of new pupils;
- managing students' examination entries;
- ensuring that staff receive the correct pay.

The 'examinations' system consists of a set of procedures. One such procedure is invoked when a teacher wishes to withdraw a student from an exam. The following procedure may be followed:

1. the teacher fills out a slip with details of the student and the exam which s/he will be withdrawn from;
2. the teacher hands the slip to the Examinations Officer who confirms that all the necessary information is present;
3. the examination officer sends a letter to the examinations board requesting that the student be removed from the list of entries;
4. the examinations officer amends his own list of entries;
5. a print-out is produced informing the teacher and student of the changed entry.

Note that **people** (the teacher and the examinations officer) have used **resources** (slips, letters, lists, a word processor, etc.) and followed **procedures** (the routine set out above) to accomplish a **task** (the removal of the student from the specified exam).

## What is an Information System?

Systems are involved in every aspect of human life. We have systems for cooking a meal, maintaining a car, and travelling to work or school. Information systems are systems that have, as a central activity, the collection, manipulation, storage and distribution of information. The exams system described above is an information system because its core activity is the management of information regarding the exams that students are entered for, the results they achieve, the overall performance of the school, etc. Information systems have the following structure:

The exams system of a school **inputs** data (about available examinations, student entries, student results, etc.), **processes** it (this may include collation, sorting, aggregation of results, etc.) and **outputs** the results (as exam entry lists to teachers, results slips to students, etc.). The **feedback** may then influence the consequent input. For example, a student who does poorly in one module may need to be entered for a re-sit.

## What is Information Technology?

A technology is a tool designed to perform a task. Information technology is a set of tools to assist in the processing of information. Information technology may refer to a wide range of devices – a 'pen' is an example of information technology – but generally it refers to computerised devices that utilise the power of microprocessors to manipulate data in a digital format.

In the above example, the procedure describes the Examinations Officer sending a letter to the examinations board. In fact, the Examinations Officer is more likely to use a computer program to communicate the change electronically and to generate an amended print-out. This is an example of information technology acting as a key resource in an information system.

# Capabilities and limitations of computer-based systems

## Capabilities

| Benefit | Explanation | Application |
| --- | --- | --- |
| The facility to undertake repetitive processes | Not only can computers perform some tasks more quickly and more precisely than humans; they can also repeat their operations without becoming 'tired' or 'bored'. This makes them ideal for performing tasks that need to be endlessly repeated. | • Querying a database entails a repetitive checking of individual records in order to find a match between the search criteria and the content of the records. This iterative procedure is something that a computer will do much more efficiently than a human. |
| Increased speed of data processing | The microprocessors found in today's computers can perform thousands of millions of logical operations every second. Many processes that once would have been completed by humans can now be reduced to a series of logical operations and completed in a fraction of the time. | • The chess-playing computer Deep Blue was able to play – and beat – the world champion because of its ability to process the several million possible move combinations in a very short time. |
| Increased data storage capacity | As the technology for storing data in digital form has steadily improved, more data can now be stored on media of ever-decreasing size and cost. The first hard drive consisted of fifty 24 inch disks, weighed several tons, and could hold 5Mb of data. The latest IBM hard drive is one inch in diameter and can store 340Mb of data. | • Text- and image-based data can be held in a compact and transportable form. Some libraries have begun to store their catalogue in digital form, thus allowing for more efficient storage and faster access. |
| The facility to locate instances of stored data quickly | One of the prime functions of databases is to facilitate searches for specific pieces of information. Because a search is, in essence, a series of logical steps, this can be performed by the computer very quickly. | • Police forces often need to search for individuals who match a set of specified criteria, e.g. those with prior convictions. This can now be achieved at much greater speed on computers. |
| The facility to combine data from different sources | Data is stored on an increasing number of private, commercial and government-run databases. As a result of computer technology, it is now a fairly straightforward task to combine data from different sources to create new information. | • Commercial companies can combine their own data with that of other companies in order to target new customers more accurately. |
| The facility to manipulate and transform data | When data is stored in digital format it can be reordered quickly and effectively. This can take place at a simple level, e.g. the editing and formatting facilities of a word-processing application, or at a more complex level, e.g. editing and adding special effects to video files. | • In medicine, scanners such as MRI devices collect data as a series of values representing different magnetic reflections. This data is then transformed into a visual image that can be easily read by a doctor. |
| Increased accuracy | Computers can perform a variety of processes more consistently and with greater precision and accuracy than humans. This facility, however, is dependent on correctly written programs and accurately inputted data. | • Machines can be computer-controlled. These machines can perform repetitive actions with great precision, without tiring and without making mistakes. |
| Increased speed of data communication | The Internet and all associated developments in communications have been made possible by computer technology. Digital processing enables not just voice but text and images to be communicated with increasing speed and across vast distances. | • The Internet itself is the most visible consequence of this facility. Millions of people now have the capacity to access information from around the world cheaply and quickly. |

## Limitations

**Hardware** The speed at which a system can perform tasks will depend on its various hardware components – especially those connected with the Central Processing Unit and the computer's primary memory. As software grows more complex, it places greater memory demands on a system's resources. If the memory and processing components are insufficient, the software will not run as it should.

**Software** Software – whether it is systems software or application software – is of variable quality. Some software packages can be 'bug-ridden' (i.e. be insufficiently tested and therefore liable to throw up errors) and cause problems; some can be badly designed and inappropriate for the needs of the organisation; and some perfectly good software can become outdated as an organisation's needs change.

**Communications** Most computer systems are part of a network. The quality of the networking media will affect how quickly and securely data is transmitted. This effect is multiplied when the network is spread across a wide area and/or is based on existing telecommunications media (e.g. the Internet). This is especially the case when memory-heavy files (e.g. video files) need to be transmitted.

**Input** A computer system is only as good as the data and instructions that are put into it. Although computers have the facility to complete certain tasks at incredible speed, they are still confined to what human operators tell them to do. Also, while they are capable of processing data quickly and accurately, if the initial data is inputted incorrectly, the output will be correspondingly erroneous.

**Inflexibility** Computers perform certain tasks far more quickly and accurately than humans could ever do, e.g. millions of mathematical calculations in a second. They cannot, however, respond imaginatively and intuitively to a situation as humans can. Nor can they adjust their processes when there is an environmental change they have not been programmed to expect.

# Why systems fail

## Examples

There have been a number of well-publicised examples of ICT systems failing spectacularly and creating acute problems for the organisation and its clients. For example:

In 1999 the UK Passport Agency had severe problems processing passport applications. At one stage there were 565 000 applications awaiting processing. A National Audit Office report on this matter concluded that the implementation of a new but inadequately tested computer system was a key causative factor. The cost to the UK taxpayer was £12.6 million.

## Causes

Small-scale system failures can be the result of a single problem, e.g. a network crash. Significant system failures result from the combined effects of a number of interdependent causes. The diagram below sets out some of the key factors in system failure:

### The nature of computer software

Software design is 'non-linear'. This means that a minor error in a line of code can have a disproportionate effect. A minor typographical error – a misplaced decimal point for example – can affect the way that the whole program behaves. Indeed, the effect of the error grows exponentially as it interacts with the rest of the system. The interdependency of computer systems means that this error can then spread in a viral manner into other systems.

### Commercial/political pressures

Organisations can find themselves under pressure to implement a new system more quickly than is advisable. This pressure can be commercial, e.g. the threat of a competitor gaining a market advantage; or political, e.g. to fulfil a promised policy initiative. This pressure can force the pace of system implementation and lead to corners being cut at one or more of the critical stages, i.e. system design, compatibility assessment, testing, etc.

### Change in circumstances during development

Complex systems can take a significant amount of time to develop. Changes that affect the organisation will also be taking place during this period. These changes may be technological (e.g. new hardware), commercial (e.g. the collapse of certain markets), legislative (new laws to conform to), etc. It is difficult for the system to keep assimilating these changes when it was originally designed without them in mind.

### Insufficient testing

Complex software requires stringent testing in order to identify any errors – or bugs – which may lead to a system failure. The testing has to take into account not only each task that the software has to perform, but also the 'real world' circumstances in which it will have to operate. On occasions, the time and resources committed to testing are inadequate and errors go unnoticed. The first time that the error is spotted is when it causes a system failure.

**SYSTEM FAILURE**

### Compatibility issues

New systems often have to interact with older (legacy) systems. In some instances inadequate consideration has been given to the compatibility of these two systems. Compatibility problems can occur when a new system has to interact with a system which has been created by a different software provider. A new system can also be incompatible with operating system software. All of these compatibility problems can cause a system to fail.

### Inadequate communication with users

There are two problems that may occur here. If, during the analysis/design stage, the developers do not take sufficient account of the needs of the final users, those users are less likely to use the system efficiently. Mistakes are then more likely to occur. This is also the case if users are inadequately prepared for the implementation of the new system. They must therefore be trained sufficiently in its correct use.

### Costing issues

When an organisation decides that it needs a new system, it will calculate the likely cost of it. However, during the period of development costs can escalate and, at the same time, the funds that the organisation has available may decline. The organisation then has to choose whether to abandon the project or cut costs in some areas. Cost-cutting can lead to inadequate development of key aspects of the system. This can lead to system failure.

### Hardware issues

Hardware malfunction is a key factor in system failure. Hardware malfunction can occur as a result of age, damage or an inherent problem. Some hardware has 'bugs' which do not become apparent until it is widely used. There have been recent cases where computers have been sold with flawed microprocessors. There can also be compatibility problems between a system and existing hardware, e.g. inadequate memory resources.

### Insufficient post-implementation support

If users do not know how to operate a system correctly, they are likely to make mistakes. Individually these mistakes may not be critical, but cumulatively they may cause the breakdown of the system. It is therefore important that users are fully trained in the use of the system prior to its implementation. Additionally, there should be reliable post-implementation support (e.g. from a help desk) to deal with problems encountered by the users once the system has 'gone live'.

# ICT in business

A business is an organisation that sells products and/or services to customers in order to make a profit. Businesses of all kinds, ranging from small family concerns to multinational corporations, use computer-based systems in different areas of their work. ICT has the capacity to make a business more efficient, more cost-effective and more responsive to the needs of its customers. Below is an indication of the ways in which ICT can aid each stage of the process involved in creating, marketing and selling a new product.

## How ICT can assist business activities

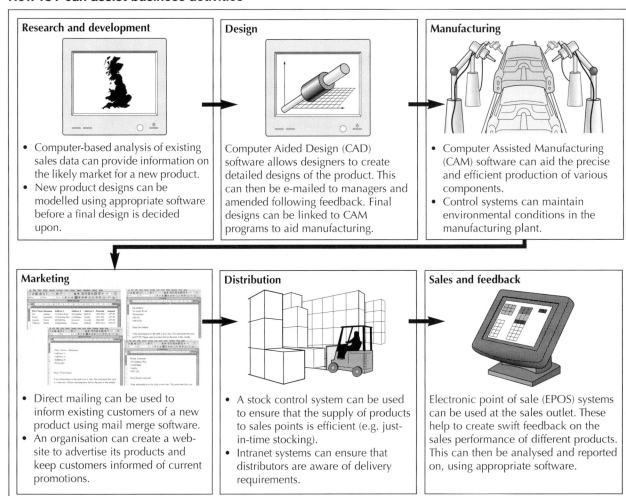

**Research and development**

- Computer-based analysis of existing sales data can provide information on the likely market for a new product.
- New product designs can be modelled using appropriate software before a final design is decided upon.

**Design**

Computer Aided Design (CAD) software allows designers to create detailed designs of the product. This can then be e-mailed to managers and amended following feedback. Final designs can be linked to CAM programs to aid manufacturing.

**Manufacturing**

- Computer Assisted Manufacturing (CAM) software can aid the precise and efficient production of various components.
- Control systems can maintain environmental conditions in the manufacturing plant.

**Marketing**

- Direct mailing can be used to inform existing customers of a new product using mail merge software.
- An organisation can create a web-site to advertise its products and keep customers informed of current promotions.

**Distribution**

- A stock control system can be used to ensure that the supply of products to sales points is efficient (e.g. just-in-time stocking).
- Intranet systems can ensure that distributors are aware of delivery requirements.

**Sales and feedback**

Electronic point of sale (EPOS) systems can be used at the sales outlet. These help to create swift feedback on the sales performance of different products. This can then be analysed and reported on, using appropriate software.

Meanwhile the organisation will continue with those processes which keep the business going:

| Activity | Application of ICT |
|---|---|
| Analysis of feedback | The feedback provided by sales data can be stored centrally and analysed by spreadsheet software. Charts showing sales patterns can be created and amendments made to distribution/marketing procedures. Profit/loss analysis can be undertaken to establish which areas need attention. |
| External communication | The business may use the Internet to communicate with suppliers of raw materials, distribution companies, external outlets, etc. DTP/word processing applications may be used to create press releases, share-holder information, direct mailing documents, etc. These can be distributed using mail merge facilities and/or the Internet. |
| Financial procedures | Spreadsheet/accountancy software can be used to manage company finances. This may involve distributing and processing invoices, managing wage bills, calculating profit/loss, etc. |
| Human Resources management | Database software can be used to store and maintain company records of employees. Analysis of staffing requirements can be undertaken using this data. |
| Internal communication | A company-wide intranet can be used to aid communication between members of the same organisation. |
| Strategic planning | The management of the organisation can interrogate the data that it holds to produce information that will help it make decisions about future planning. Modelling software can be used to see what effects changes in business activity might have. Expert systems can be used to draw on the expertise of other similar organisations. |
| Display of data | Some businesses need to keep a constant check on data associated with their operations. For example, a distribution company may wish to view the progress of a particular package and the location of delivery drivers. Communication and display technology can be used to facilitate this. |

# ICT in business: feedback

### What is feedback?

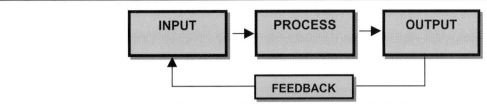

In an information system outputted information is 'fed back' to appropriate individuals within an organisation. This feedback allows them to correct or amend the input process as necessary. There is also a broader concept of feedback in ICT. The speed of processing facilitated by computer-based systems means that organisations can constantly monitor changes in core operations. This enables them to be more responsive to situations and take more effective actions.

For example, those working in the financial markets use computer technology to monitor information about stock values. Transactions that take place are quickly processed and fed back into the system so that traders can base their actions on up-to-date information.

### Just-in-time stock maintenance

Another example of the use of feedback in business is the practice of just-in-time stocking, an example of which is illustrated below.

#### The standard method of stock maintenance

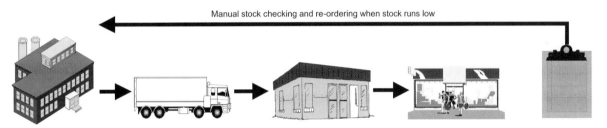

An organisation, a shop selling electrical goods for example, keeps its stock in a retail outlet and in an attached warehouse. When stock in the shop area runs low it is replenished from the warehouse. A check is kept on how much stock is in the warehouse. When the warehouse stock needs replenishing, an order is placed with the appropriate suppliers – or with the organisation's main warehouse – and the goods are delivered.

#### Just-in-time stock maintenance

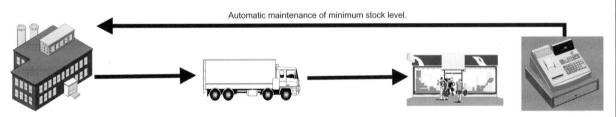

This system takes advantage of a stock control information system. As products pass through the electronic points of sale (EPOS), the relevant data is sent to a database containing information about stock levels. When stock falls below a set level more is ordered. Thus only a bare minimum of necessary stock is ordered and there is no need to maintain a large, fully stocked warehouse. In some cases the system is fully automated, working out how what stock is needed and electronically processing and communicating the order.

| ADVANTAGES | DISADVANTAGES |
|---|---|
| • Money is saved because less warehouse space needs to be purchased and maintained.<br>• Economies can made in regard to labour costs, i.e. because fewer staff are needed.<br>• The business is more aware of and more responsive to changes in supply and demand. | • If there is disruption to the road haulage system, shops and businesses will quickly run out of stock.<br>• Shops can still be caught out by sudden changes in buying patterns. In such cases they often find themselves without the stock that customers are asking for.<br>• An ICT system can be costly to set up and maintain, and expertise – which may also be costly – will be needed to run it. |

# ICT in education

## Beneficial impact of ICT in the education sector

| Source of information | Learning assistance programs | Communication of information | Distance learning | Administration |
|---|---|---|---|---|
| | | | | |
| • If skilfully navigated, the Internet is a fertile source of information for students at all levels. It facilitates access to specialist sites, databases, libraries and journals. The international dimension ensures that the information covers a broad range of perspectives.<br>• CD ROMS have been published which contain information on a wide range of topics. Some have multimedia capacity, containing not just text and image but audio and video files that can be played. | • Some companies have produced programs that help students learn, e.g. applications designed to improve spelling. These programs have an interactive capacity whereby students can test their knowledge by undertaking quizzes and tests. A scoring system allows them to gauge their progress. This approach has proved useful for a number of students, especially those with learning difficulties.<br>• There are a number of interactive revision programs to be found on the Internet. | • Teachers are able to use computer projectors to improve the presentation of their material. They can show a whole class material contained on a CD or on a web-site. Electronic white boards have been developed which can be used interactively.<br>• Teachers and students are able to use word processing, DTP and spreadsheet software to enhance the presentation of their work. Teachers can create effective learning materials and students can produce project work which combines text, images, charts, etc. | • As a consequence of developments in ICT, students no longer have to be in the same location as the teacher. This can be especially beneficial for students living in remote areas and for those suffering from disabilities. Videoconferencing can be used for lectures and assignments can be submitted via e-mail.<br>• Other distance learning schemes use a combination of teaching programs stored on CDs and interactive 'help lines' accessed via the Internet.<br>• Intranets and remote-working technologies allow students and teachers to log into systems based in educational establishments and work from home. | • The staff of schools have a large number of administrative duties to perform. These include: registering pupils, reporting to parents, managing exam entries, etc. Such tasks can be time-consuming and take staff away from what should be their core activity, i.e. teaching.<br>• There are a number of ICT systems that can assist in the process. Database applications can be used to store pupil records, spreadsheets can help to manage budgets and word-processing packages can aid communication with parents and outside agencies.<br>• Using an intranet or Information Management System, staff can share information – e.g. about student progress – with each other. |

## Some problems

ICT is an integral aspect of education today, whether functioning as a medium for learning or as a subject in its own right. For the reasons stated above, the introduction of ICT has been valuable in many areas of education. There are, however, some concerns about the developments. They include:

• ICT requires significant amounts of capital investment for the initial setting up of networked systems and a steady flow of funds for the maintenance and upgrading of those systems. Some schools are cash-starved and find it difficult to achieve this. This can lead to the unfair distribution of resources between different schools.
• Some educationalists have questioned the value of computer-oriented learning. They have suggested that it can lead to a decline in the ability of pupils – especially young ones – to learn collaboratively and thus develop valuable social skills. Others have suggested that the nature of computer interactions leads to a lowering of attention span which, in turn, can have a detrimental effect on a student's capacity for disciplined learning.
• Some educationalists have argued that the use of text messaging, with its characteristic use of abbreviated language, will lead to a diminishment in literacy.
• While distance learning has its uses, a computer cannot provide the personal support, advice and guidance of a skilled teacher. In some situations, where the learner lacks confidence for example, the presence of human interaction is a necessary aspect of the learning process.

# ICT in health

## Beneficial impact of ICT in the health sector

| Medical equipment | Patient records | Web-based support/diagnosis | Communication between health professionals | Modelling new drugs |
|---|---|---|---|---|
|  | John Anybody |  |  | |

**Medical equipment**

- CAT and MRI scanners are advanced imaging devices which allow clinicians to diagnose patients' conditions. They depend on computers to process their data into readable formats.
- Microprocessors are used to control a wide variety of patient support devices. Many people who suffer from heart conditions wear computer-controlled pacemakers. These miniature defibrillators maintain the heart's regular rhythm.
- Computer-guided lasers have been used in operations, including the removal of brain tumours.

**Patient records**

There has been a gradual move to store all patient records in digital format. Benefits include:

- Doctors will not have to read unintelligible handwriting.
- It will enable more economical storage of data.
- Access will be quicker and more efficient.
- Transfer of records between different providers will be easier, e.g. between GPs and a hospital.
- Data can be interrogated to provide analyses of medical conditions, e.g. regional patterns of certain cancers.

**Web-based support/diagnosis**

There is a wide range of medical information available on the Internet, including:

- Symptom diagnosis, for people who wish to identify their condition before – or instead of – visiting a GP.
- Information about available treatments, especially those categorised as alternative therapies.
- Information about support groups for people suffering from particular conditions, e.g. diabetes.
- Access to medical research and professional journals for clinicians.
- Information about the side effects of various drug therapies.
- Expert systems to aid diagnosis.

**Communication between health professionals**

- It is important that the latest advances in medicine are shared as widely as possible. Access to the Internet facilitates this (e.g. drug companies' websites).
- Teleconferencing has been used to share expertise. Surgeons based in one country have provided advice as surgeons in other countries perform operations.
- Resources can be shared. For example, in the US there are four high-voltage electron microscopes. Doctors can send samples for analysis and then view the results via a video link.

**Modelling new drugs**

Most drugs do their job by binding to target molecules and inhibiting their activities. Finding drugs to do this used to be matter of 'happy accident' or 'trial and error'. Now, increasingly, drugs are designed to do a specific job. The atomic structure of the target is analysed and the effects of different chemical compounds on this structure are examined. This process has been made possible through the use of advanced computers which, by repeating processes with minor variations, can model the effects of different drugs. The output can be shown visually to the researchers.

## Some problems

While it is undoubtedly the case that the impact of ICT in health care has been a largely beneficial one, there have been some concerns. These include:

- The move to put all patient records on to a computer system has faced a number of difficulties. These include: establishing nationally (and, in due course, internationally) agreed codes for different conditions, treatments, parts of the body, etc; inputting the enormous number of existing paper-based records; establishing sufficiently robust security systems to protect data which, for obvious reasons, must remain confidential.
- Some medically oriented websites have been established by well-informed and responsible bodies. Others are less trustworthy. There is a danger that people will access incorrect information about their condition and this could lead them to self-diagnose inaccurately. This, in turn, could lead to false complacency or unnecessary anxiety.
- Computers have flaws and, on occasions, break down. There is a danger to patients of an over-reliance on computer-controlled equipment. This was the case in America when the software-controlled radiation therapy machines accidentally gave patients overdoses of radiation, leading to the death of three patients.
- Health providers do not always belong to the same organisation. For example, in the UK, there are the NHS, a number of private companies, and some independent practitioners. There may be disputes between these groups about the sharing of information and resources, thus making centralised patient records impossible.

# ICT in manufacturing and industry

## How ICT can be used in manufacturing

There are a number of ways in which ICT can be used to improve the efficiency of the manufacturing process, including:

- Automated stock control systems may be used to ensure that the amount of raw materials purchased and stored is matched precisely to the immediate needs of the organisation, thus saving on space and cost.
- Modelling software can be used to test different approaches to manufacturing processes, thus creating an optimised system.
- Tracking systems can be used to provide managers with feedback on what stage of manufacturing a particular order has reached. This can help with the monitoring of systems and employee work-rate.
- One significant impact of ICT has been the introduction of computer-aided design and manufacturing (CAD and CAM) systems. These terms cover a variety of systems in which the actions of machines are controlled by computer mechanisms.

## How a computer-controlled machine works

In this system a set of instructions can be programmed into a computer (**1**). This might be a PC-sized computer separate from the machine or a small keypad built into the machine. There is, built into the computer, an 'industrial interface' (**2**). This device translates the low voltage signals of the microprocessor into voltages large enough to control heavy machinery (**3**). There may also be some form of feedback, e.g. a sensor on the arm of the machine (**4**) may send back a signal indicating how close it is to an object. This feedback can help the computer make any necessary adjustments to the program.

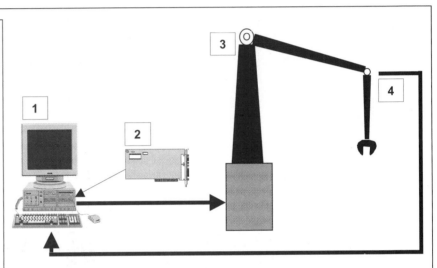

## What are robots?

The word 'robot' comes from the Czech word *robota*, meaning 'slave'. Robots are machines that are able to perform tasks either automatically or with a small amount of human assistance. Typically, they will perform repetitive mechanical tasks – e.g. spray painting a car – or tasks that may be hazardous for humans – e.g. handling radioactive waste. A robot can be programmed to perform a designated task. A human must first work out what sequence of operations needs to be performed and then write a computer program that will instruct the robot to perform these actions. Most industrial robots are reprogrammable, i.e. their original task designation can be changed when the need arises.

## Advantages and disadvantages of computer-controlled machines

| Advantages | Disadvantages |
|---|---|
| <ul><li>They can perform monotonous, repetitive tasks without becoming 'tired' or 'bored'. Individual parts may need to be replaced but this will be predictable and easy to account for.</li><li>They can cut labour costs considerably. The usual estimate given is that, on average, they can replace six workers.</li><li>They can work in low lighting and temperature conditions, thus saving on energy bills.</li><li>They can work to a greater degree of precision than humans and this level of precision will be more consistent.</li><li>They can work in environmental conditions which would be hazardous for humans, e.g. where high levels of radiation are present.</li></ul> | <ul><li>They can only do what they are programmed to do. It is unlikely that they can be programmed to deal with every eventuality that they will encounter. This makes them inflexible and, unlike humans, unable to respond to unexpected events.</li><li>They require large amounts of capital investment and incur maintenance costs. This cost is a 'constant' for the company, i.e. it is incurred even if a shortage of orders leads to the machines being inactive. In a similar situation, human workers could be temporarily laid off.</li><li>Although cutting labour costs might be advantageous to the organisation, its impact may be negative both on individual workers who lose their jobs and on the surrounding community.</li><li>There may be a need for high-tech support in the event of a software crash.</li></ul> |

# ICT in the home

## Embedded systems

In a typical modern home one can find many examples of embedded systems. These are microprocessor-based systems that are embedded in (i.e. hard-wired into) electronic consumer devices. The system is programmed to perform a designated task, e.g. to perform a wash cycle or microwave a meal. Typically, these systems rely on input information from a touchpad or dial. This information is then processed and sent to a control mechanism that instructs the equipment to perform in a certain way. There may also be output devices that are designed to give feedback to the user, e.g. a temperature readout display panel on a washing machine, and sensors that allow the system to make adjustments in response to environmental changes. Embedded systems, which can be found in cookers, washing machines, DVD players, televisions, etc. have improved the performance and efficiency of many domestic devices.

## The personal computer

At the moment there are PCs in (approximately) 50% of British homes. They are used for a variety of purposes, including:

**Working from home** Many people do some of their work at home, taking advantage of the PC's ability to communicate with other computers (e.g. workplace-based) through the Internet or remote access systems. Some people work entirely from home, setting up an office with ICT facilities, i.e. teleworking.

**As a learning tool** Students use the Internet to gather information, and word processing, spreadsheet and DTP packages to produce assignments. There are resources, available both on CD-ROMs and via the Internet, that offer specific help with different subjects.

**Shopping from home** There are websites that allow people to use the Internet to order and pay for goods which are then delivered to their house. This is of particular value to people who are house-bound, e.g. people with disabilities.

**Domestic accounts** Spreadsheet programs and on-line banking facilities may be used by householders to manage their personal finances more efficiently.

## Communications

There are now a wide range of communication devices that people have access to. These include mobile phones, e-mail, text messaging, instant messaging, voice mail, etc. This developing technology has created new possibilities in the field of human communications. Perhaps the most dramatic change has been in the way in which people are able to communicate with each other over vast distances. Not only has it become cheaper to communicate with someone on the other side of the world, it has also become possible to send them electronic images, sound files and video clips. With the advent of cheap mobile phones, it is no longer the case that all members of a household are reliant on a single means of communication.

## Smart homes

At the cutting edge of domestic technology is the concept of the smart home. The smart home is wired up with a vast array of sensors, processors, control devices and communication systems. The house constantly monitors its own environment and makes adjustments in order to maintain optimum comfort (consistent with the owner's criteria). Simple systems like this already exist – a thermostat adjusts the level of a central heating system to maintain a predetermined temperature – but the smart house takes this a stage further. The smart fridge, for example, will know what is in the owner's fridge, when something has reached its sell-by date and will even 'instruct' another system to order fresh supplies via an online shopping service. Another system will 'know' when the owner's car is approaching. It will then instruct control systems to open the garage door, turn on the appropriate lights and turn on the music system in the house.

## Entertainment

One of the most common uses of early computers was game-playing. Computer games are now a multi-billion dollar industry, an industry which, in its relentless quest for market domination through innovation, has driven many hardware and software developments. Increasingly, games are not played on PCs but on dedicated game-playing consoles. These consoles, which are constantly increasing in sophistication, allow players to use TV screens as monitors and offer a range of input devices such as joy sticks, 'steering wheels' and multi-function game-playing devices. Additionally, there is increasing convergence of analogue and digital technologies in the provision of music videos, television programmes, films, etc. In some areas of America there are video-on-demand systems where customers use a cable connection to download digital versions of films that they have selected from an online menu. Music can be downloaded from the Internet, possibly via file-sharing systems, and played through the speakers on one's computer or via a personal MP3 player.

## Possible drawbacks

**Dependency**  An increasing dependency on embedded systems can be a problem. It used to be the case that a typical householder could effect minor repairs to a malfunctioning washing machine. This is no longer the case. The more complex the electronics in these systems become, the more dependent we become on – sometimes expensive – specialists to maintain and repair our equipment.

**Isolation**  Home-based systems make it increasingly possible to live one's life without leaving the house. People can work from home, shop from home, download whatever videos they want to watch and communicate via e-mail. This can be of value to those who live in rural areas or who have mobility problems. It can also, as some commentators have suggested, lead to a greater degree of social isolation, with fewer people participating in communal activities.

**Cost**  All of the possibilities offered by digital technology come at a price. Although computer-based systems are becoming more and more affordable for an increasing number of people, it is still the case that many are excluded from the 'technology revolution' due to lack of resources. This is even more the case when one compares households in the developed and the developing world.

# Data, information and knowledge

| DATA | INFORMATION | KNOWLEDGE |
|---|---|---|
| • Data may be defined as a collection of values.<br>• This collection of values – sometimes referred to as raw facts and figures – may take many forms: combinations of letters and numbers, sound waves, image elements, etc.<br>• The meaning of the data may not be apparent when it is in its raw – i.e. unprocessed – form. At this stage it may just appear as a stream of random items.<br>• However, data has *potential* meaning because it represents events, objects, individuals, dates, times, amounts, etc. | • Information is data that has been made meaningful, i.e. the potential meaning of the data has been realised.<br>• Two stages are involved in this. First, there must be a context for the information, a specific use to which it will be put, e.g. providing the answer to a particular question.<br>• Secondly, the data will need to be processed into a form that is accessible to users.<br>• This may involve transforming the data into a different format, sorting and grouping it, organising it into a table, etc. | • Knowledge may be defined as a broad understanding of the context in which a particular piece of information occurs.<br>• Knowledge is something that develops gradually and over time. It involves understanding the formal and informal rules that exist in a certain field. This understanding may be gained through experience and/or instruction.<br>• Knowledge enables somebody to make sense of a piece of information, to grasp its significance and to use it to draw conclusions, identify problems, aid decision-making, etc. |

## The relationship between data, information and knowledge

Information systems collect **data** from various sources, perform processes on it and output it as **information**. This information can then be used by individuals with **knowledge** of the wider context to draw conclusions and make decisions.

*For example:*

This set of numerical values (i.e. **data**) does not appear to have any meaning:

> 1400,140/80,1500,140/80,1600,120/60

To render the data as information, it must first be given a context. In this instance the context is a medical one. The data represents the blood pressure readings of a hospital patient taken at different times. The patient's doctor wants to know how the patient is doing. Before the data is presented to her as information, it needs to be processed into a recognisable format. In this case it will need to be transformed, sorted and tabulated.

| Reading 1: Time: 14.00 | Patient's BP = 140/80 |
|---|---|
| Reading 2: Time: 15.00 | Patient's BP = 140/80 |
| Reading 3: Time: 16.00 | Patient's BP = 120/60 |

It is now **information** and can be presented to the doctor as a report. The doctor is able to apply her **knowledge** to this information. She has an understanding of the context in which the information appears, i.e. an understanding of the patient's condition and the medical significance of blood pressure readings. She is therefore able to draw conclusions about the patient's state and decide upon an appropriate course of action.

## Data, information and knowledge in action

| DATA | INFORMATION | KNOWLEDGE |
|---|---|---|
| A retail business collects data from Electronic Point of Sale terminals in all its branches.<br><br>The resulting data consists of sets of values that represent sales of individual products, date and time of sales, branch locations, stock levels, etc. | The analysts who work for the business wish to ask questions about the data.<br><br>The data is therefore processed into a form that will be meaningful to them, e.g. a series of charts showing how well each branch has performed relative to its sales targets. | The analysts have developed both a general knowledge of the retail trade and specific knowledge of their own organisation.<br><br>They can now apply this knowledge to the sales charts in front of them and draw conclusions about the relative performance of each branch. |
| The data is stored in various data files. | The data can now be used purposefully by the analysts. It is now information. | This in turn may help them make decisions, e.g. which branches are due for expansion. |

Processed into → ← Applied to

# Information: value and cost

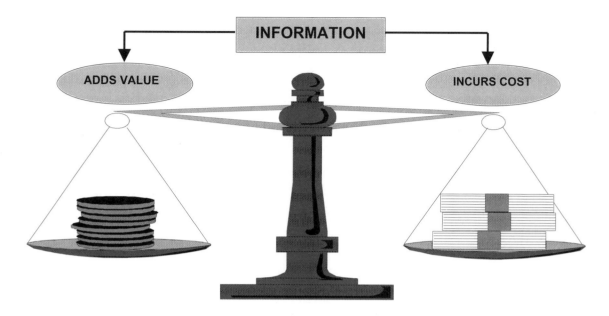

| | |
|---|---|
| Good information, i.e. information that is timely, accurate, up-to-date complete, etc. adds value to organisations in the ways described below: | Producing good quality information incurs costs in terms of money, time and human resources. |

**To aid decision-making** The quality of a decision depends, to a significant degree, on the quality of information that it is based on. Decision-making is an essential feature of the management of an organisation and the more effective the decision-making, the more successful the organisation is likely to be.

**Data collection** If data is collected directly, individuals may have to be paid to produce, send out and collect questionnaires. Companies that want customers to respond to requests for information often have to offer prize incentives (e.g. holidays) to guarantee adequate returns. If the data is collected indirectly, the organisation may have to pay a third party in order to gain access to data in their possession.

**To monitor and control** Information can help an organisation stay informed about how well it is doing. Information derived from market research and sales figures can help to achieve this. An organisation can also look at the performance of different employees to determine who is the most – or least – effective. This process can help to ensure that the use of resources is cost-effective.

**Data entry** If the data is keyed in, this will take time and operators will have to be paid to do it. There are automated methods of data entry – Optical mark readers (OMR), optical character recognition (OCR), bar code readers, etc. – but they still need to be operated by someone and they need to be purchased in the first place.

**To target resources** Organisations have limited resources and their efficient use will be a key determinant of success. For example, an organisation should ideally target its advertising and marketing at those customers who are most likely to be interested in its products. Information about customers' buying habits is extremely valuable in this process and can lead to an organisation becoming more profitable.

**Data processing** Once the data has been inputted it needs to be processed into information. This requires hardware and software resources. The software may have been purchased 'off-the-shelf' or it may have been a customised development; either way it will have cost money. Large-scale processing can tie up a good deal of an organisation's ICT resources.

**To gain competitive advantage** Information can tell an organisation how well it is doing in relation to its competitors. Information about, for example, gaps in a particular market, can help it take action ahead of its competitors. Identification of strengths and weaknesses will also help to improve its competitive edge.

**Data maintenance** There are costs involved in ensuring data remains accurate and up to date. For example, an organisation might maintain a database of its customers. The database will only remain accurate and up to date if any changes to customers' details are reported and the appropriate records amended. This involves communicating with customers and verifying that their details are correct.

# The quality of information

- Organisations and individuals use information to improve the quality of their decision-making. A decision that is made with inadequate or poor-quality information is likely to be a bad decision. This can have negative consequences for the organisation or individual concerned. In some instances these consequences can be disastrous.
- The better the quality of the information, the greater the likelihood of a good decision being made. This is what gives information its value. It can help produce decisions that will add value to the organisation.
- Not all information is of equal value. It is possible to evaluate the quality of information by using the criteria set out below.

## The qualities of good information

### ACCURATE

Information should be error free and a <u>true</u> reflection of what it represents. Even minor inaccuracies can lead to poor quality decisions being made.

**Example** A bank keeps records of its customers' accounts. This information must reflect truthfully the transactions that the customer has undertaken. Both the bank and the customer rely on the accuracy of this information to make decisions about future spending plans, loan requests, etc. If there were errors in the information, it might lead to bad decisions being made, e.g. the customer spending money that they don't in fact have.

### CORRECTLY TARGETED

Information should be presented to the people who need it. Giving information to people who have no need of it can contribute to 'information overload'. It can also create confusion and may lead to information that was meant to be confidential being in the wrong hands.

**Example** A report containing information about possible relocation sites is disseminated throughout an organisation. This creates a climate of anxiety and makes the actual decision-making process more difficult.

### UNDERSTANDABLE

Information should be set out in a clear, accessible format and communicated in a manner that is appropriate for the user. The level of detail included and the language used should reflect the specific needs and expertise of the user.

**Example** A company's financial managers are investigating the feasibility of a building project. They receive a report from engineers that uses terminology that only other engineers would understand. The decision cannot be made because the relevant information, though present, cannot be understood.

### COMPLETE

Information should include <u>all</u> the data which the user needs to make his decision. There should be no significant absences. (Absence of information is just as misleading as inaccurate information.)

**Example** A company wants to look at its sales performance during a specific period. It therefore needs the figures from <u>all</u> of its branches. If the data relating to the branches in one region was missing, it would lead to the wrong conclusions being drawn. This, in turn, could lead to serious errors in future planning.

Interim report

### TIMELY

Information should be made available at the time when it is needed. It must be presented at the appropriate moment in the decision-making process if it is to aid that process.

**Example** A company is making a decision about where to locate a distribution point. There is relevant information about changes to rail links available. Such information would have to be presented at the right point in the decision-making process. If it were presented too early, its relevance would not be apparent; if it were presented too late, the decision might already have been taken.

### RELEVANT

Information should not include data that has no bearing on the user's informational needs. A user receiving more information than she needs can lead to 'information overload'. The specific information that the user needs becomes lost amongst data that is not needed.

**Example** A company manager asks for details of one client's account and receives a report with all clients' details on. The information is not particularly useful to her because she would have to waste time finding the information that was relevant to her needs.

### HAS USER CONFIDENCE

Information should have the confidence of the users. If the user believes the underlying data is inaccurate or the original source of the data is not reliable, then the information will be useless to them. They won't feel able to make a decision based on such information.

**Example** A report is presented to an organisation's executive. The underlying data comes from a source which, in the past, has provided inaccurate data. The integrity of the information is questioned by the executive and it is either sent back for verification or else discarded.

### UP TO DATE

Information should be accurate at the point when it is presented. It should not be a reflection of an earlier state of affairs.

**Example** A furniture warehouse stores data on stock levels. Information produced from this data is used to make decisions about re-stocking. Unfortunately this type of data ages quickly, because stock levels can change daily, even hourly. Consequently, the information might be out of date by the time it is presented. This, in turn, might mean that incorrect stock orders are made.

# Different characteristics of information

| Category | Headings | Explanation | Example |
|---|---|---|---|
| SOURCE | Internal | Information generated from data produced within the organisation | Work schedule, indicating which employee will be working when |
| | External | Information generated from data produced outside the organisation | Government document indicating a new legal requirement |
| | Primary | Information collected directly from an original source | Market research involving questioning the organisation's clients |
| | Secondary | Information collected via another organisation/individual | Market report indicating general consumer trends |
| NATURE | Quantitative | Information largely or wholly presented in numerical terms | Sales report indicating the value and volume of sales in one week |
| | Qualitative | Information largely or wholly text-based description | Description of an employee's productivity in an appraisal report |
| | Formal | Information communicated via prescribed and authorised procedures | Minutes of a departmental meeting |
| | Informal | Information communicated without reference to predefined protocols | Telephone conversation between the heads of two departments |
| LEVEL | Strategic | Information used by high-level management to aid decision-making | Report forecasting the likely outcome of a rise in interest rates |
| | Tactical | Information used by middle managers to aid policy implementation | Weekly report for a warehouse manager indicating stock levels |
| | Operational | Information used by junior managers to aid day-to-day operations | Printout of daily price changes for a shop manager |
| TIME | Historical | Information relating to events, transactions, etc. that are in the past | Record of an ex-employee used to write a reference |
| | Current | Information relating to ongoing events, transactions, etc. | Printout indicating current atmospheric conditions in a workshop |
| | Future | Information forecasting the consequences of future developments | Modelled outcome for a proposed future development |
| FREQUENCY | Real-time | Information constantly updated as new data is processed | Temperature readout on a piece of machinery |
| | Scheduled | Information produced at fixed intervals, e.g. hourly, daily, weekly, etc. | Daily transaction report for the manager of a bank |
| | Ad hoc | Information made available on request | Report showing employees with more than five days' absence |
| USE | Planning | Information used to make decisions about future needs | Report indicating what funds are available for stock purchase |
| | Control | Information used to monitor current procedures to ensure efficiency | Report showing the time taken for a specified task to be completed |
| | Decision | Information used to support the decision-making process | Report that compares the prices of different suppliers |
| FORM | Written | Information presented in a written format | Research document about current market trends |
| | Visual | Information primarily visual in format | Chart showing current and projected sales figures |
| | Aural | Information communicated aurally, i.e. by being heard | Face-to-face briefing by a departmental head to a senior manager |
| TYPE | Disaggregated | Information presented with individual data items intact | Printout of the hours worked by each employee in the department |
| | Aggregated and sampled | Information summarised and sampled to make it more concise | Summary report showing the weekly labour costs of a production department |

EXAMPLE 1 A purchase order produced within the organisation

| SOURCE | Internal |
|---|---|
| NATURE | Formal |
| LEVEL | Operational |
| TIME | Current |
| FREQUENCY | Ad hoc |
| USE | Decision (implementation) |
| FORM | Written |
| TYPE | Disaggregated |

EXAMPLE 2 A presentation to senior managers by potential suppliers

| SOURCE | External |
|---|---|
| NATURE | Formal |
| LEVEL | Strategic |
| TIME | Future |
| FREQUENCY | Ad hoc |
| USE | Planning |
| FORM | Visual/aural |
| TYPE | Aggregated |

# Internal and external information

One way of characterising information is to define it as **internal** or **external**. These categories can then be further subdivided into **source** and **requirement**. If information is internal, it has either been produced or is required within the bounds of the organisation, i.e. it is related directly to the resources (human and non-human), procedures, transactions, etc. of the organisation. If information is external, it has either been produced or is required by individuals or organisations that lie outside the boundaries of the organisation.

## Internal ⟶ Internal

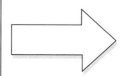

### SOURCE

- Information produced by Transaction Processing System, e.g. sales figures
- Human Resources database
- Stocks and supplies database
- Internal accounting
- Hours and pay rates
- Monitoring and control devices
- Capital assets
- Organisation policy documents
- Knowledge and expertise of organisation members
- Archived data

### REQUIREMENT

- Accounts, e.g. profit and loss, wage bill, stock value, etc.
- Performance reports: how well the organisation is currently performing, e.g. sales figures per month.
- Reports on staff, e.g. appraisal, hours worked, performance, etc.
- Development plans: setting future objectives for individual areas.
- Analyses of organisation's current position and future prospects.
- Historic analysis, i.e. whether the organisation's performance is improving over time.

## External ⟶ Internal

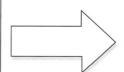

### SOURCE

- Market research reports on customer/client needs
- Suppliers' details, including details of product availability, prices
- Government documents, e.g. relating to changes in legislation
- Secondary data, collected for another purpose, e.g. population trends, social trends
- Information about the organisation's environment, e.g. competitors' performance, stock market, interest rates, etc.
- Information about news events that might impact on the organisation
- Invoices from suppliers

### REQUIREMENT

- Reports on customer/client preference, likely impact of marketing strategies, popularity of products, etc.
- Reports that would aid decision-making about which suppliers to use, which products to buy, etc.
- Reports on general trends and how they might impact on the organisation's potential market.
- Performance indicators, showing how well the organisation is doing relative to other similar organisations.
- Analysis of the threats and opportunities presented by changes in the organisation's business environment, e.g. changes in legislation, news events, etc.

## Internal ⟶ External

### SOURCE

- Information produced by Transaction Processing System, e.g. sales figures
- Human Resources database
- Stocks and supplies database
- Internal accounting
- Hours and pay rates
- Monitoring and control devices
- Capital assets
- Organisation policy documents
- Knowledge and expertise of organisation members

### REQUIREMENT

- Accounts, required by auditors to check that the organisation is conducting its finances legally.
- Financial institutions to whom the organisation is financially obligated, e.g. investment banks need to know how the organisation is performing.
- Shareholder need to be kept informed on current plans and future developments.
- Government bodies require information returns, e.g. tax paid, number of employees, etc.

# Presenting information: 1

Information may be presented in a range of different formats and via different media. A successful information system will ensure that information is presented in the most appropriate format for the intended audience. For example, if the information is in summary form and has to be communicated quickly, a graphical presentation may be the most appropriate. Factors that will need to be taken into account include:

- The nature and complexity of the original information: some information cannot easily be translated into a different format. The nature of the information determines the output.
- The time available for the recipient to study the information: busy managers sometimes need to have information summarised for them so that they can tell at a glance what the situation is.
- The needs of the recipient of the information: sometimes the recipient will need to understand a situation in detail; at other times they may just need to receive a general impression.
- The 'life-span' of the information – will it soon be supplanted by new information or will it need to be regularly referred to? Some information – a policy statement for example – does not change very often, whereas other information – such as stock market figures – is constantly changing.
- How long the recipient needs to study the situation. If information needs to be referred to over a period of time, then it needs to be presented in a 'permanent' format (e.g. a written report) rather than a temporary one (e.g. a verbal presentation).

## Different methods of presentation

**Tabulated summary** This would be an effective means of presenting largely quantitative (i.e. numerical) data in an accessible format. In general, the higher up in an organisation the recipient is, the greater the need for the information to be summarised. If mathematical calculations were included on the report they would need to be consistent with the ability of the recipient to understand their significance. Tabulated summaries can be set up as standard reports in Management Information Systems and thus be regularly produced without any investment of time.

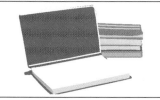

**Written report** Sometimes it is not sufficient to present the information in summary form. The information may require the kind of detailed explanation and commentary that can only be provided by descriptive text, i.e. a written report. This form of report may be of use to someone who needs to understand the meaning behind the figures and has sufficient time to read through a more extensive document. Such documents are also useful if the information does not change quickly and/or if it needs to be accessed regularly, e.g. policy documents.

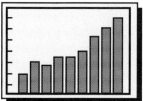

**Graphs, charts, diagrams, etc.** Visual presentations of this kind are valuable for highlighting trends, showing relationships/comparisons between different blocks of data, and summarising complex numerical data. They are helpful for demonstrating quickly and simply the underlying meaning of the information, e.g. 'the sales figures regularly improve during the summer months'. Spreadsheet software is becoming increasingly sophisticated in its ability to translate numerical data into graphical format, so the process need not be labour-intensive.

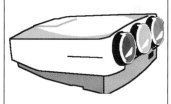

**Slide show** The slide show, created using presentation software and shown using a computer projector, is a lively and engaging means of presenting information to an audience. It can incorporate graphs, diagrams, simple numerical data and short pieces of text. More sophisticated systems can create multimedia presentations incorporating audio/video-based material. It is not a satisfactory medium for presenting complex numerical or detailed textual information. Slide shows are often used when there is a larger audience, e.g. a meeting of Heads of Department, a presentation to prospective students of a college. They take time to prepare and often need to be supported by information in document format.

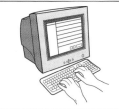

**Computer access** Information can be made available online. Applications may be developed which allow different users access to regularly updated information. Decision Support Systems and Executive Information Systems allow managers to access relevant information to support them in their work. Traders in the financial markets often use applications of this kind. They need to ensure that they have up-to-date information on the screen in front of them. They do not have time to order a printed report and wait for it to be delivered.

**Oral presentation** Sometimes information is presented orally, e.g. a manager addressing a meeting of colleagues, a CEO addressing a meeting of shareholders. The advantage of this format is that the information can be explained and there can be some interaction with the audience. The disadvantage is that if the recipients do not document the information, it may be forgotten or mis-remembered. For this reason oral presentations are often supported by visual or document material.

# Presenting information: 2

## Features of an effective report

Printed reports are a popular method of presenting information. In order to communicate the information effectively, printed reports should have the following qualities:

**Sensible organisation**  Reports are often used by managers who need to be able to assimilate information quickly. The layout of information on the page should therefore be arranged so that it can be read easily. Elements of page layout such as dividing lines, blocking, tabulation, etc. should be used to optimise ease of access.

**Clear labelling**  Both the report itself and individual items of information on it should be clearly labelled so that there is no ambiguity about what is being referred to. Reports should always indicate their date of production and their place of origin (i.e. which member of the organisation produced it).

**Appropriate detail**  The level of detail contained within a report should be consistent with the use to which it will be put. People at different levels within an organisation have different information needs. For example, a manager making a strategic decision will need information that has been summarised, whereas a manager working at an operational level will need it in more detail.

**Appropriate complexity**  The language used within the report should be at an appropriate level for the end-user. For example, a summary of technical processes may need to be simplified if it is to be used by a person without the appropriate technical knowledge. The same is also true of numerical data: some users can deal with high level statistical analyses; others may need it presented at a simpler level.

**Standardisation**  It is useful if all the reports in an organisation have common elements, e.g. font, header identifications, etc. This will help those organisation members who need to access information from many different sources.

## Elements of a report

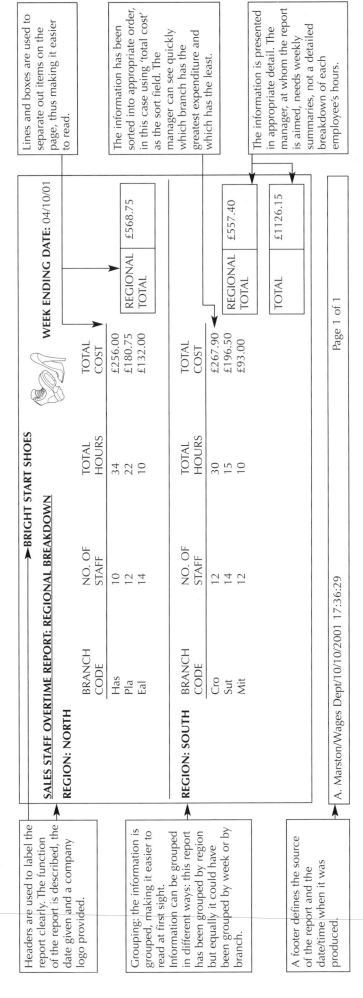

Headers are used to label the report clearly. The function of the report is described, the date given and a company logo provided.

Grouping; the information is grouped, making it easier to read at first sight. Information can be grouped in different ways: this report has been grouped by region but equally it could have been grouped by week or by branch.

A footer defines the source of the report and the date/time when it was produced.

Lines and boxes are used to separate out items on the page, thus making it easier to read.

The information has been sorted into appropriate order, in this case using 'total cost' as the sort field. The manager can see quickly which branch has the greatest expenditure and which has the least.

The information is presented in appropriate detail. The manager, at whom the report is aimed, needs weekly summaries, not a detailed breakdown of each employee's hours.

### SALES STAFF OVERTIME REPORT: REGIONAL BREAKDOWN

**BRIGHT START SHOES**

**WEEK ENDING DATE:** 04/10/01

**REGION: NORTH**

| BRANCH CODE | NO. OF STAFF | TOTAL HOURS | TOTAL COST |
|---|---|---|---|
| Has | 10 | 34 | £256.00 |
| Pla | 12 | 22 | £180.75 |
| Eal | 14 | 10 | £132.00 |
| | | REGIONAL TOTAL | £568.75 |

**REGION: SOUTH**

| BRANCH CODE | NO. OF STAFF | TOTAL HOURS | TOTAL COST |
|---|---|---|---|
| Cro | 12 | 30 | £267.90 |
| Sut | 14 | 15 | £196.50 |
| Mit | 12 | 10 | £93.00 |
| | | REGIONAL TOTAL | £557.40 |
| | | TOTAL | £1126.15 |

A. Marston/Wages Dept/10/10/2001 17:36:29                    Page 1 of 1

# Data collection: 1

### Different ways in which data may be collected

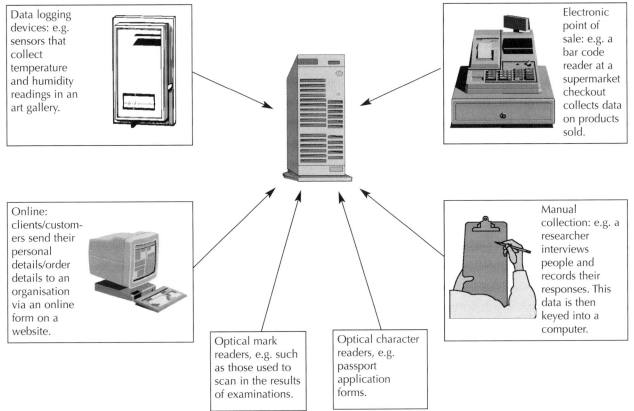

Data logging devices: e.g. sensors that collect temperature and humidity readings in an art gallery.

Electronic point of sale: e.g. a bar code reader at a supermarket checkout collects data on products sold.

Online: clients/customers send their personal details/order details to an organisation via an online form on a website.

Optical mark readers, e.g. such as those used to scan in the results of examinations.

Optical character readers, e.g. passport application forms.

Manual collection: e.g. a researcher interviews people and records their responses. This data is then keyed into a computer.

### Direct/indirect collection of data

*Sources of data can be categorised as direct and indirect*

**Direct**  The data is collected to fulfil a specific purpose. For example, when a video store swipes the bar code on a video and links it to the customer who is taking it out, they are collecting data that will inform them of who has taken out what video, when it is due back, whether a fine has been imposed, etc.

**Indirect**  The data is used to create information that is not directly related to the original purpose of the data collection. For example, the video store data could be used to create customer profiles, e.g. which customers are particularly interested in romantic comedies. This information could be then be used for targeted promotions. Furthermore, because such information has commercial value, it could be sold to another organisation who may use the information for purposes of its own, e.g. a publishing company trying to identify the market for romantic novels. There are some legal restrictions on the use of data for secondary purposes – data subjects have to give their consent to secondary usage – but it is still common commercial practice.

### The quality of the data source

The quality of information is dependent on the quality of the data it is derived from. This concept is usefully encapsulated in the phrase 'garbage in – garbage out'. If, for example, when a client fills out their details on a membership form, they make a mistake writing out their address, all subsequent information based on this data will be erroneous. At a very basic level, this will mean that letters are sent to the wrong address. In order to be of value data should be:

- accurate;
- up to date;
- complete.

There are many reason why this might not be the case:

- If the data has been collected via a data capture form, it might not have been accurately written down. Equally, a correct entry may be inaccurately transcribed by a data entry clerk. Validation routines should pick this up, but these may not be in place.
- An automatic system might have an undetected fault that results in it recording inaccurate data. A sensor, for example, might be logging readings that are erroneous.
- Data might be out of date because changes have not been recorded. If, for example, a person changes address but does not inform their employer, the employer's database will produce information based on non-current data.
- If someone, when filling in an online form, omits a particular piece of data (e.g. a second income), the data will not be complete. This will have a detrimental effect on any information subsequently produced.

Because ICT systems are complex, interdependent and often hide their processes, even minor data inaccuracies can have a catastrophic effect at a later stage. It is therefore important to ensure that the source of the data can be trusted.

# Data collection: 2

## Desirable features of a data collection system

Data capture refers to a set of procedures whereby raw data is inputted into a computing system prior to being processed. It is a critical phase in any information system. If the data capture is not performed successfully, the quality of the final output will be negatively affected. This principle is summarised in the well-known phrase 'garbage in – garbage out' (GIGO). The following criteria may be used to determine the quality of the data capture system:

**Efficient**  Capturing data always incurs costs, both financial and in terms of human resources. A successful system will complete the operation in the most cost-effective manner.

**Timely**  The time taken to complete the data capture, and the intervals at which it is completed, will need to be consistent with the requirement that information systems should deliver their output to the right person at the right time.

**Secure**  In common with all other phases of an information cycle, the data capture process must ensure that the data it captures is held securely.

**Accurate**  If the original inputted data is inaccurate, then the final output will also be inaccurate. This can lead to managers making business-critical decisions based on false information.

## The different stages of data capture

### The nature of the original data

The data may be in a variety of formats (text, numerical, verbal, etc.) may consist of a few items or many thousands of items and may be of variable quality. These factors will all have to be taken into account when undertaking the processes that follow. For example, if the data consists of many items and is in text form, it may be necessary to utilise an OMR/OCR system.

### Transcription/translation

Before the data can be inputted it may be necessary to translate it into another format or to transcribe it from one medium into another. For example, verbal responses may need to transcribed on to an OCR capture form before input. Inevitably the process of transcription/translation has implications for the accuracy of the data. It is a stage in the process where simple errors can occur.

### Choice of data capture method

There are a wide range of data capture techniques (bar code scanners, OCR, OMR, magnetic strip, etc.). Each of them have their strengths and weaknesses (see pages 32–3). In choosing a method, one must take into account the nature, volume and quality of the original data. These factors will determine which method is the most efficient in terms of cost and time taken.

### Validation

There are several methods of validation that can be performed, either at the point of input or subsequent to it. These are defined by the types of check they perform (e.g. range, length, presence, etc.). Though valuable, validation checks can only determine whether the data is valid, i.e. whether it falls within predefined parameters. They cannot determine whether or not the data is accurate.

### Verification

Verification is the process of double-checking the data that has been entered. A standard means of verification is double entry: the data is entered twice and inconsistencies followed up. This method will only identify simple transcription errors. A more time-consuming method involves printing out the inputted data and checking it (or a random sample of it) against the original data source.

### Auditing

Audits are systematic checks that ensure the accuracy of organisational data. Their primary purpose is to prevent fraud, but they are also used to determine the effectiveness of a system. The standard approach is to use an 'audit trail' that follows a data sample from its original source to its final output. The process – which is often automated – involves looking for inconsistencies in the data.

# Data input: encoding data

### What is encoding?

- Sometimes, in order to facilitate an efficient inputting procedure, information has to be encoded as data. For example, the names of countries may be stored as codes (e.g. UK, FRA, AUS, etc.).
- Encoding involves translating all the original items of information into an agreed format. Sometimes this involves restricting data items to a predetermined range of values, e.g. only allowing 'gold', 'silver' or 'bronze' for 'Medal status' on an athletics meeting sheet. It may also involve shortening the original data item, e.g. male becomes 'M', female becomes 'F'.
- Sometimes encoding happens before the data is captured; sometimes it happens after capture but before entry; sometimes at the point of entry.

### Example

A company wants to establish the marital status of its employees. Its application forms therefore contain a box with the heading 'Marital Status'. Because applicants are free to write what they wish, many different responses are returned, including the following:

- Living with someone
- Living with partner
- Live-in lover
- Live with girlfriend.

The database administrator decides that these entries all belong in the same category. She decides that 'Living with Partner' will be the category for all of the above. She now needs to define a new code. There are already codes for married (M), widowed (W) and divorced (D). The new category will be P. She amends the data entry screen so that the data entry clerks now have P as a value that can be entered in the Marital Status field.

### The advantages of encoding

- **Fewer transcription errors** There is less chance of an error if the data entry clerk has to key in only one or two letters.

- **Less time spent on data entry** It does not take as long to key in shortened codes.

- **Greater data consistency** If data conforms to pre-established codes, it is more likely to be consistent and therefore easier to interrogate.

- **Less memory required** Although the saving might seem to be a small one, databases holding significant numbers of data items need to be as economical as possible.

### Problems associated with encoding

- **Encoding can coarsen data** Encoding requires data to fit into pre-established categories. However, some data does not easily fit into one category. To use the example above, 'long-term cohabitee' is not the same as 'just moved in with boyfriend' but the two entries would end up in the same category. This loss of precision is an inevitable effect of encoding and must be weighed against its advantages.

- **Subjective judgements** There is a particular difficulty when the data being encoded relates to value judgements. For instance, someone may be asked "Was your hotel: 'Excellent', 'Very Good', 'Good' or 'Poor'?". Apart from the problem of having to fit the data into a category, there is the additional problem of 'subjectivity'. One person's 'Excellent' hotel is another person's 'Good'. Such problems can have an effect on the value of the resulting information.

### When does encoding take place

| Before data is captured The data capture form is designed so that only certain values can be entered. | After capture and before entry The data is amended and the appropriate codes written on the form. | At the point of entry The screen data entry form allows only prescribed values to be entered. This might be achieved through the use of validation rules and/or drop-down boxes. |
| --- | --- | --- |
| Title: (underline one of the following) Mr / Mrs / Miss / Ms / Dr  Other (please specify) ___ | Office use only  Ethnic origin: Black African  Religion: Islam  Country of origin: UK  B | Sex: Male / Female |

# Validation and verification: 1

## How do data errors occur?

Data accuracy is critical in all information systems as even minor inaccuracies can have serious consequences. Errors can occur at different points in the information system cycle.

**General input error**    There are various errors that fall into this category, e.g. customers filling in the details on the data entry form incorrectly, forms being lost or mistakenly entered twice, problems with automatic data collection devices, e.g. a malfunctioning bar code reader.

**Transcription error**    This is a specific type of error that can occur when a data entry clerk is keying in data, i.e. copying from a data capture form or via telephone instructions. A number of mistakes can occur during this process, e.g. transposing two numbers in a date of birth or mis-spelling a street name.

**Processing error**    Even if the data has been correctly inputted, errors can occur as it is being processed. For example, the program responsible for the processing could contain a mathematical function that calculates percentage totals. If an error were made (and left undetected) at the program writing stage – a miscalculation would be made every time it was run. The resulting inaccuracies may not be discovered for some time.

**Transmission error**    At various points in the system the data will need to be transmitted from one location to another. If, for example, a networked system were being used, the data would have to be transmitted from the client terminal to the server. During this process data can be lost or corrupted.

## Validation routines

Validation is a means of reducing data errors, especially at the inputting stage. Validation routines ensure that the data being entered conforms to prescribed rules, rejecting it if it does not. Validation may be completed at the point of entry, e.g. by not allowing the operator to enter invalid data into a text box, or subsequent to data entry, e.g. by running a program which returns a list of all invalid entries. There are many different types of validation checks. Some of the most commonly used are set out in the table below.

| Type | Description | Example |
|------|-------------|---------|
| Presence | A presence check requires that a value must be entered, i.e. there cannot be a null value. | The details of an order are being inputted. The order cannot be processed unless an order number has been included. The validation routine returns an error if the operator tries to leave the input box empty. |
| Format | The data must conform to a prescribed layout, i.e. a specific pattern of letters and numbers. | An employee code consists of a particular pattern of number and letters, e.g. SY//3480/C. If the operator tries to enter a different arrangement of letters and numbers, an error is returned. |
| Range | The data must be a value that falls between two predefined values. | The date of birth of a student at a secondary school must be between 01/09/83 and 31/08/95. Any date that falls outside this range is rejected. |
| Data type | The data must be of a specified type, i.e. numerical, text, Boolean, image, etc. | The data entered for a 'number in stock' item must be numerical. If the operator entered any value that was non-numerical, e.g. a text item, it would be rejected. |
| Fixed value | The data must conform to one of the values in a predefined list. | The only entries that can be made for the 'gender' item on a form are Male and Female. Any attempt to enter anything other than these values will result in an error message. |

## Check digits

This is a particular type of validation check that is used to check for transcription errors in long, numerical identifiers, e.g. the ISBN number on the back of this book. The check works by performing a mathematical calculation on the code number and returning an error if there is a discrepancy between the expected and actual outcome. The most commonly used test is called 'modulus 11'. In this system each number in the code is multiplied by a number (10 for the first number, 9 for the second and so on). The multiplied numbers are summed and the total divided by 11. The remainder from the division is then subtracted from 11. This is the check digit. If the remainder is 10, this is written as $X$, to restrict the outcome to one digit.

# Validation and verification: 2

### Checking for transmission errors

One form of checking that is used to detect errors that might occur during the transmission of data is the 'check digit' system. It works by using the binary digits that are used to transmit data. For example:

1   The letter 'A' is represented by the ASCII code 1000001.
2   When this combination of digits is transmitted a parity bit is added to the end of the sequence. The parity bit is either a 0 or 1, depending on whether the sum of the bits is an even or an odd number.
3   In an even-parity system, the total of all the bits (including the parity bit) must be an even number. In the case of the letter A, the bits already add up to an even number so a 0 will be added.
4   If they didn't add up to an even number (e.g. a 'C' which is 1000011), then a 1 would be added.
5   This then provides a means of checking whether that particular byte of data has been correctly transmitted.

This is by no means a flawless system. If, for example, there were two errors in the transmission they would cancel each other and the data would be accepted as correct.

Another, similar, system that is used is the 'checksum' system. When data is transmitted in packets a checksum – i.e. a total of the numeric value of the transmitted bytes – is included in the transmission. This can then act as a checking value at the point of reception.

### Validity and accuracy

Just because data has been accepted as valid – i.e. it has passed through a system's validation routines – it does not mean that it is accurate. To be valid, data has to be reasonable and fall within a system's accepted parameters; to be accurate it has to be a truthful representation of an original source.

**Example**   *A customer completes a data capture form with 05/07/68 as their date of birth. The operator who enters this makes a transcription error: instead of 05/07/68 being entered, 07/05/68 is keyed in. This entry passes through all the system's validation routines – because, though erroneous, it is in the correct format for a date of birth – and is duly processed. The data is valid but inaccurate.*

Validation then is no absolute guarantee of accuracy. In order to increase the level of data accuracy verification routines must be used.

### Verification

Verification refers to routines that might be used to establish the accuracy of inputted data. These routines include:

• proofreading the screen entries against the original document;
• reading back details to a customer whose data had been inputted via telephone;
• sending printouts of inputted data to the data source (e.g. a customer) and asking them to confirm the accuracy of the data.

One – rather time-consuming – method of verification, involving double inputting of data is shown below.

| ERRORS | |
|---|---|
| Record 1: | Name field |
| Record 35: | DOB field |
| Record 42: | Town field |
| Record 56: | DOB field |
| Record 69: | PostCode field |
| Record 75: | PostCode field |
| Record 92: | DOB field |
| Record 105: | HomeTel field |

The first data entry clerk enters the data, copying from the source document.

The second data entry clerk repeats the routine, copying from the same document.

The verification program compares the two sets of data and identifies discrepancies that require further checking.

# Data storage: text and numbers

## Binary data

Computers and other digital devices operate on binary principles, i.e. they store and manipulate all data as combinations of two digits, 0 and 1. Regardless of whether the data represents sound, images, text or numbers, it will eventually be reduced to a series of 0s and 1s for storage and processing. This is because it is (relatively) easy to build electronic circuits that recognise two states, i.e. 'on' and 'off'. These two states can then be used to represent 0s and 1s.

The smallest unit of data is a bit (short for Binary Digit). A bit can represent one of only two values: 1 or 0. Bits are represented in different ways in different parts of computer systems:

**Fibre optical cable:**   as pulses of light
**Compact disks:**   as 'lands' (flat areas) and 'pits' (depressed areas) that reflect light
**Microprocessor:**   as the absence or presence of an electrical charge in an integrated circuit
**Hard drive:**   as polarities of magnetically charged particles

A bit is a limited unit to work with and so computer storage tends to be structured into and measured in terms of **bytes**. A byte comprises 8 bits and this allows for up to 256 values to be created in this format. This is sufficient to represent the extended ASCII character set (see below). Multiples of bits and bytes are used as units of measurement when discussing processing power, data transmission and storage capacity. The most common multiples are:

1 kilobyte (kB)   =   approximately 1000 bytes
1 megabyte (MB)   =   approximately 1 million bytes
1 gigabyte (GB)   =   approximately 1 billion bytes
1 terabyte (TB)   =   approximately 1000 GB

## STORING TEXT

When computers first began to store text-based data a question emerged: how exactly will text be represented in binary format? What, for example, will be the binary equivalent of the letter 'A'? Not only did there need to be a standard for this procedure, it had to be one that different manufacturers conformed to. Without conformity, the transfer of text-based data between systems would be impossible. One of the standards that did emerge was the ASCII (American Standard Code for Information Interchange) system. In this system, each alphanumeric character (i.e. the letters of the alphabet plus numbers, characters such as '?', '#', etc.) is given a 7- or 8-bit code, depending on which system is being used.

| Character | ASCII binary code |
|---|---|
| A | 10000001 |
| B | 10000010 |
| C | 10000011 |
| ! | 00100001 |
| & | 00100110 |
| 1 | 00110001 |
| 2 | 00110010 |

Once converted, the data can be stored and transmitted digitally. When it needs to be displayed, i.e. on the screen or on a printout, it is converted back into standard English notation.

The extended 8-bit ASCII system can represent 256 characters which is sufficient for most of the tasks one would need to perform using English. However, as the need for international communication becomes more pressing, a system that can cope with different languages, including those with large character sets such as Japanese, is needed. The 16-bit Unicode system is currently the favourite for taking on this role. The 16-bit capacity means that it is capable of storing 65 536 characters.

## STORING NUMBERS

Sometimes it is perfectly acceptable to store numerical data as text. For example, if one were entering a telephone number into a database record, it could be stored as a text data-type using the ASCII code. This is because telephone numbers are not (generally) used in calculations. Therefore, the number will always act *as if* it is text. If, however, a piece of numerical data is to be used in calculations it must be stored as a binary number (which does not have a leading zero).

Binary numbers work differently to the denary, base-10, system that we use on a daily basis. In the denary system the number 225 would be represented as follows

| 100's | 10's | 1's |
|---|---|---|
| 2 | 2 | 5 |

Moving right to left across the columns, each digit has a value ten times greater than the one before it, hence base-10. The binary system works in a similar way but replaces 10 with 2. In other words, moving left to right across the columns, each digit is worth twice as much as the previous one. In this system the number 225 would be represented thus:

| 128 | 64 | 32 | 16 | 8 | 4 | 2 | 1 |
|---|---|---|---|---|---|---|---|
| 1 | 1 | 1 | 0 | 0 | 0 | 0 | 1 |

i.e.

$$(1 \times 128) + (1 \times 64) + (1 \times 32) + (1 \times 1) = 225$$

In order to represent higher numbers, two or sometimes four bytes are stored next to each other. Once numerical data has been stored using this system, any calculation can be performed on it. If decimals are required, a somewhat different system is needed, but the binary principle still applies.

# Storing graphics data: 1

### Bit-mapped files

Bit-mapped images work on the same principle as 'painting by numbers'. The image (usually a picture but it could be a piece of text or a combination of the two) is divided into a grid format. Each 'box' in the grid is an addressable element referred to as a pixel (or picture element). A pixel has two key properties associated with it: a position on the grid and a colour value. These properties are stored as data in the computer's memory. When the image needs to be displayed, the data held in the bit-mapped file is used to reconstruct the image. Bit-mapped files appear in a number of different formats. These are listed below. Collectively, these file formats represent the most popular means of storing graphical information.

### How bit-mapped files work

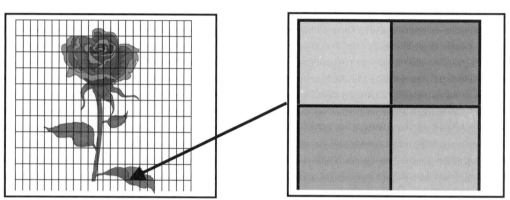

The bit-mapped graphic, sometimes called a raster graphic, is composed of grid of small squares or rectangles, called pixels. The image only becomes clear when the grid is viewed in its entirety.

Each pixel has a location in the grid and a colour value. In a colour image, the colour value consists of a combination of three values, one each for red, green and blue.

| R190 G215 B66 | R200 G245 B73 |
|---|---|
| R190 G240 B90 | R186 G236 B99 |

The graphics program translates the pixel colours into numerical values that can be stored. With a 24-bit system, 16.7 million colour values are possible. This is called 'true colour'.

| BMP | Width XXXX | Height XXXX | Palette |
|---|---|---|---|
| 42D2BE | | 49F0C8 | |
| 5AF0BE | | 63ECBA | |

The file also contains a header that specifies what file format is being used, the height and width of the image and the particular palette that is being referred to by the stored value.

### Different bit-mapped formats

Bit-mapped graphics come in a range of file formats, some of which are more widely used than others. They include:

**.BMP**  Bit-Mapped Picture. The standard file format used with Windows applications.

**.GIF**  Graphics Interchange Format. These files are often used on websites, especially in their animated form (animated GIFs). They have a 256 colour limit (i.e. 8 bits per pixel) and use a lossless compression algorithm to save on memory.

**.JPEG**  Joint Photographic Experts Group. Again, frequently used on the Internet. JPEGs are often used when good-quality photographic images need to be stored. This is because they can store 24 bits per pixel and therefore have the capacity for 16 million colours. There are different JPEG formats, the difference relating to the level of compression used.

**.TIF**  Tagged Image File Format. The file structure is more complex than some of the other formats but it can be used on several different platforms.

# Storing graphics data: 2

### Vector-based graphics

Vector-based graphics – also known as object-oriented graphics – work on a different set of principles to bit-mapped images. The file for a vector-based graphic contains mathematical data that defines the key properties of every element of the image. If, for example, there is a straight line in the graphic, the data in the file will define its length, thickness, location, fill pattern, etc. The file data – referred to as the display list – will also specify the hierarchy of the objects, i.e. which picture element will be displayed first, second and so on. Although a vector graphic is stored according to its mathematical properties, it is still displayed as a temporary bit-mapped image. Vector graphics have certain advantages over bit-mapped graphics (see below) and are favoured by designers using CAD programs. Vector-based graphics are also essential when CAD/CAM systems are being used, i.e. where the graphical object is being used, in part, as the basis for instructions to automated machines.

### How vector-based graphics work

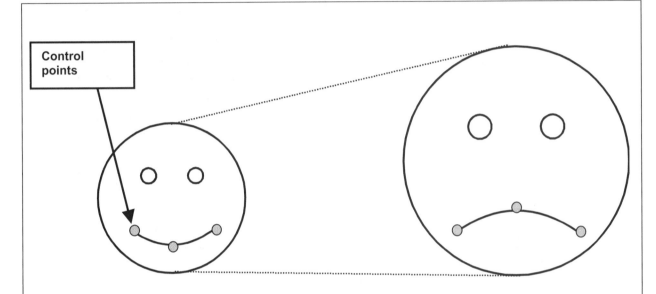

Control points

The user creates the graphic using a pointing device and a set of predefined objects: lines, squares, circles, curved lines, etc. As the different elements are drawn the program stores key pieces of information about them. For example, in order to create the 'smile' in the above image, the program would store the start and end point of the curved line (i.e. as sets of coordinates that define their position on the page). It would also use an additional control point to define how far the curve is pulled away from a straight line. When the image is rescaled – i.e. made larger or smaller – the formulae that define the coordinates change, thus creating a newly sized object. In this case the coordinates of the central control point have also been changed, thus transforming the smile into a frown. The coordinates can be defined with a high degree of exactitude and this contributes to the overall precision of vector-based graphics. In addition to the positional data, the file would also define the thickness of the lines, the type of fill used and the relationship of one picture element to another, i.e. whether an object should be displayed over or under another object.

### Vector graphics versus bit-mapped graphics

| VECTOR | BIT-MAPPED |
|---|---|
| • The key advantage of vector graphics is their 'scalability', i.e. unlike bit-mapped graphics they keep their shape and precision level when resized. This makes them ideal for designers and architects who need to constantly adjust the size, perspective, proportions, etc. of their objects.<br>• The facility for producing simple vector-based graphics is often included as part of a word-processing program. They allow the user to create simple drawn objects, such as squares and lines, that can enhance the presentation of a document.<br>• The size of a vector graphics file is, relatively speaking, smaller than an equivalent bit-mapped graphic file. | • The main problem with bit-mapped graphics is that, when they are resized, there is a diminishment in image quality. This is because, the process of resizing involves stretching or constricting each pixel so that it fits the new size. This leads to the image having jagged edges and so losing clarity of definition. This is known as 'aliasing'.<br>• Bit-mapped graphics remain popular because they deal well with complex, highly detailed images such as photographs. Because each pixel is an addressable unit, it is possible to make subtle changes to the properties of an image.<br>• Bit-mapping is also more consistent with the general computing environment, i.e. both display and printing devices tend to use a series of dots to define images and text. |

# Importing images

Images can be used in conjunction with a variety of different applications, including spreadsheets, word-processing and DTP packages, slide-show presentations and web-page compilers. There is a variety of methods that may be used to import pages into a document. The method used will depend on the nature of the document, its intended audience, the memory resources available and access to image-capturing hardware.

## CLIP ART

- Clip art refers to pre-packaged electronic images that the user can import as required. They vary in quality: some are highly detailed graphics, others are merely crude line drawings.
- They are usually stored in bit-mapped format (e.g. .BMP, .JPEG, .GIF), making it easy for the user to import them into documents.
- They are available from different sources: word-processing and graphics programs tend to include a folder of clip art files; they are packaged into commercially available sets of CDs; and there are websites that offer access to clip-art libraries.
- Clip art is easy to access and straightforward to use. It is seen by some, however, as rather amateurish and inappropriate for serious, business documents.

## DIGITAL CAMERA

- A digital camera works by reading the light reflected by the image being focused on. The readings are converted by an array of light sensitive diodes into an analogue signal. An ADC converter transforms these varying signals into digital pixels. These values are then processed, compressed and stored as a bit-mapped file, either on a disc or a flash memory chip.
- Digital cameras are coming down in price, though the top-of-the-range devices are still expensive. Good-quality colour printers and special paper are required if professional grade results are to be obtained.
- Digital cameras are portable, easy to use and provide an efficient means of capturing an image that can then be digitally manipulated.
- Professional photographers complain that digital photography does not achieve the same results in terms of image quality: the subtler effects of light and shade are lost in the digital process.

## GRAPHICS PROGRAM

- Graphics programs allow users to create their own images. These programs gives the user access to a wide range of drawing tools that mimic the actions of real drawing implements. For example, a 'spray paint' function will apply colour in a similar manner to a spray gun.
- The quality of the image will depend on the skills of the user and the quality of the program, with only the more expensive, top-end graphics packages offering professional grade drawing tools.
- Graphics programs often require the use of specialist input devices such as light pens and digitiser tablets.
- They are most suitable for professional graphic artists or designers who wish to use a CAD program to create a precise and specific design image.

## SCANNER

- Scanners can be used to capture an image that is in hard-copy format, e.g. a photograph in a magazine. The scanner first reads the amount of reflected light from each small section of the image. It then translates the readings first into analogue values and then into digital pixels. A bit-mapped file is created from these values. The computer is able to use this file to create a replica of the image on the computer screen.
- Scanners are relatively cheap to buy and easy to install. The quality of reproduction varies according to the specification (and therefore the cost) of the scanner and the computer it is linked to.
- There are three main categories of scanner: flat bed (where the user has to place the image face down on a glass plate); hand-held (the user moves a hand-held device across the image); and sheet-feed (where a number of documents can be fed through automatically).

# How computers process sound

An increasingly wide range of applications require computers to process sound. Multimedia programs and computer games, whether stored on CD ROMS or accessed via the Internet, require audio playback devices; speech recognition systems entail the conversion of sound signals inputted via a microphone, and there is a trend towards people using their PCs as part of their home entertainment system, including the place where they record, store and play their music files. Sound processing technology is, relatively speaking, still in its infancy and there are a number of problems associated with it. Those users who download their MP3 files from file-sharing sites, store those files on their PCs and create their own CDs, complain that download time is slow and the resulting sound quality still doesn't match older, analogue technology. Most PCs that have the capacity to process sound do so via a sound card, the role of which is to:

- communicate with input/output peripheral devices such as microphones and speakers;
- convert analogue signals to digital data and vice versa;
- complete some essential processing tasks on the sound data;
- communicate with the CPU and, through this, secondary storage devices.

## How a sound card works

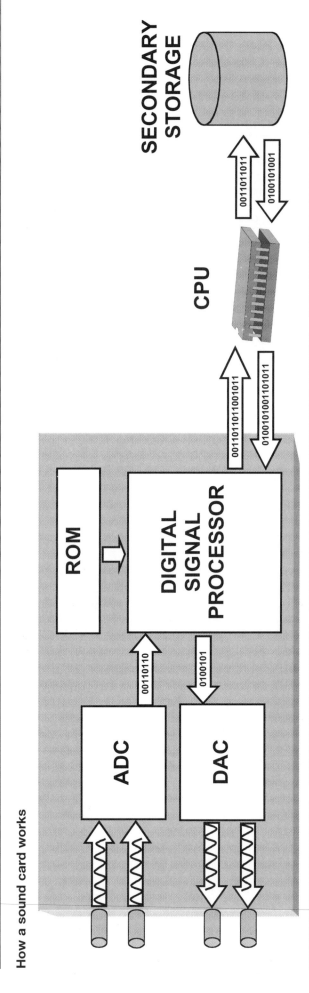

**SECONDARY STORAGE**

**CPU**

0011011011

0100101001

0011011011001011

0100101001101011

**ROM**

**DIGITAL SIGNAL PROCESSOR**

00110110

0100101

**ADC**

**DAC**

Sound is inputted via a microphone or another external source, such as a CD player. The sound signals are, at this stage, in analogue format. When the sound needs to be outputted, e.g. to a set of speakers, the signal must, once again, be in an analogue format.

Two chips, the ADC and the DAC are responsible for converting the incoming signal from analogue to digital format and converting the outgoing signal from digital to analogue format. The signal must be in a digital format for the computer to be able to process and store it.

A ROM chip (which may or may not be rewritable) contains the instructions that the Digital Signal Processor (DSP) needs to process the sound data. If the sound card uses wave table synthesis, the ROM chip will contain recorded samples of actual instruments playing different sounds. The DSP completes the processing work on the sound. One of its tasks may be to compress the data so that the resulting file will not be too large to be efficiently stored and retrieved.

In most modern sound cards the DSP is powerful enough to do all the processing required, thus freeing up the CPU to perform other tasks. The CPU is responsible for sending completed files to be stored and for retrieving files that are requested.

The final file may be saved in a number of different formats. The most commonly used are .wav, and .MP3. Another sound file sometimes referred to is a MIDI file. Such a file comprises a set of instructions for how an electronic instrument should play the stored piece of music.

# Portability

One of the properties of a data file is its portability, i.e. how easily it can be transferred from one application to another. There are many occasions when it is desirable for a user's data files to have a high degree of portability:

- a user may wish to transfer a file they have been working on at home to their PC at work;
- a student may wish to submit a piece of work to his teacher on disc or via an e-mail attachment;
- a user may wish to import a graphic produced in one application into a document produced in another;
- a user may need to update a document created in one version of an application on a later version of the same application.

Most users have encountered portability problems but, fortunately, there are a number of ways in which portability can be enhanced. These are set out below.

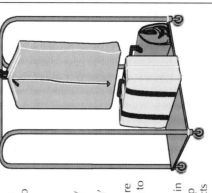

## Factors that create portability problems

**File types**
Applications oblige the user to save their data in specific file formats. These formats, usually identifiable by the three-letter extension that follows the file name, define the way in which the data is stored in the file. Some file formats will only open in certain applications. An attempt to open the said file in a different application will result in a collection of nonsense characters appearing on the screen.

**Hardware issues**
The problem may result from using a hardware device that is incompatible with another piece of hardware or the software/OS it is running. For example, the user may take some photographs with a digital camera and then find that there is no way of downloading the images to their PC.

**Version issues**
This is a common problem. A file may be created on an up-to-date version of an application but the user may need to edit it on an earlier version. The earlier version has problems recognising, and therefore opening, the file created in the later version.

## Factors that mitigate portability problems

**File types**
Though some proprietary file formats (i.e. formats that only open in a particular application) can cause portability problems, most applications allow the user to save a file in a range of formats, including formats that are easily transferable. Text based documents, for example, can be saved as text files (.txt). Such files will port to a wide range of applications, though the user may have to sacrifice some of the original formatting. Similarly data files can use the 'comma separated values' (.csv) file type to port data between different databases.

**Standards**
Whether they have been imposed by a regulatory body or have emerged through market domination, protocols and industry standards are increasingly in evidence. Whilst some companies will try to 'lock in' their users by making it difficult to move data in and out of its applications, it is more often the case that manufacturers conform to generally accepted models, protocols and standards, particularly where data communication is concerned. It is usually in the manufacturers' best interests to develop products that can connect with the products the user already has.

**Integration**
One way of improving portability is to use integrated packages (such as MS Office). Such packages make it easy for the user to import (and/or dynamically link) into one document objects created in another application.

# Integrating data

### Integrated packages

One way of dealing with the problem of moving data between different applications is to use an integrated package. An integrated package provides the user with a 'suite' of applications which perform different tasks while sharing many of the same features. Most domestic users, when they buy a computer, find an integrated package already installed, the most popular being Microsoft Office and Lotus SmartSuite. These integrated packages provide access to a select range of generic software, including a word-processing package, a spreadsheet program, a database, a graphics program and presentation software. The advantages and disadvantages of such an approach are set out below.

| ADVANTAGES OF AN INTEGRATED PACKAGE | DISADVANTAGES OF AN INTEGRATED PACKAGE |
|---|---|
| • The movement of data between applications is made easy. The separate modules are specifically designed to link with the other components in the package.<br>• It is generally less expensive to purchase the integrated package than to purchase all the components separately.<br>• There are often many common features (e.g. user interface design, keyboard shortcuts, etc.) which makes it easier for the user to learn how to use the different components. | • The user, almost inevitably, pays for functionality that they don't need and will never use.<br>• If a user purchases an integrated package, they are obliged to use all the modules. While some modules may be effective, others may be less so. The user may have been better advised to purchase those applications separately.<br>• Running an integrated package will require more memory resources than would be the case if the user only installed those applications he needed. |

### OLE/COM technology

One way in which data residing in different applications can be linked is using OLE/COM technology. OLE stands for Object Linking and Embedding and refers to the practice of inserting data stored in one application in another application. COM, Component Object Model, is the updated version of this. The difference between the two, which is not especially noticeable to the general use, has helped developers create programs that allow users to share resources in organisation-wide networks. OLE/COM technology maintains the distinction between linking and embedding. This is demonstrated below:

**LINKING**

**EMBEDDING**

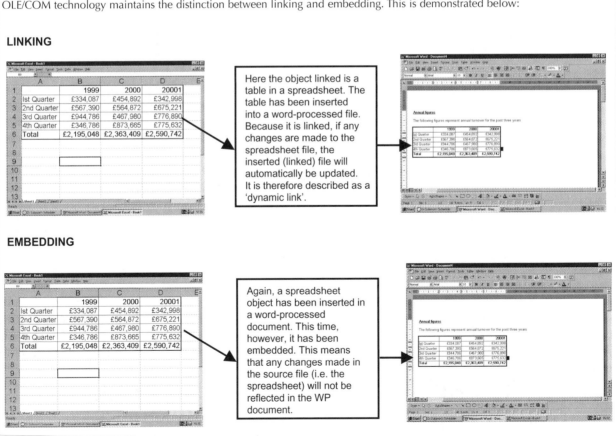

# File compression

Compression entails reducing the size of files so that they take up fewer memory resources. In the early days of computing, when disc space was both limited and expensive, the emphasis was on compacting data so that more of it could be held by the storage medium. The development of the Internet, with its need to send large files over long distances in the shortest possible time, has meant that compression technologies have shifted their focus from storage to transmission. Internet files and web pages for example, often contain memory-hungry multimedia components. Without effective compression techniques these files, already slow to arrive in some cases, would have interminable transmission times. Compression techniques fall into two categories: 'lossless' and 'lossy'.

## Lossless compression

Both lossless and lossy compression techniques use algorithms – programs comprising a set of step-by-step instructions – to convert a file into a smaller version of itself. Lossless compression, as its name suggests, undertakes this process without losing any of the original data. There are a number of different lossless algorithms that may be used, many of which are based on a technique devised by Lempel and Ziv in 1977 and called LZ77. The LZ77 algorithm is based on the principle of redundancy. It searches for data that is repeated in a file (e.g. the word 'the' in a document file) and finds a way of (a) storing the first instance of that data and (b) providing a more compacted code for storing future instances of that data. Below is an example based on the LZ78 algorithm.

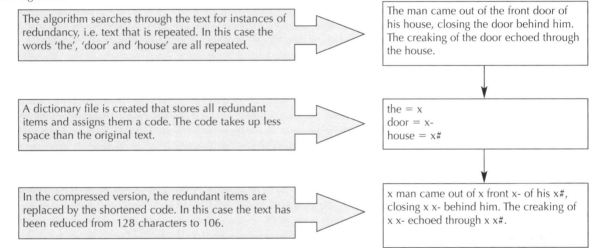

The algorithm searches through the text for instances of redundancy, i.e. text that is repeated. In this case the words 'the', 'door' and 'house' are all repeated.

> The man came out of the front door of his house, closing the door behind him. The creaking of the door echoed through the house.

A dictionary file is created that stores all redundant items and assigns them a code. The code takes up less space than the original text.

> the = x
> door = x-
> house = x#

In the compressed version, the redundant items are replaced by the shortened code. In this case the text has been reduced from 128 characters to 106.

> x man came out of x front x- of his x#, closing x x- behind him. The creaking of x x- echoed through x x#.

Lossless compression is particularly suited to text based files and is used in popular utilities programs like WinZip and PKZIP. It has also been used by modem manufacturers (in a version known as V.42bis) to speed up data transmission. It is valuable for compressing files where any loss of data would be problematic, e.g. program files.

## Lossy compression

Lossy compression works on the principle that the human senses do not necessarily need every item of data in order to perceive a sound or an image as complete. It is a technique that entails storing/transmitting only the minimum data required. Each lossy algorithm is oriented to the type of file it is designed to compress. The Motion Picture Experts Group have developed standards for compression that are widely used. The MPEG-1 standard is used to compress video and audio files. It is particularly well known in its MP3 format (which is a shortened version of MPEG-1 Level III) as a technique for compressing music files so that they can be transmitted via the Internet and played on portable devices. It works on the principle of removing sound data that the human ear would be unable to detect and looking for redundancies. Lossy compression works well with multimedia files but is not suitable for any files where data integrity is critical. An example of how lossy compression might be used with a moving image is shown below:

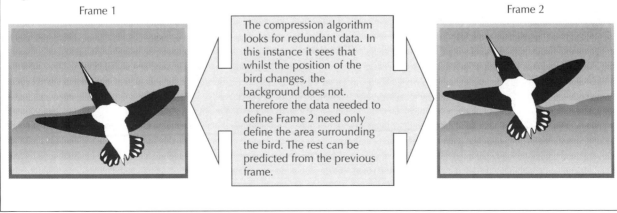

Frame 1

The compression algorithm looks for redundant data. In this instance it sees that whilst the position of the bird changes, the background does not. Therefore the data needed to define Frame 2 need only define the area surrounding the bird. The rest can be predicted from the previous frame.

Frame 2

# Analogue versus digital transmission

### What is the difference between analogue and digital?

| ANALOGUE | DIGITAL |
|---|---|
| 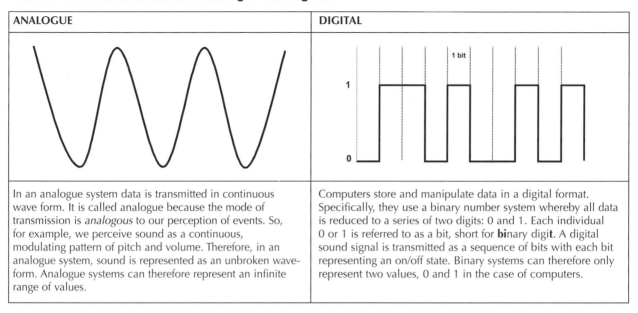 | |
| In an analogue system data is transmitted in continuous wave form. It is called analogue because the mode of transmission is *analogous* to our perception of events. So, for example, we perceive sound as a continuous, modulating pattern of pitch and volume. Therefore, in an analogue system, sound is represented as an unbroken wave-form. Analogue systems can therefore represent an infinite range of values. | Computers store and manipulate data in a digital format. Specifically, they use a binary number system whereby all data is reduced to a series of two digits: 0 and 1. Each individual 0 or 1 is referred to as a bit, short for **bi**nary dig**it**. A digital sound signal is transmitted as a sequence of bits with each bit representing an on/off state. Binary systems can therefore only represent two values, 0 and 1 in the case of computers. |

### Interfacing between analogue and digital systems

Recording, communication and transmission devices are increasingly designed to operate in digital mode. This means that when such devices need to interface with a computerised system it is a straightforward matter, i.e. a digital-to-digital connection. There are still occasions, however, when computers need to interface with analogue systems. In such cases there has to be a process whereby signals are converted from analogue to digital or vice versa. An example of this process is shown below.

A user speaks into a microphone, when using a voice input system for example. The sound is converted into analogue electrical waves. These are transmitted to the computer.

Before such signals can be processed by the CPU they have to be converted to digital signals. This is achieved via a device called an analogue–digital converter (ADC)

The signal, which now comprises a set of values in digital format is ready to be processed by the CPU.

The ADC samples the analogue signal at set frequencies. The precision of the conversion will depend on how often the signal is sampled and how sensitive the ADC is.

VOLTAGE

TIME

001001011100101000101111010101010101000101010100101010

# Connecting peripheral devices

A computer will need to interface with a wide range of peripherals, i.e. input and output devices that can send data to and receive data from the CPU. At the moment, this is largely achieved through the use of external ports. This involves cable connections from the peripheral device plugging into sockets that are usually located on the rear face of the computer. There are different types of connection that can be used and these are set out below. It should be noted that, while cable connections are still the norm, there is a gradual move towards peripherals communicating in a wireless mode.

---

**SERIAL PORTS**

Serial connector

Serial ports – also known as COM ports – are external ports that attach directly to the computer's motherboard. They transmit data one bit at a time, usually via a round, 9-pin interface. One line is for grounding the connection, the others transfer data signals between the Data Terminal Equipment, i.e. the computer, and the Data Communications Equipment, i.e. the peripheral device. Serial connectors are relatively slow at transmitting data and some have limitations on the length of cabling allowed, though these limitations are not as stringent as they are for parallel ports. Serial ports tend to be used for devices where the volume of data to be transmitted is small, e.g. a mouse, a keyboard, an external modem, etc.

---

**PARALLEL PORTS**

Parallel connector

Unlike serial ports which transmit one bit at a time, parallel ports transmit eight bits (i.e. one byte) of data along parallel wires. This means that in the same time it would take a serial port to transmit the letter 'C', the parallel port could have transmitted the word COMPUTER. On most domestic systems, the parallel port is used to connect the printer. It is well suited to this purpose because of its ability to transmit data quickly. A parallel port comprises 25 lines, 8 of which are used for grounding and 17 for the transmission of data. The transmission lines are divided into three further categories: control, status and data. The control lines are used to establish and maintain a connection between the two components; the status lines are used to send messages, for example when the printer needs to indicate that it is out of paper; the data lines transmit the data that tells the printer what needs to be printed. Parallel ports are generally limited in terms of cabling distance and number of connected devices.

---

**USB**

USB connector

At the time of writing the USB (Universal Serial Bus) is the connection device that is making other approaches redundant. USBs first appeared on computers in the mid-1990s and are now found on all new computers. The USB cable contains just four lines. One line sends electrical power to the device, a second acts as a grounding line, the third and fourth lines – referred to as D+ and D- – are used to transmit data and commands. USBs have a fast transmission rate but their main advantage is that they can be used to connect large numbers of peripheral devices. Hubs may be connected to the ports in the back of the computer and these can be used to connect further devices. Inside the computer a USB controller acts as an interface between the devices and the computer's software, including device drivers. USBs can be used for almost every type of computer peripheral and so have the potential to become an industry standard. Another – similar – approach is the FireWire connector. Also with fast transmission speeds – in may cases faster than USBs – and also able to connect multiple devices, FireWire is in competition with USB to become the standard connection mode for all peripheral devices.

---

**SCSI**

SCSI connector

SCSI stands for Small Computer System Interface, often referred to as 'scuzzy'. The SCSI is a quick and flexible way for a computer to connect to a wide range of peripherals. A SCSI can generally connect up to seven devices at once. Inside the computer the SCSI controller identifies the devices that it is communicating with and provides an interface between that device and the CPU. Each device has an ID number and, when more than one device needs to transmit or receive at the same time, the ID number is used to establish a priority order. The cabling comprises 50 lines, some of which are used to send and receive data and commands, the rest of which are used to manage the connections with the various devices. SCSIs are often found in networked environments or with servers that have to connect multiple hard drives as well as other peripherals. There are, however, different varieties of SCSIs, some of which are incompatible with others. This lack of a single standard limits its general use.

# Input devices: 1

| | HOW IT WORKS | EXAMPLES OF APPLICATIONS | STRENGTHS AND LIMITATIONS |
|---|---|---|---|
| **Bar code reader** | • Uses a laser to read the light reflected from an arrangement of lines (or bars) of different widths.<br>• The lines represent a number which represents information about the product. This information is stored in a database. | • Product sales in the retail trade<br>• Loan systems in libraries<br>• Package tracking in delivery firms<br>• Stock management in warehouses<br>• Some identification cards | ✓ Bar code readers are fast and accurate when dealing with product identification.<br>✓ The data can be scanned in a fraction of the time it would take to key it in.<br>✗ They are limited to 'fixed' data, i.e. details cannot be changed. |
| **Digital camera** | • The pattern of light associated with the image is stored digitally rather than on film.<br>• The image, now stored in a standardised format, can be imported into a range of different applications and modified to suit the user's needs. | • Everyday personal use, e.g. weddings, holidays, etc.<br>• For engineers to communicate to clients the progress of a project<br>• For estate agents to update websites using digitally captured images<br>• Speed cameras and number plate recognition | ✓ The image can be used flexibly in a wide range of applications.<br>✓ It can be modified using specially designed applications.<br>✓ It can be attached as a file to an e-mail.<br>✗ Image files can be 'memory-heavy'.<br>✗ Quality of output will depend on quality of printer and paper. |
| **Keyboard** | • The keyboard translates key selections into digital format text/number values.<br>• It also contains a number of 'function' keys which allow the user to send instructions to the computers, e.g. 'delete', 'scroll down'. | • To enter data that must be copied from a document or audio source<br>• To input text directly into the computer<br>• To send instructions and commands to computer-based control systems | ✓ Keyboards remain the most common method of inputting text-based data.<br>✗ Transcription errors are common.<br>✗ Data entry is time-consuming and dependent on typing skills.<br>✗ They can contribute to repetitive strain injury if overused. |
| **Magnetic ink character recognition (MICR)** | • The data is printed in the form of specially designed characters. The ink used to print these characters contains a magnetic substance.<br>• This can then be read by an appropriately sensitive input device. Software then translates the patterns into text/numerical values. | • Banks use this approach to process cheques. Cheques are designed to have key data (branch details, account number) printed in magnetic ink across the bottom. This can then be read in using the input device and the data processed by the bank's computers. | ✓ For the processing of cheques, MICR is quick and highly efficient.<br>✓ Unlike bar codes, humans as well as machines can make sense of the data.<br>✓ It is resistant to forgery.<br>✗ It only has limited applications and, with the decline of cheques as a means of payment, its use is in decline. |
| **Magnetic strips** | • A magnetic strip – usually placed on a plastic card – contains encoded data about the card's user.<br>• When the card is swiped through a sensitive reader it is translated into data which can be processed by a computer. | • To store personal details on debit and credit cards, identification cards, loyalty cards, etc.<br>• To store data on phone cards, travel tickets, etc. | ✓ Personal cards are increasingly used for financial transactions and the magnetic strips help to speed up these transactions.<br>✗ They can be forged and are susceptible to damage.<br>✗ There is a trend to replace magnetic strips with embedded microchips.<br>✗ Magnetic data can fade/be deleted. |
| **Mouse** | • The mouse is a flexible input device which allows the user to communicate a wide range of commands to the computer.<br>• The mouse ball sends positional information to the computer which is then translated into the movements of a pointer on the screen.<br>• Other information is sent via clicking of buttons. | • For the user to communicate with a graphical user interface<br>• To select icons and, through them, activate commands<br>• To issue commands to the computer directly (e.g. 'scroll down')<br>• To allow the user to select from a range of menu items and activate specified commands | ✓ With the advent of graphical user interfaces, a means of pointing to various places on the screen became necessary. The mouse fulfils this function well.<br>✓ There are constant developments in the functionality of these devices and their use is likely to continue for some time.<br>✗ Some users dislike having to shift constantly from keyboard to mouse and will tend therefore to use keyboard short-cuts.<br>✗ Hand-to-eye coordination is an issue for some users. |

# Input devices: 2

| | HOW IT WORKS | EXAMPLES OF APPLICATIONS | STRENGTHS AND LIMITATIONS |
|---|---|---|---|
| **Optical character recognition (OCR)** | • A scanner device reads the reflected light from characters on a page. These may have been typed or hand-written.<br>• The scanner creates an image of the character. Software then tries to match it against a 'library' of similar character shapes.<br>• When a match is found, it inputs the appropriate character. | • This method is used to input large blocks of text held in 'hard copy' format.<br>• It is also used to input data captured on forms. Often these forms require the person filling it in to write each character in a box. This is because OCR systems need to be able to read each character individually. An example of this is the passport application form. | ✓ This method can speed up an otherwise lengthy process of keying in.<br>✗ It often misreads letters, and documents captured in this way almost always have to be proof-read afterwards.<br>✗ For capturing hand-written text, the cursive style must be clear and the document must be 'clean', i.e. not contain any marks or smudges that could be interpreted as characters. |
| **Optical mark recognition (OMR)** | • This method works on the same principle as OCR but, instead of trying to interpret characters, OMR systems read marks made at specified points on a specially designed form.<br>• These marks equate to pre-set values and, once read, can be sent for processing. | • The most popular application of this method is the filling in of National Lottery forms.<br>• It is also used for examination papers where multiple choice questions are used and for submitting grades to examination boards.<br>• School registers | ✓ Avoids need for file transfer.<br>✓ This can be an extremely quick way of entering large amounts of data.<br>✗ The input forms necessarily limit the range of permissible responses.<br>✗ Incorrect marking of the sheet will lead to the data being rejected. |
| **Sensors** | • Sensors are devices which read changes in the environment around them.<br>• There are a wide range of sensors which can detect changes in: light, air pressure, temperature, humidity, speed, etc. | • Sensors are frequently used in control systems. They can be used to measure the temperature of a room. This input can then be used to trigger a control system which adjusts the heating.<br>• Other examples include: humidity sensors in an art gallery and movement sensors in a security system. | ✓ Sensors are a necessary element of any control system and can also be used for data logging.<br>✓ Data can be captured cheaply and with little human effort.<br>✗ They are limited in the type of data they can collect.<br>✗ They can 'misread' environmental changes, e.g. a car alarm activated by a strong gust of wind. |
| **Touch screens** | • Values are associated with different positions on a VDU via a 'grid' of infrared beams across the front of the screen.<br>• When the user touches a particular part of the screen, the associated value is sent to be processed. | • Touch screens are used by museums and galleries to communicate information.<br>• They can also be used by small children and people whose disabilities might prevent them from using other input devices.<br>• They are increasingly common in places where customers place orders, e.g. fast food outlets. | ✓ They are user-friendly. Even people who might be intimidated by computers feel comfortable using these devices.<br>✗ They are limited as input devices because only a limited number of values can be displayed at any one time. |
| **Voice recognition systems** | • The data is inputted in audio form, either directly, via a microphone, or indirectly, via an audio tape.<br>• Software analyses the inputted sound and matches it against a library of sounds.<br>• When a match is found the value is sent for processing. | • A voice recognition system allows users to dictate text straight into the computer. The resulting text can then be edited using standard word-processing applications.<br>• It has also been used in control systems, e.g. instructions to robots in the manufacturing industry.<br>• It is sometimes used in security systems. | ✓ A user can speak much more quickly than even the most skilled of typists can type.<br>✗ Interpreting human language is a complex process because meaning can be ambiguous. Software cannot, as yet, interpret meaning.<br>✗ The human voice is not uniform: we speak in different styles and different accents. Voice recognition software has to be 'trained' to recognise the voice patterns of individual users. This can take a long time. |

# Printers: 1

## Different types of printers

| TYPE | HOW THEY WORK | COMMENT |
|---|---|---|
| **Dot matrix** | 1  A printhead, consisting of a number of pins, moves back and forth on a cartridge.<br>2  Each pin – there are usually 9 or 24 – is mounted on a spring. On the head of the pin is a magnet. Above each pinhead is a small electromagnet.<br>3  The printer's microprocessor analyses the information from the computer and translates the instructions into a series of electrical impulses.<br>4  These signals are sent to the electromagnets, the effect of which is to push selected pins down towards where the paper is being fed through.<br>5  Between the printhead is an ink ribbon. The 'firing' pin heads therefore impress a series of ink dots on to the page.<br>6  These dots constitute the text/graphic being printed. | Dot matrix – or impact – printers were amongst the first on the market for home and small office use. They are relatively cheap and fairly reliable. However, the print quality is poor and they are only suitable for producing draft material where print quality is not an issue. They are also the slowest and noisiest of the printers. As the price of ink-jet printers has decreased, dot matrix printers have virtually disappeared from the market. |
| **Ink-jet** | 1  A controller receives information from the computer about what needs to be printed. This is translated into a series of instructions that are sent to the various elements of the printer.<br>2  The printhead, which moves back and forth across the pages, contains a series of nozzles. The number of nozzles will affect the print quality. A black and white printer might have 50, a colour printer up to 600.<br>3  Above the printhead is an ink cartridge, either a single one with black ink or a set of 3–6 different coloured ones for colour printing. Each nozzle takes ink from the cartridge, and heats it to produce a small bubble of ink. The bubble pushes a droplet of ink out of the nozzle and on to the paper. | Ink-jet printers are relatively cheap, reliable and can produce good quality prints. The quality of ink-jet printing has improved steadily over the past few years. The newer, colour versions are, at the moment, good, economical alternatives to expensive colour laser jets. They are slower than laser printers and they cope less well with bulk printing, but they are still cost-effective solutions for homes and small offices. |
| **Laser** | 1  The printer's processors prepare the received data and then send a series of instructions to the printhead.<br>2  The printhead contains a laser which emits a beam of light. A spinning multi-faced mirror directs the beams in a horizontal line across a rotating drum.<br>3  The drum is covered with a zinc-oxide-based film whose electrical properties change when it is hit by light.<br>4  The laser is switched on and off in a designated pattern, thus creating an equivalent pattern of positively or negatively charged dots on the drum.<br>5  On its rotation the charged area of the drum then picks up black powder from a toner cartridge, the black powder being attracted by the electrical charge.<br>6  The arrangement of toner is then deposited on to the paper as it passes by the drum. The paper passes through a 'fusing system'. This uses heat and pressure to bind the toner to the paper.<br>7  The drum then passes a thin wire, the corona wire, which emits a strong positive charge. The drum is thus prepared to receive another pattern of charged dots via the laser. | Laser printer are fast, reliable devices that can produce high-quality output. They have come down in price over the past few years and are therefore within the range of small businesses and home workers. They are quiet and can handle bulk printing. They are more expensive than ink-jets and the differential is more pronounced when colour printers are concerned. The replacement of toner cartridges is a regular, costly expense that needs to be taken into account. |

# Printers: 2

## Plotters

Plotters are specialised output devices that are used when precise, high-definition copies are needed and when the documents in question are larger than usual (typically A1 or larger). They are used by commercial art/design businesses, map-makers, architects, engineers, etc. There are different types of plotters, including:

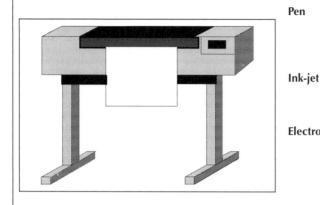

| | |
|---|---|
| **Pen** | These work by moving a pen across drafting paper. They are the least expensive plotter device but they are slow and there are some functions (e.g. detailed shading) that they cannot perform. They can also be used to cut rough film for large lettering and banners. |
| **Ink-jet** | These use a similar technology to a standard ink-jet printer, depositing a pattern of ink droplets via nozzles. They are quiet and can produce more detailed output than pen plotters. |
| **Electrostatic** | These create a pattern of electrostatic charges on specially treated paper. The paper is then run through a developer and the image is produced. Such devices produce very high resolution outputs and are faster than ink-jet/pen based devices. They do, however, use expensive chemicals. |

## Selecting a printer

*When selecting a printer the following criteria may be used:*

| | |
|---|---|
| **Quality of output** | Different printers create outputs of differing quality. If it is important to have a product that is clearly defined and professional looking, then a printer capable of producing such output will be needed. The quality of output is related to the printer's 'resolution'. This is measured in dots per inch (dpi). |
| **Bulk printing capacity** | Some printers, e.g. those used for domestic purposes, will only be required to produce one or two documents at a time. Others, based in large offices, may need to produce multiple runs more or less constantly. |
| **Cost** | Cost is always a criteria when selecting a hardware device. Printers can now be purchased quite cheaply, but such printers will not be able to produce professional standard output, nor will they be able to manage long, 'memory-heavy' print runs. |
| **Speed** | In a business where time is a critical factor, it will be important for the printer to be able to process incoming data and produce the output quickly and efficiently. |

## How a printer communicates with the CPU

When a software application produces a document for printing, it must be able to communicate instructions to the printer in a format that the printer understands. This is achieved via a printer 'driver', a piece of software that acts as a communication interface between computer and printer.

→

The instructions to the printer can be transmitted in a variety of ways. If the printer is located close to the computer, the parallel port is usually used. Transmission may also take place via a network connection, or in some offices, via wireless transmission.

→

If the printer is connected to a network, it will be necessary to have a queuing system so that the printer isn't swamped with requests. This is achieved via a technique called 'spooling': data is saved to a disc location where it is stored and placed in a 'job queue' until the printer is free. At this stage some jobs may be prioritised.

A CPU can process data much faster than a printer. So that the CPU doesn't have to 'wait' for the printer, a technique called buffering is used. Data needed for the print job is sent to a 'buffer' memory until the printer is ready to process it. This memory store may be located in the printer or in the computer.

→

A printer has to translate instructions from the computer into commands that can be sent to its different working parts. Many printers use a technique called 'Page Description Language', a code that specifies what the printer will need to do to create the appropriate marks on the page.

→

Most printers have the capacity to send 'feedback' messages to the computer, e.g. to indicate when the paper supply has run out. The message is sent back to the driver which, in turn, generates an on-screen error message to inform the user of the problem.

# Visual display units

The visual display unit (VDU) – or monitor – is a central feature of any computer set-up. It is the device via which users see the results of their interactions with the software applications. There are two main technologies used in VDUs, Cathode Ray Tube (CRT) and Liquid Crystal Display (LCD).

## CRT monitors

The first step in producing an image on a CRT monitor's screen is for a special adaptor to convert the computer's digital signal to an analogue signal, using a digital-to-analogue converter (DAC). The adaptor receives information in the form of different voltage levels for each of the three primary colours (red, blue and green). This information will determine the colour of each pixel (a pixel is an addressable picture unit). Adaptors have different memory capacities and this will determine how much information can be used to define the pixel's colours.

The adaptor sends the converted information to three electron guns located at the rear of the monitor, one for each of the three primary colours. The gun emits a stream of electrons, the intensity of which is determined by the signal sent by the adaptor.

On the inside of the screen is a coating of phosphor. Three different phosphors are used, one for each of the three primary colours. The stronger the stream of electrons that strikes the phosphor, the brighter the phosphor will glow. The combination of different intensities of the three primary colours will produce a full range of colours.

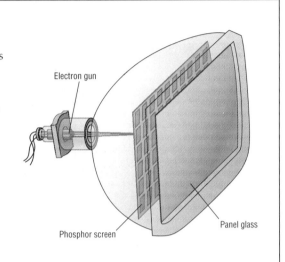

## LCD monitors

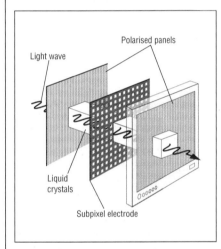

An LCD monitor is made up of multiple layers, with each layer performing an important function.

Light, emitted from a constant light source, is first passed through a polarised filter that only allows through light waves that are vibrating more or less horizontally.

These light waves then pass through a layer of liquid crystal cells. These cells are arranged in a matrix which relates to the pattern of pixels on the screen. The liquid crystals contain molecules that will change their shape according to how much electrical charge is applied to them. The light then travels along the path defined by the crystals' shape.

The light then passes through one of three filters, one for each of the three primary colours.

The light then passes through a second polarised filter, this time one that only allows through light waves that are vibrating more or less vertically. Depending on what has happened to the light as it passed through the liquid crystals, differing intensities of red/green/blue light will now emerge. The combination will create a pixel of a certain colour.

## Evaluating different monitors

| CRT monitors | LCD monitors |
|---|---|
| • CRT monitors are the older technology and have one main disadvantage, that of size. Their 'depth' requirement, i.e. the distance between the screen and the rear of the cathode ray tube, means that they take up a lot of desk space. The larger the screen, the more this is the case. This requirement means that they cannot easily be used for smaller, portable devices.<br>• Another significant disadvantage is that they require more power to run and emit small quantities of electromagnetic radiation. There can also be problems regarding heat generation.<br>• At the moment they tend to have a price advantage over LCD monitors, but, given present trends, this is not likely to last. The current trend is towards LCD desk-top monitors.<br>• They also have, at present, an advantage regarding quality of resolution and colours. This might not be important to someone performing basic computing tasks, but it will be critical to someone like a professional graphic artist. | • LCD monitors are the emerging technology and are likely to dominate the market in the coming years. They are light, adaptable, take up less space, and can be used for small portable devices like digital cameras, palm tops, etc.<br>• They do not require as much energy as CRT monitors and so can be used on battery-run portable devices.<br>• There are, however, some technical shortcomings with LCD technology. For example, as the light source is projected perpendicular to each pixel, the screen generally has to be viewed face on. The 'refresh' time is also slower than a CRT's. This is why mouse movements on an LCD monitor often show signs of 'streaking', i.e. leaving an after-image as they move.<br>• At the moment, LCD manufacturers are having difficulties maintaining image quality at a competitive price for larger screens. |

# Secondary storage

Secondary storage devices are needed to store and transfer software and data files. There are many such devices on the market and this is an area of fast-changing technology. There is a constant drive to increase the capacity of storage media while maintaining security of storage and keeping costs low. One reason for this is because applications are becoming more complex and users increasingly wish to store memory-heavy items such as sound/video files. In addition to capacity, the following criteria should be taken into account when choosing a storage medium: speed of transfer, speed of access, re-usability, cost, portability, ease of use and vulnerability to corruption.

## Floppy disc

**Description** Flexible plastic disc held in a hard plastic case. The disc is coated with a magnetic film which is formatted into tracks and sectors. It is here that the data is stored. Floppy discs can usually store 1.4Mb of data.
**Evaluation** Floppy discs are highly portable and most PCs can accommodate them. They can be over-written and so reused, though this leads to disc corruption in time. Their small capacity, slow transfer speed and liability to corruption make them suitable only for non-critical transfer/storage of small files.

## Compact disc

**Description** CDs are polycarbonate discs with a fine coating of aluminium. They have data written on to them by a powerful laser that 'burns' a pattern of 'pits' on to the surface. Another laser then reads this pattern and converts it into a sequence of binary digits. Some CDs can only have data read from them (ROM) but, increasingly, writable and rewritable CDs are being used.
**Evaluation** CDs have high storage capacity, are relatively cheap and fairly robust. They are often used for storing application software that will be sold to users, e.g. computer games. Writable and rewritable CDs are increasingly being used to store user-created data.

## Hard drive

**Description** Hard drives usually consist of a series of metal discs, mounted on a spindle. They each have a read/write head which accesses the magnetically stored data. The discs rotate continuously while the computer is in operation.
**Evaluation** The standard means of storing data in a PC, hard drives provide good capacity, are relatively robust and offer fast access times. They can, however, crash and so back-up systems are required. In a network this usually takes the form of a RAID system (see page 123 for more information about this).

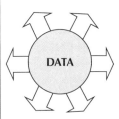

DATA

## Magneto–optical disc

**Description** Combined magnetic/optical technology. The surface of a disc is coated with a special alloy which can only be written to when heated to a certain temperature. A laser heats up a spot on the disc which can then be written to using a magnetic head. Data is read using a standard laser, in the same way as with a compact disc.
**Evaluation** This is a developing technology which may supersede current approaches. The discs can be reused without significant loss of quality, they cannot have their data wiped by electromagnetic fields, and they have high capacity. At the moment they are still an expensive medium, though they are a popular medium for long-term storage.

## Digital tape

**Description** Digital Audio Tape works by storing data on Mylar film coated with iron oxide. Sections of the tape are magnetised to represent bits. The tape is held in a plastic cassette and played through a device which may be externally or internally located. Digital Linear Tape is a more expensive, more advanced version of this technology. It has greater capacity and faster access time.
**Evaluation** Tape storage uses 'sequential access' which means that access to data can be slow (the whole tape must be played, up to the point where the required data is stored). However, tape has a high storage capacity and is cheap. It is therefore a popular back-up medium.

## Zip drive

**Description** Plastic container encases a single hard drive of the same diameter as a floppy disc. This stores data in the same way that a standard hard drive does. Zip drive cassettes are either used with a drive located in the computer or via a hand-held device which is plugged into the parallel port. They can store between 100 and 250 Mb of data.
**Evaluation** Good capacity, portability and reasonably fast transfer rates make zip drives a good alternative to floppy discs for the transfer of data. Unfortunately, many PCs do not have built-in zip drives and using the hand-held devices can be cumbersome. They are good for individual back-up but are rarely used for network back-up systems.

# The central processing unit (CPU)

## What is the CPU?

The central processing unit (CPU) is at the heart of the computer. It is usually contained on a single chip called a microprocessor which, in turn, is contained within a cartridge that plugs into the computer's motherboard. It is, in effect, the control centre of the computer. All other components serve the CPU:

- Every time a key is depressed on the keyboard or a mouse button is clicked, a signal is sent to the CPU. The CPU must translate this instruction into binary code and then execute it. What the computer does to process the instruction will depend on what software is being run at the time.
- The hard drive is where the software is stored. The software is, in essence, a set of instructions for the CPU to follow. When the computer runs this program, the CPU checks the hard drive for the required instructions and loads them into the main memory.
- The main memory, or RAM, is what the CPU uses as a temporary store for all the software instructions. The more RAM a computer has, the less time the CPU will have to spend waiting for instructions. This will have the effect of speeding up the performance of the computer.

The job of the CPU is to manipulate data in binary form. It has to **fetch** the instructions it requires from the appropriate source, **decode** the instructions into binary code, **execute** the commands it has been given and **store** the results in an appropriate memory location. These actions are completed in a fraction of a second so that when you press the A key on your keyboard the letter A appears on your screen more or less instantaneously.

The speed of the microprocessor – which is a key indicator of how quickly a computer will perform its functions – is measured in cycles per second. This equates to the number of cycles a processor completes within the span of one 'tick' of the computer's internal clock. The first processors created for PCs, the Intel 8088 series, operated at a speed of 4.7 MHz (i.e. 4.7 million cycles per second). At the time of writing the latest Pentium 4 processors offer speeds of up to 1,700 MHz (or 1.7 Giga Hertz). Industry specialists agree that these speeds will increase still further in the future.

## The components of the CPU

The **control unit** coordinates all the CPU's activities. It send instructions for decoding, sends the data that needs processing to the ALU and FPU and ensures that the processed data is stored in appropriate memory registers.

The **Arithmetic and Logic Unit (ALU)** completes mathematical and Boolean logic (i.e. true/false) processes. It can only handle binary digits that represent whole numbers.

The **Data Cache Unit (DCU)** temporarily stores data. It holds it in a 'queue' until the necessary processing resources are available.

The **Floating Point Maths Unit (FPU)** deals with those calculations that involve decimal points and fractions. If the ALU comes across such a calculation it passes it to the FPU.

**Registers** are small, dynamic memory stores that are located at various points around the processor. They temporarily hold data while it is 'waiting' between processes.

The **Instruction Cache** is a dynamic, temporary memory store that holds instructions in a queue until they are required by the control unit. These instructions might come from the CPU's own instruction set or from software sources.

The **Prefetch Unit** checks all incoming data and then looks in the instructions cache to find out what should be done with it. It then passes along the instructions together with an address showing where the data can be found.

The **decode unit** takes the instructions from the software and from external commands and translates them from program language or machine code into binary digits that can be processed.

The **Instruction Set** is the CPU's own built-in set of instructions. It tells it how to respond to external commands and how to manage all the tasks it performs.

# Different types of computer memory

Memory, in computer terms, is any area where data is stored on a semiconductor chip. A computer uses different categories of memories, with different categories fulfilling different functions.

**Read Only Memory (ROM)** is non-volatile, i.e. it consists of a combination of circuit states (0's and 1's) that are fixed and therefore not lost when the computer is switched off. ROM is where the computer stores data and instructions that do not change, e.g. the instructions that control the computer's start-up system.

**Programmable Read Only Memory (PROM)** is used when the stored instructions may need to be customised, meaning, therefore, that the chips cannot be mass produced. Once the chip has been programmed it behaves like any other ROM chip, i.e. it does not change.

**Erasable Programmable Read Only Memory (EPROM)** is a programmable memory chip that can be changed using a PROM programmer or special software application. This might be used in a CAM system where the manufacturer has to regularly update a fixed set of instructions for an industrial robot.

**Random Access Memory (RAM)** is a volatile store of data, i.e. when the computer is switched off it disappears. It is used to store data and programs that the user needs, e.g. a spreadsheet application and the particular file the user is working on. It is therefore dynamic, its content changing as the needs of the user change. It takes its name from the way that the CPU accesses the data that it holds, i.e. in a direct, non-sequential manner. There are a number of different types of RAM that might be found in a computer.

**Dynamic RAM (DRAM)** is so called because the data it contains is refreshed at regular intervals. There are several types of DRAM (e.g. SDRAM) available, with varying level of performance.

**Static RAM (SRAM)** does not need to be continuously refreshed in the same way as DRAM. This gives it increased speed and stability but means that it costs more. It is used for cache memory.

**Printer memory** is usually referred to as the printer buffer. This temporarily holds data sent for printing so that the CPU can continue processing without having to 'wait' for the printer.

**Video RAM** is a memory store that is used specifically for the computer display. It is usually contained on a video/graphics card though it might be built into the motherboard.

**Extended Data Out RAM (EDO RAM)** increases the speed of data transfer by allowing the CPU to request a second piece of data as soon as the first has been sent on its way.

## Cache memory

Cache (pronounced 'cash') memory is a specific type of Random Access Memory that is used to speed up processing. There are usually two cache memories in a PC, Level 1 (L1) and Level 2 (L2). They act as holding bays and sit between the CPU and the main memory. They hold the most frequently accessed data so that it can be retrieved more quickly by the CPU, thus improving processing speeds. The primary cache (L1) is usually a memory chip that is built into the CPU whereas the secondary cache (L2) is located on a separate chip, located between the CPU and the main memory. When the CPU needs a piece of data it searches first the primary cache and then the secondary cache before going to the main memory. Cache systems use SRAM which is more expensive than DRAM but more suitable for this purpose.

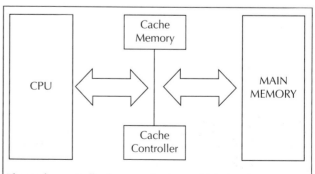

The cache controller keeps a check on which data is most frequently accessed. It then determines which data will be held in the cache memory. The CPU then has 'less far to go' to retrieve the data that is most likely to be in demand.

# Application software

## Different types of application software

Applications are software programs that are designed to perform a range of related tasks. Application software falls into three main categories:

| | |
|---|---|
| **Generic/general purpose software** | This category includes popular packages that allow users to process text, create spreadsheets, build databases, manipulate graphics, create slideshows, etc. These applications can be used by a wide range of businesses as well as by domestic users. They are flexible and can be put to a variety of uses, from the commonplace (writing a homework assignment) to the highly professional (producing a legal document). |
| **Specific task software** | Software in this category is not as flexible as generic software. It is designed to perform a specific task and may only be useful to people who are working in a particular field. For example, accounting programs share many characteristics with standard spreadsheet programs, but they are too specialised to be used by the general user. They are aimed at accountants and others working in the financial sector. |
| **Bespoke software** | Bespoke software has been custom-made to fulfil a client's specifications. The application will only be of use to the individual/client who has had it designed. A laboratory, for example, may engage a software vendor to produce a program that will analyse scientific data in a very particular way. |

Whatever the prime function of the software, there are some features that are desirable in all packages. These are set out below.

## Desirable features of software packages

### Help files

Good software will provide the user with a comprehensive set of help files. These files should cover all queries a user – even an inexperienced one – is likely to have. They should be easy to search and should set out their responses in a clear, accessible format.

### Search facilities

The user should be able to search through files to find a particular item of information. The search process should not be over-complex and should allow for a range of different criteria to be used, e.g. using Boolean operators such as 'and', 'or', 'not', etc.

### Editing facilities

The software should allow the user to make changes to existing files, to add new information, amend existing data and delete unwanted data. Standard cut/copy/paste operations are useful editing tools that can be used in a variety of contexts.

### Upgrade paths

If the software is a newer version of an existing software package, it should allow the user to upgrade existing files without any loss of data. Upgrade releases should be managed so that they cause the user the minimum of disruption.

**Desirable features of software**

### Macro capabilities

A macro is a short program that the user creates. It consists of a set of coded instructions that automate an action or procedure. The macro can then be activated when a keyboard shortcut is pressed or an icon is clicked on.

### Data portability

There are often problems when data has to be transferred from one application to another. A good application will provide facilities to transfer data to other programs, without the user having to go through a complicated process.

### Report generators

A report is a printed summary of information. There are a range of applications that need to be able to generate customised reports, e.g. databases, accounts packages, data analysis programs, etc.

### Application generators

Some programs allow the user to create their own customised applications. Database programs, for example, let the user define the file structures and user interfaces to create an 'application within an application'.

# Approaches to acquiring software

When an organisation needs a software application to perform a specified task, it has to choose how it will acquire that application. There are four basic choices and they are outlined below. In making the choice, the organisation will apply the criteria set out on page 52.

| Approach | Customising existing off-the-shelf software | Purchasing a specifically designed, off-the-shelf application | Paying for a customised solution by an external software provider | Developing the application using an in-house team |
|---|---|---|---|---|
| **What is involved** | Many generic applications allow the user to develop customised programs, e.g. a spreadsheet application can have user-designed workbooks. This process entails creating data structures and user interfaces, writing modules, developing macros, etc. | Specialist applications are developed and marketed with specific end users in mind. These applications have the functionality to complete business-specific tasks, e.g. a package designed to manage the end of year accounts of a small business. | Software providers are companies whose business is to sell customised solutions to different organisations. The provider would work alongside the organisation to determine its needs, design the solution and implement the finished application. | Some organisations have 'in-house' development teams. These teams develop applications to meet the needs of the organisation. Some of their work will involve the customisation of generic applications, some of it will involve developing applications from scratch. |
| **Strengths of this approach** | **Cost** Because commercially available generic packages have such a large market, the purchase cost is relatively low. **Reliability** The application will have been through an extensive testing procedure, including testing in a variety of business environments. **Upgrading** If improved releases of the package become available, it will be easy to install them. **Time** The application has already been tested, so it can be implemented quickly. This will, however, depend on how many customisations are required. | **Cost** The relative cost of such packages is low, though there is less functionality for the money than with a generic package. **Fitness for purpose** An application can be chosen which will fit closely with user requirements. As more specialist applications become available, the easier this becomes. **Time** The application can be implemented straight away. However, it will take time to configure it for the specific data structures of the organisation. | **Fitness for purpose** The user is paying for the application and so can determine exactly what is produced. It is therefore likely to fit closely with the user requirements. **Minimal change** Sometimes, with an off-the-shelf application, organisational procedures and policies have to change in order to fit in with the limitations of the applications. With a customised system this can be avoided. **Support** The extent and type of support can be geared to the needs of the organisation. | *The strengths of 'Customised solution by external provider' apply. Additionally:* **Close liaison** The developers and users work alongside each other. A constant dialogue can be created where the user requirements – including changes to these requirements – can be quickly communicated to the developers. **Strengthening of organisational resources** Some organisations feel that having an in-house development team can give them a competitive edge, i.e. because they are able to respond more quickly to changes in the market. |
| **Weaknesses of this approach** | **Fitness for purpose** Even with customisations, the application is unlikely to fulfil precisely the organisation's requirements. There is also likely to be 'waste functionality', i.e. tasks that the application can perform but which will never be needed. **Inherent weaknesses** Despite extensive testing, some commercially successful packages have inherent problems or bugs. Without access to the source code there is little the user can do about this. | **Lack of flexibility** Applications of this kind tend not to allow the user to customise extensively. This can mean that the application determines how information is processed. This can be restrictive. **Support** The quality of post-implementation support can vary considerably and will depend on the calibre of the vendor. In some cases it can be minimal. **Documentation** This is likely to be restricted to what the vendor provides. | **Cost** Costs tend to be high. The more complex the requirements, the higher the cost. **Time** The process can be a slow one and this can create its own difficulties. In the fast-changing world of business, changes in requirements can occur during the development period. **Reliability** Because testing is necessarily limited, problems can occur after implementation, i.e. when the application is being used in a live business environment. | *The weaknesses of 'Customised solution by external provider' apply. Additionally:* **Continuity** Development teams keep changing, especially in today's climate where ICT professionals change jobs regularly. This can lead to problems, e.g. the originator of a piece of coding is no longer available to explain how an aspect of the application works. |

# Word-processing applications

Word-processing programs are among the most commonly used pieces of computer software. This is true both of the domestic market and the business environment. Fast, efficient text-processing programs have largely replaced all forms of typewriter and paper-and-pen technology in office environments. They allow the user to enter data, usually via a keyboard or a speech recognition system, and for that data to appear in text format on the screen, as if it were being typed on to paper. The text can then be formatted (i.e. its appearance changed), edited, saved as a document and printed. Most word-processing programs have WYSIWYG (what-you-see-is-what-you-get) functionality, i.e. the appearance of the page on the screen is the same as that which will be printed out. This helps the user determine precisely the desired configuration of the page.

Word-processing programs are valuable for a wide variety of users, including secretaries who have to produce letters and other documents, students who have assignments to write, authors creating manuscripts for books and articles, etc.

## Some key functions of a word-processing application

### Editing

This is possibly the greatest advantage of word-processing programs over other methods. The user can keep returning to a document, amending it, adding new text, deleting old text, etc. without having to worry about starting the whole document again or damaging the presentation of the finished copy. The program allows the user to move blocks of text around, either by clicking and dragging or by using the cut/copy/paste facility. If, for example, the user wished to copy one block of text into a number of different documents, she could copy it to the clipboard (a temporary store) and then paste it into the appropriate documents.

Other tools that help the user edit a document include the facility to find and replace a specific word or phrase in the document, a function for checking the spelling and a word-count function.

### Templates

Templates are predefined documents that can be used to create documents that conform to a basic format but differ in detail. Many companies have a range of form letters that they send out, e.g. a payment reminder. The message and the layout of the document remains the same (i.e. it provides the template) but the details of the customer and how much he owes changes every time the letter is sent.

Templates can also be used for data capture forms, generic report writing, memos, etc. They are often used in conjunction with a facility that allows the user to merge data held in a data source (e.g. a database) with a word-processed document. This facility may be used if a business wants to send the same form letters to all the clients in their database. Users can create their own templates or use the ones provided by the application.

### Formatting

Formatting means altering the appearance of the text on the page. This can entail changing the size of the text, its colour, its alignment on the page, whether or not it is emboldened/italicised/underlined, etc. Most word-processing programs come with a set of fonts – i.e. styles of writing – installed. The user can choose the font that is most appropriate for the document that they are creating. Other aspects of formatting include setting the paragraph style, determining the line spacing, establishing the style that will be used for bullet points, inserting page numbers, headers/footers, etc. All of these formatting elements can be used in conjunction with each other to create a document that has an appearance consistent with its purpose and audience.

### Importing objects

When word-processing programs were first produced all they could do was process text. As they have developed, so they have grown in sophistication and now rival Desk Top Publishing programs in terms of the functionality they offer. For example, the user is now able to import a wide range of different objects into a document. A graph created in a spreadsheet program can be inserted into a document, as can images downloaded from a digital camera or retrieved from a clip-art library. Graphs and tables created in another application can be inserted as linked objects. This means that when they are updated in the source application they are also updated in the word-processed document. The inserted object can be formatted in a number of different ways, e.g. its properties can be set so that text 'wraps' around it.

## Advantages of word-processing programs

| Advantages | Disadvantages |
|---|---|
| • The main advantage of word-processing over type-written or hand-written documents is the user can keep going back to the document and amending it. Previously this would have meant retyping/rewriting the whole document or spoiling its appearance with crossings-out and/or correction fluid.<br>• Large documents can be saved economically and searched for quickly.<br>• If correct security and back-up procedures are followed, the data held in a word-processed document will be securely stored.<br>• The quality of the final presentation far outstrips any comparable method, especially if imported graphics are used to enhance the appearance of the document. | • The only real disadvantages are generic, i.e. concern about security and loss of data.<br>• There are those who suggest that the ease with which form letters can be produced has led to a decline in the personalised letter and a concomitant growth in the 'pseudo-personalised letter'. |

# Mail merge

'Mail merge' is a commonly used facility that can be found in most word-processing applications. It allows the user to insert merge fields into a template. These merge fields then draw upon data held in a data file, thus creating a number of individualised documents from one template. Typically, this facility will be used for addressing letters to a group of individuals whose details are held by an organisation, e.g. a customer list. This is more efficient than having to address each letter individually and so is widely used by organisations that regularly send letters to clients or customers, e.g. banks, schools, hospitals. The system allows the user to draw on data held in different applications and so is a good example of a way in which data held in separate programs can be integrated. This integration is easier to achieve when working with an integrated 'office' suite.

## How mail merge works

**DATA SOURCE**

| Title | F.Name | Surname | P.Code |
|-------|--------|---------|--------|
| Mr | Alan | Wright | PV3 6YH |
| Miss | Sophie | Jones | PV16 9KT |
| Mr | Adam | Paul | PV5 8TY |
| Mrs | Helen | Lamb | PV16 8RD |
| Ms | Nisha | Omar | PV3 7PY |
| Miss | Kelly | Peake | PV16 6RE |

The data may be held in a **database**, either in a table or in a query that combines related tables and sets parameters for what data should be included.

| Title | F.Name | Surname | P.Code |
|-------|--------|---------|--------|
| Mr | Alan | Wright | PV3 6YH |
| Miss | Sophie | Jones | PV16 9KT |
| Mr | Adam | Paul | PV5 8TY |
| Mrs | Helen | Lamb | PV16 8RD |
| Ms | Nisha | Omar | PV3 7PY |
| Miss | Kelly | Peake | PV16 6RE |

The data may be held as a distinct **data file within the word-processing application**. It may be in tabulated format or a comma separated values (.csv) file.

| Title | F.Name | Surname | P.Code |
|-------|--------|---------|--------|
| Mr | Alan | Wright | PV3 6YH |
| Miss | Sophie | Jones | PV16 9KT |
| Mr | Adam | Paul | PV5 8TY |
| Mrs | Helen | Lamb | PV16 8RD |
| Ms | Nisha | Omar | PV3 7PY |
| Miss | Kelly | Peake | PV16 6RE |

The data may be held in a **spreadsheet**. Although not primarily designed to act as a text-based data store, spreadsheet applications can function in this way.

A querying function may be used to determine which of the records held in the data file will be used as the source of the document, e.g. by selecting only those customers that live in certain postcode district.

A template is created that contains the information to be communicated, together with 'merge fields'. These will be populated with the names, addresses, etc. from the selected records when the document is merged. This template can be saved and re-used as required.

Shureshine Cleaning Co.
Unit 3b
Warwick Rd
London
SW26 5TG

17th March 2002

Dear <<Title>> <<Surname>>

Please find enclosed
details of .......

Shureshine Cleaning Co.
Unit 3b
Warwick Rd
London
SW26 5TG

17th March 2002

Dear Mr Wright

Please find enclosed
details of .......

The template is merged with the source data and either sent directly to the printer or used to create a new document file. The document file will consist of one individualised copy of the template for each of the records contained within the data source.

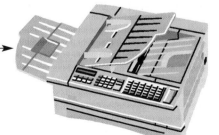

# Spreadsheets

## What is a spreadsheet?

The spreadsheet is generally credited with being the application that first persuaded business users that the PC could run programs that would be of use to them. In 1982 Lotus introduced Lotus 1-2-3, a spreadsheet program that allowed users to store and process numerical data. Its main appeal lay in the fact that it looked like an electronic version of the ledger books that accountants, and other business users who worked with figures, were used to. Its introduction led to a massive growth in the market for IBM PCs and began a decade of unprecedented growth for the computer industry.

A spreadsheet is an information processing tool that organises data into rows and columns. Modern spreadsheet programs are extremely versatile and may be used for creating graphical displays or as simple databases. Their predominant use, however, remains the storage and processing of statistical – and especially financial – data. Their facility for embedding automated mathematical and statistical functions makes them the ideal electronic replacement for the accounts book, inventory sheet and budget summary.

## The uses of spreadsheets

### ACCOUNTS
Accountants use spreadsheets to keep a record of financial transactions. A template can be set up to allow simple entry of new data and embedded mathematical functions can be used to create summaries and totals. Another beneficial feature is dynamic updating: if the user changes the data in one cell, all the data in associated cells will be automatically updated. Specified regions of the spreadsheet can be formatted to produce a report in hard-copy format.

### DATABASE
Although not ideally suited to functioning as a database, spreadsheets can be used in this way. The tabular format can be used to store the data and there are functions that will sort data and perform simple queries. The results of these queries can then be used as the basis of a report.

### STATISTICS
Spreadsheets are ideal for processing statistical data. The data drawn from a data logging device, for example, can be stored in the tens of thousands of available cells. Once stored, a wide variety of statistical analyses can be applied to it. Spreadsheets are capable of employing complex statistical instruments and producing instant results for the user. In addition to standard statistical functions, most spreadsheets allow the user to create customised formulae.

### MODELLING
Businesses need to use the data they have collected to make effective decisions. In particular, they need to know the likely effects of changes they are planning. Spreadsheets can help by providing the functions needed for modelling. If, for example, a company wanted to know the probable effects on sales of a projected price rise, they could use the spreadsheet to model different scenarios, e.g. how would the volume in sales be affected by a 5% price rise?

### PRESENTATION OF DATA
Although not primarily designed for this purpose, spreadsheets can be used to present tabulated data effectively. Program functions allow the user to format grid lines, change the width of columns and height of rows, shade in cells and use different colours to present the data clearly.

### GRAPHICAL DISPLAY
Spreadsheets can transform numerical data into graphical displays. Graphs of different kinds help to simplify data and summarise trends. The user can choose the most appropriate graphical format (e.g. pie charts, scattergraphs, etc.) and use formatting functions to alter the look of the final display, e.g. by changing the colour key used. Graphical displays can be printed out from the spreadsheet program or imported into a word-processed document or a presentation slide.

## Spreadsheets – evaluation

| Advantages | Disadvantages |
|---|---|
| • The use of spreadsheets has become ubiquitous in environments where financial and/or statistical data has to be managed.<br>• They can perform a full range of mathematical calculations with a high degree of precision in a fraction of the time it would take a human.<br>• Cells, spreadsheets and workbooks can be dynamically linked, so that updating of associated data is automatic.<br>• Properly protected and regularly backed-up, they can be used to provide a secure and economical store for large volumes of statistical data.<br>• They can provide a user-friendly means of creating graphical representations of statistical data.<br>• They can be used for modelling scenarios based on 'what-if' projections. They can thus aid decision-making. | • There are no obvious, intrinsic disadvantages to using spreadsheet software over traditional, manual methods. The problems that might be faced are generic to computing, i.e. vulnerability to loss of data, virus attacks, unauthorised access, etc. There might be some concern about keeping critical data in an environment that isn't 100% secure, but this was equally the case with the traditional methods.<br>• Some users may find it difficult to adapt to working with electronic spreadsheets and this may lead to errors being made. |

# Presentation software

Presentation software is used to create slide-show presentations that can be shown to audiences. Such presentations used to be created with projected photographic slides and (possibly) a linked tape recorder to provide a sound track. An alternative, less complex approach, involved overhead transparencies projected onto a screen. Presentation programs have enabled the user to create more sophisticated, multimedia presentations, involving graphics, animation, sound and video clips. The finished file can be stored, edited as necessary and shown again when required.

Software of this kind is used by anyone who may wish to give information to an audience, including: business people, teachers and lecturers, demonstrators, visiting speakers, etc.

## Some key functions of presentation software

**FORMATTING**

The appearance of each individual slide can be changed in a number of different ways. Formatting allows the user to determine the properties of any text that is used: the slide background, borders, bullets, graphics, etc. Properties that can be changed include: size, position on the page, colour and order priority. Many programs also offer formatted templates. These provide a colour-coordinated outline that the user can customise as necessary. The whole slide show can be formatted so that it looks the same or each individual slide can be formatted differently.

**IMPORTING OBJECTS**

The program not only allows the user to insert any text that they wish but also to import different objects. These objects may include graphs created in a spreadsheet document, images taken from a clip-art library, a table from a word-processed document, etc. The object may be embedded in the slide-show or linked so that it automatically updates. The more sophisticated presentation programs allow the user to import video clips and sound files. By using these facilities it is possible to create an exciting multimedia presentation.

**CREATING A SHOW**

The user can customise, to some degree, the way in which the slide show runs. If it is necessary for the person giving the presentation to control the pace of the show, the transitions can be made to occur on a mouse click or a key stroke. Alternatively, if the slide show can run automatically the transitions may be set to a timer. This approach might be used if the show is being set up to run on a TV monitor in a continuous loop. The way in which the show starts and ends can also be defined by the user.

**ANIMATED TRANSITIONS**

One set of functions to be found in a presentation package relate to the way that text and graphics appear on the screen. Instead of the text just appearing, it can be made to 'fly' in from one side, emerge gradually in a 'chequerboard' pattern, spin in from the centre, etc. Such effects liven up the slide show and make it more interesting for the audience. Similar functions can be used to define the way in which one slide transmutes into another, e.g. as one slide finishes it 'dissolves' into the next.

## Advantages and disadvantages of using presentation software

| ADVANTAGES | DISADVANTAGES |
|---|---|
| • The quality of presentation is superior to that which can be produced by photographic slides and overhead transparencies. | • Some files, especially those that contain multimedia elements, can take up a lot of memory resources. |
| • It has the potential to utilise full multimedia facilities, thus expanding what material can be included in the presentation. | • In order to show the presentation effectively, a good quality computer projector is required. These can be costly. |
| • The finished document can be economically stored, easily edited and used again as often as necessary without any diminishment of quality. | • The whole system can be complicated to set up, requiring a computer with the file on, a computer projector, screen, cabling, etc. This is especially difficult if one has to show the presentation in different locations. |
| • The user has much more control over the final appearance of the slide show. | • As with all computer-based technology, there is the danger of the document being lost or corrupted as the result of a system crash or security breach. |
| • It can run automatically – in 'loop' mode – on a TV monitor, e.g. as used in exhibits, etc. | |

# Graphics software

## Characteristic features of graphics software

Graphics software is designed to allow the user to store, manipulate and print graphical images. There are different varieties of graphics software, each designed for a different purpose, but they share some common characteristics:

**Manipulation** The user can move images around the page, resize them, 'crop' them (i.e. extract sections) and, depending on the sophistication of the program, change their perspective, e.g. 'flip' the entire image from right to left.

**Modification** The properties of the image (line width, colour, texture, brightness, etc.) can be adjusted, either in relation to individual components of the image or to the image as a whole. In this way the user can alter the overall look of the image.

**Importing** The user should be able to import images from various sources and work with them in the document. Programs usually allow importing from scanners, digital cameras and clip-art libraries. Some programs are particular about what file formats can be used. In such case the image files will need to be converted before they can be used.

**Stored files** In addition to allowing users to import their own images, many programs come with their own image banks. These may consist of general clip-art libraries or specialist graphic objects that could be needed for the specific program, e.g. software to help people design gardens will have available graphical representations of fences, lawns, plants, etc.

**Graphical tools** Those programs that allow users to create their own images provide computerised versions of typical graphical tools, e.g. brushes, pencils, spray paints, etc. that create analogous effects.

## Varieties of graphics software

### COMPUTER-AIDED DESIGN (CAD) PROGRAMS

- CAD programs are designed to be used by professional designers, architects, engineers, etc. The level of sophistication in such programs makes them unsuitable for the general user.
- They use vector-based images rather than bit-maps as this allows for a greater level of precision, especially when the image needs to be manipulated.
- They allow the user to view objects from different perspectives and to model them at different stages of development, e.g. a car may be shown both as a skeletal design and as the finished product.

### PHOTO-MANIPULATION PROGRAMS

- Increasingly, people are using digital format cameras to take their photographs and computers to store them on. This is true both for professionals and general users.
- Photo-manipulation software has grown in popularity. Consequently, there are a variety of programs on the market, some aimed at the professional, some at the home user. The functionality is broadly the same but the level of sophistication differs.
- The programs work with bit-mapped files, allowing the user to manipulate the size and shape of the image. A bank of effects facilitates modification of the image, e.g. a colour image can be made to appear in black and white.

### DESK TOP PUBLISHING (DTP) PROGRAMS

- DTP programs allow the user to combine image and text to create magazine pages, posters, leaflets, etc. They are used by both general users and professionals and there are products on the market aimed at both groups.
- There are similarities with word-processing packages, and the latest versions of WP software have many of the same features as DTP programs. The difference is one of emphasis: WP programs focus on the creation of text-based documents; DTP programs focus on the manipulation of graphical objects on the page (including text) to create a composite image.

### PAINT/DRAW PROGRAMS

- Paint/draw programs facilitate the creation of images by the user. The program provides a 'blank canvas' and a set of graphical tools to work with. These tools are computerised equivalents of pencils, brushes, crayons, paint sprays, etc.
- The image is built up by the user, using different colours and textures. It can then be edited and modified, with elements changed and new effects added.
- Programs of this kind are used by both the general user and professional artists working in computer-generated formats. There are a number of programs aimed at young children.

## Hardware needs

**Memory store** Graphics programs generally use more memory resources than text-based programs. If this is not allowed for, computer performance will be affected as more and more images are stored on the system.

**Input devices** Specialist input devices can be used to gain a great degree of precision (e.g. a digitiser tablet) or to mimic the effects of real graphical tools (e.g. a light pen).

**Printers** Specialist printers (e.g. graphical plotters) may be needed by professional users and even home users will need a good-quality printer and specially formatted paper if they are going to achieve good-quality finished products.

# Computer-modelling software

There are a number of different programs that can be used to create computer models. A model is a simplified representation based on computed data of a real phenomenon. A simple example of a model is a bar chart showing temperature values for a city over a year, such as might be used in a holiday brochure. The chart is a model because (a) it is a graphical <u>representation</u> of a real situation (i.e. the actual temperatures of the city), (b) it is a <u>simplified</u> version of the real phenomenon (not every minute temperature change is represented), and (c) it is <u>based on data</u> (i.e. temperature values) that has been processed. The ability of computers to (a) undertake fast, repetitive processing of large volumes of data and (b) transform data into different representative formats makes them well-suited to this kind of work.

## Different applications of computer modelling

### WEATHER PATTERNS

As with many modelling programs, the computation of weather patterns is based on three elements: **constant values** (e.g. the orbit of the Earth around the Sun); **variable values** (e.g. temperature, wind speed, atmospheric pressure, etc.); **accepted rules** based on scientific principles (e.g. the relationship between tidal activity and lunar cycles). Models can then be produced that either represent current conditions in a simplified form (e.g. on a weather map published on a website) or predict future events, (e.g. the impact on sea levels of global warming). In the latter case the model is predictive, i.e. it models the effect on dependent variables (sea levels) of changes in independent variables (rises in aggregate temperatures).

### CAR CRASH ANALYSIS

Car manufacturers need to know the likely effects of crashes on their vehicles. The standard method for collecting this information is to 'crash' prototype vehicles with crash test dummies in them and use monitoring equipment to judge the outcomes. Computer models offer a cheaper alternative to this expensive process. The data associated with the car (i.e. constant values) is inputted, and modelling software simulates the effects of crashes at different speeds (i.e. variable values), taking into account the properties of materials such as metal and plastic and the physics of force and acceleration (i.e. accepted rules). The outcome is displayed graphically. Such programs are supplanting some vehicle test procedures, though not replacing them entirely.

### ECONOMIC FORECASTING

Both governments and commercial organisations rely heavily on economic forecasting models to make decisions. Data based on productivity, sales, volume turnover, capital assets, etc. are inputted and then represented, often in graphical form. This allows organisations to judge their present performance. Models can also be used to predict future scenarios. What is likely to happen to a company's profit margins, for example, if interest rates go up by 1%, 2%, 3%, etc? Such models can be used to influence decisions about the future. If for example, a company knows that a demographic model predicts a rise in active, elderly people, it can develop – and then market – new products accordingly.

### DESIGN

Those involved in designing products want to see the likely outcomes of design changes before they actually build projects. Computer Aided Design (CAD) software can be used to produce models of a variety of objects. Data associated with the design can be inputted and applied to a range of pre-loaded design elements, e.g. cubes, globes, lines, etc. The model can be manipulated on the screen to demonstrate the different effects of minor changes, it can be represented in different formats (e.g. as a skeletal model or as a prototype) and it can be viewed from different perspectives. This facility enables designers to test different ideas without having to worry about constructing expensive prototypes.

## Issues associated with computer modelling

- Computer modelling brings with it many benefits: it is cheaper than building prototypes; it can represent complex phenomena in a simplified format; it can compute data in a fraction of the time it would take humans; it can suggest future trends in business, society, the natural world, etc.
- Some programs oversimplify complex phenomena by computing some but not all of the relevant data. Consequently, models are produced that don't take into account all the variables involved.
- Some phenomena are bound by rules and laws that are well understood, e.g. the relationship between mass and energy. Other phenomena are less well understood, e.g. the factors affecting population growth. None the less, some computer models are based on incompletely understood rules and laws. Moreover decisions are made on the basis of the predictions such models produce. A good example of this is the debate about global warming: different countries are making different commitments to the reduction of greenhouse gasses (partly) on the basis of which predictive model they adhere to, yet all of these models are based on an incomplete understanding of major climatic change.

# Global positioning systems (GPS)

### What is GPS?

GPS is a system developed by the American military in the 1970s and the 1980s. It comprises 24 satellites positioned 11 000 miles above the Earth in geosynchronous orbit, which means that, relative to the Earth and each other, they maintain a constant position. They are distributed such that, at any one time, at least four are visible from any point on Earth. The satellites send out constant signals on predetermined frequencies. These signals can be captured by any GPS-enabled device and used to determine the exact location (in some cases with a precision level of a few centimetres) of the receiver. In recent years the military has made the technology commercially available and it has thus been used for a wide range of applications.

### How does GPS work?

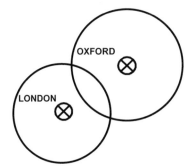

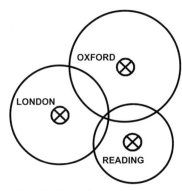

Using the principle of triangulation, GPS technology allows you to identify your precise geographical location if you know your distance from three different points. If, for example, you know that you are 50 miles from London, you also know that you must be at one point on the perimeter of a circle with a 50-mile radius.

If you know that you are also 60 miles from Oxford, you must be located at one of two points, i.e. the two points where the circles intersect.

Finally, if you know that you are 25 miles from Reading, you can identify exactly where you are, i.e. the point where all three circles intersect.

GPS uses satellite transmission to identify the three points required for triangulation, plus a fourth satellite to calculate altitude. The transmissions are picked up by a GPS device, which uses the data to calculate the longitude and latitude of its position and then applies that data to stored map data to display the result to the user.

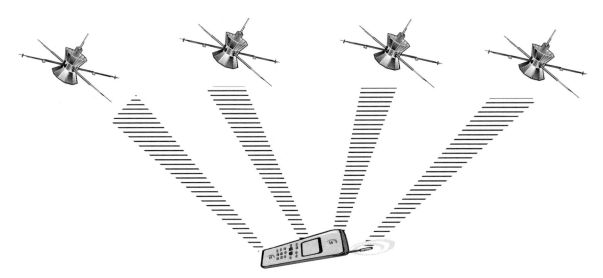

### WHAT APPLICATIONS ARE THERE FOR GPS?

GPS-enabled devices are found in a wide variety of applications:

- Travellers who are exploring remote areas can use them to identify their precise location and transmit this information to others if they find themselves in difficulty.
- Car manufacturers offer 'SatNav' facilities so that drivers can see where they are by combining GPS data with pre-loaded map-based information. The same system can be used as a security device to track stolen vehicles.
- Farmers in America have begun to use driverless tractors. These utilise GPS data in combination with pre-programmed route information and can be used to used to cover predefined areas.
- Delivery firms can use GPS to track the location and speed of any one driver.
- It has been suggested that GPS technology could be used to monitor drivers on British roads. The resulting data would then be used to determine what level of road tax an individual driver should pay.
- They are used to replace terrestrial systems for ships at sea. They can also calculate speed and distance covered.

# Web-browsing software

## How web browsers developed

The World Wide Web had its inception at the end of the 1980s at the Geneva base of the European Organisation for Nuclear Research. It was designed (by scientists Tim Berners-Lee and Robert Cailliau) to be a communication tool that would help physicists all over the world share their data and ideas. It took a while for this idea, generally considered to be one of the most revolutionary of the twentieth century, to take hold. By June 1983 there were just over 100 websites, mostly based in scientific centres and universities and accessed by only a few informed academics. What was needed for the idea to gain widespread acceptance was an application that would allow the general user to access and read websites.

In 1993 Marc Andreesen, a student at the University of Illinois, led a team that developed the first web browser application. The browser, which was called Mosaic, was an immediate success. In 1994 he developed it as commercial application and launched it as Netscape Navigator. Its widespread acceptance by general users led to the explosive growth of the World Wide Web. By January 1996 there were 100 000 registered websites, and to date there are over 32 million. Netscape Navigator became the market leader in browser software but, at the time of writing, they have ceded this position to Microsoft's Internet Explorer.

## The main function of a web browser

The primary function of a web browser is to use the Internet to request web pages. The web page arrives as an HTML file. The browser interprets this and displays the results.

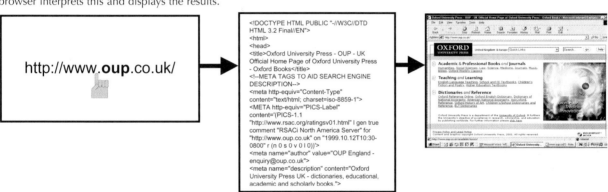

The user requests a web page by clicking on a hyperlink or typing in the website's URL into the address box. The browser sends the request to the user's Internet Service Provider or to a direct network link. The request is then made to the server hosting the desired website. The host sends back an HTML (Hyper Text Mark-up Language) file that contains all the information needed to create the web page.

The HTML file is read and interpreted by the browser. It uses the detailed instructions embedded in the code to construct the requested page. Some sections of the code relate to the overall appearance of the page, other sections contain addresses of files (e.g. graphics files) that need to be downloaded.

The page is gradually constructed on the screen. Some aspects of the page 'arrive' more quickly than others which is why web pages construct themselves in stages. The browser also needs to be able to launch helper applications (or plug-ins) in order to include certain types of files, e.g. audio files. If certain components of the page (e.g. a specified colour) are not available, the browser uses appropriate substitutes.

## Other facilities offered by web browsers

Web browsers have grown in sophistication and now offer a number of additional functions to support the user. These include:

| | |
|---|---|
| **Favourites** | A way of storing the addresses of those websites the user visits most often. |
| **History** | A function that allows the user to maintain a record of recently visited sites. |
| **Navigation** | There are a number of navigation options available, including the facility to return to a previous web page, to return to the home page, to cancel the downloading of a page, etc. |
| **Search** | Most users go to a search engine site (e.g. Google) to search for a particular item, but web browsers come with their own search facility. |
| **Security** | The user can determine their own security settings, ensuring, for example, that only websites that have been approved are downloaded. |
| **Links** | Browsers display links to popular websites, or to a page with links that come under a certain category heading (e.g. music, news, sport, etc). |
| **E-mail** | The user can access and compose e-mails via the browser. |

# Web-authoring software

One of the most revolutionary aspects of the Internet is the way it allows users with varying levels of experience and only minimum resources to create their own websites. This facility has led to an increase in small-scale enterprises challenging the market domination of established companies and, indeed, creating entirely new markets. It has also meant that special interest groups have been able to express their views and communicate with like-minded people around the globe, by-passing the commercially controlled mass media. In order that individuals with little or no programming experience can produce websites, software has been developed that facilitates this in a user-friendly way. This is referred to as web-authoring software.

## Functionality of web authoring-software

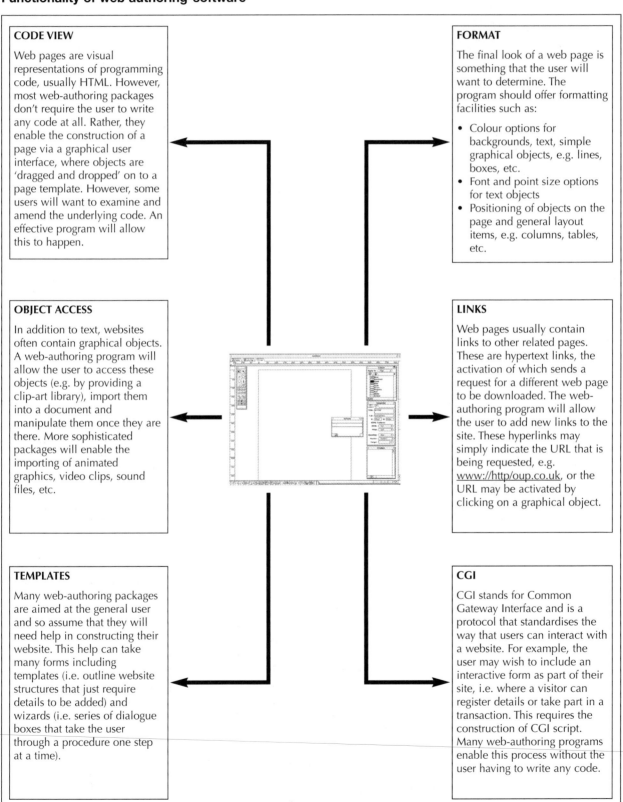

**CODE VIEW**

Web pages are visual representations of programming code, usually HTML. However, most web-authoring packages don't require the user to write any code at all. Rather, they enable the construction of a page via a graphical user interface, where objects are 'dragged and dropped' on to a page template. However, some users will want to examine and amend the underlying code. An effective program will allow this to happen.

**FORMAT**

The final look of a web page is something that the user will want to determine. The program should offer formatting facilities such as:

- Colour options for backgrounds, text, simple graphical objects, e.g. lines, boxes, etc.
- Font and point size options for text objects
- Positioning of objects on the page and general layout items, e.g. columns, tables, etc.

**OBJECT ACCESS**

In addition to text, websites often contain graphical objects. A web-authoring program will allow the user to access these objects (e.g. by providing a clip-art library), import them into a document and manipulate them once they are there. More sophisticated packages will enable the importing of animated graphics, video clips, sound files, etc.

**LINKS**

Web pages usually contain links to other related pages. These are hypertext links, the activation of which sends a request for a different web page to be downloaded. The web-authoring program will allow the user to add new links to the site. These hyperlinks may simply indicate the URL that is being requested, e.g. www://http/oup.co.uk, or the URL may be activated by clicking on a graphical object.

**TEMPLATES**

Many web-authoring packages are aimed at the general user and so assume that they will need help in constructing their website. This help can take many forms including templates (i.e. outline website structures that just require details to be added) and wizards (i.e. series of dialogue boxes that take the user through a procedure one step at a time).

**CGI**

CGI stands for Common Gateway Interface and is a protocol that standardises the way that users can interact with a website. For example, the user may wish to include an interactive form as part of their site, i.e. where a visitor can register details or take part in a transaction. This requires the construction of CGI script. Many web-authoring programs enable this process without the user having to write any code.

# The process of evaluating software

When an organisation decides that it wishes to acquire new software, it will be the task of an individual or team to evaluate available software solutions. The aim of this process is to ensure that the software chosen will meet all of the users' needs in a cost-effective manner. In a centralised system, this task will fall to the ICT department. They will need to establish the users' needs, evaluate possible solutions and advise management on the best purchase.

## Matching software to different users' needs

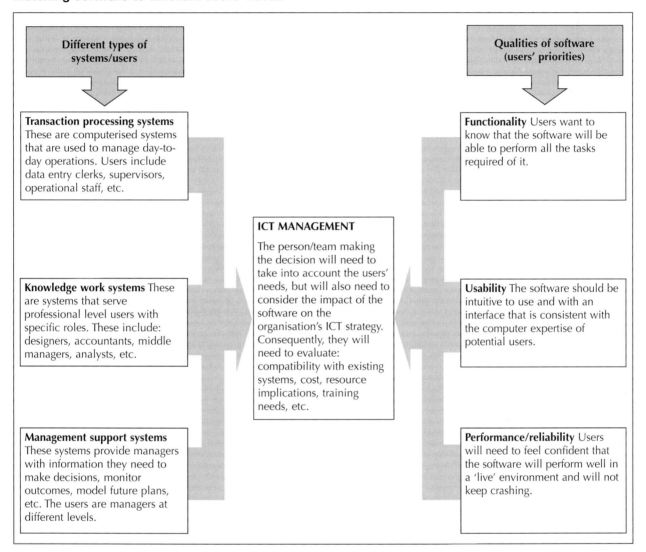

## The process of evaluating software

| | |
|---|---|
| **1. Determine criteria** | In order to evaluate anything systematically, the first step is to determine what will be the relevant criteria for making the decision. In the case of software this will include: cost, reliability, compatibility, etc: These criteria may then be placed in a rank order to determine their priority or weighted according to how critical they will be in reaching the decision. |
| **2. Gather information** | Information about what products are available will need to be collected. The software vendors will send out their own promotional material and in some cases will contact directly those in charge of software acquisition. Further information may be found on the Internet, in magazines and newspapers and by speaking to users in other organisations. |
| **3. Evaluate possible choices** | Once the possible choices have been established, each choice needs to be evaluated using the established criteria. This may be achieved by taking a demonstration copy through a series of benchmarks tests designed to assess its performance. It would also be valuable to gather comments from potential users and to assess the likely impact on the organisation's ICT infrastructure. |
| **4. Make decision** | Having been through the above processes, the individual/team is in a position to make a decision. The decision may take the form of a 'recommendation to buy' report which would be sent to a senior manager. In this instance, the report should also justify the choice, indicating how the choice was arrived at and what criteria were used. |

# Criteria for evaluating software

✔ **Agreed problem specification**

Is the software the right solution for the specific problem it will have to solve? There should be the closest possible match between what the software does and what it will be required to do. There should be no shortfall in functionality and there should be a minimum of surplus functionality, since this represents waste. The better the software's 'fitness for purpose', the more effective its acquisition will be. In order to reach this judgement it is critical that a precise analysis of need has taken place.

✔ **Functionality**

Functionality refers to what the software is capable of doing. In some instances, the software will be designed to perform a designated task and nothing else. In other instances, the software will have a degree of flexibility. It will enable the user to customise – to some extent – data structures, interfaces, functions, etc. The level of functionality must be measured against the tasks it will be required to do.

✔ **Performance**

Different pieces of software will demonstrate different levels of performance when measured against each other. Typically, one would be looking for speed of processing, accuracy, quality of output, etc. In order to help users make judgements against these criteria, benchmark tests have been designed to measure the performance of software packages against defined standards.

✔ **Usability**

Is the software user-friendly? An ideal user interface is intuitive – that is, the user should only require a general familiarity with computing software and a modicum of common sense to perform the majority of operations. The software should take into account the needs of users with different levels of 'computer literacy'. For example, novice users tend to prefer the facilities offered by a graphical user interface (e.g. icons), whereas more experienced users tend to make more use of keyboard short-cuts. There should be easily available – and easy to search – help files and the interface should be 'easy on the eye', i.e. not overcrowded nor designed using garish colours.

✔ **Compatibility**

It is critical that the software is compatible with existing software and hardware. There shouldn't be any problem about running it on whatever operating system is in use and it shouldn't require any significant modification to hardware. It should also be possible to transfer data between the new software and existing software. In some instances, the program files of a new piece of software can cause 'crashes' in other parts of the system.

✔ **Transferability of data**

The software should permit the user to import data from and export data to other applications with relative ease. The new piece of software may have to accept data from a range of different sources and the user may need to merge the information produced by the software into another application. Most software packages allow for this. Many of them allow the user to put data into a 'portable' form, e.g. a csv data file, an unformatted text file, etc.

✔ **Robustness or stability**

All software is tested, but sometimes the testing does not sufficiently take into account the day-to-day needs of a live business environment. The software should be tough enough to withstand pressured usage, i.e. where it is expected to perform quickly, in a networked environment in conjunction with other applications, and with users not always operating it as they should. If, in this environment, it regularly crashes, users will quickly lose confidence in it.

✔ **User support**

Whatever the source of the software, there should be good post-implementation support. This can take many forms – online help files, documentation, telephone help desk, etc. – but it should be easily accessible and appropriate for users of all levels. The nature of the support should be compatible with the working environment, i.e. in a fast-moving, pressured environment – e.g. the stock market – users will not be able to consult a book every time there is a problem.

✔ **Resource requirement**

In calculating the overall cost of the software package – another important criterion – it is necessary to take into account any other resource implications. The software may require specific hardware (e.g. it might require a bar code reader for data input) and/or additional software (e.g. an attached database package to store data). There may also be implications in terms of staffing. Users may need to be trained in its use and this has cost implications for the organisation.

✔ **Upgradability**

There should be a clear upgrade structure for the software. Changes to other linked applications and/or operating systems, changes to the business environment (e.g. a change in legislation) and changes in business requirements can all create demand for an upgraded system. It should be clear from the provider's profile, whether their practice is to provide regular upgrades or not.

# Systems software

## The difference between applications software and systems software

Broadly speaking there are two categories of software: applications software and systems software.

**Applications software**  These are programs that are designed to perform a specific range of tasks for the user. Spreadsheet, database and desk top publishing programs all fall into this category.

**Systems software**  This refers to programs that enable the computer to function effectively, to interact with the user, to communicate with peripheral devices and to manage the demands made upon its resources by applications software. The most important program in this category is the operating system but the category also includes utility programs such as virus checkers, file management programs, etc.

## Functions of the operating system

The operating system acts as an intermediary between the user and the hardware. It has a user-friendly interface to enable the user to run programs, save files, communicate with peripheral devices, etc. Whereas computers can function effectively without applications, they cannot easily function without an operating system.

Operating systems provide a common platform for applications to run on. Without them each application would need to define its own way of communicating with the user, saving files to secondary storage, communicating with peripheral devices, etc. There are a number of competing operating systems on the market, the most commonly used one being Microsoft Windows. UNIX is an alternative system popular with some business users and LINUX is a free system developed by an Internet-linked community of programmers.

### Interrupt handling

Various hardware events such as mouse clicks, keystrokes, a message from an external source, etc. generate a particular type of signal called an interrupt. It is a signal that needs an immediate response, so the OS has to manage any ongoing processing jobs while dealing with it.

### Memory allocation

The OS ensures that adequate memory resources are available for the task being performed by the user. This task has become more critical as multi-tasking (i.e. the ability to perform two or more different actions at the same time) has become the norm.

**Application software**
**Operating system**
Hardware

### Backing storage

The OS organises the storage and retrieval of data from the hard disc drive and other secondary storage devices. In order to maintain efficiency it must be able to locate specific files quickly. It maintains a directory for this purpose.

### Communicating with peripheral devices

A computer may be linked with any number of peripherals, including: a mouse, keyboard, printer, scanner, etc. The OS ensures that device drivers are in place and the computer can receive and send instructions to these devices effectively.

## Examples of utility software

| | |
|---|---|
| **Virus checkers** | A virus checker is a valuable piece of software that maintains an updateable directory of the 'signatures' – i.e. tell-tale sections of code – of known viruses. If noticed, a warning can then be sent to the user. |
| **File management** | Software of this type helps users to keep their files in logical order, ensuring optimal use of disc space and speed of retrieval. It might also offer facilities for compressing files and repartitioning the hard disc drive. |
| **Security** | Usually associated with network systems, software of this type allocates passwords, defines user access rights, maintains a log of computer usage, etc. |

# Databases: introduction

## What is a database?

A database is a systematically organised store of data. Increasingly, the term database refers to computerised systems, but databases can also be manual. Before computers, manual systems such as card index files, filing cabinets, libraries, etc. were used to organise data and so can be defined as databases. Computers have the ability to store large amounts of data in a compact space and to process it speedily. These two facilities make them ideally suited for database work and organisations of all sizes now use computers to manage their data. Databases vary enormously, both in terms of scale and architecture, but there are certain elements that are common to almost all database systems:

- Data is organised in tabular structures where each row constitutes one record and each column defines a field.
- Users are able to add new records, amend existing records, and delete unwanted records.
- Users are able to interrogate (or 'query') the database, i.e. ask it to show which records fulfil certain criteria.
- Users can output the results of queries as reports. These can be viewed on-screen or printed out as hard copy.

## How does a database work?

| ID | Forename | Surname | Dept |
|----|----------|---------|------|
|    |          |         |      |
|    |          |         |      |
|    |          |         |      |
|    |          |         |      |
|    |          |         |      |
|    |          |         |      |

A file structure is created that organises the data into fields (e.g. ID, forename, etc.) and records (each row is one record).

**DATA ENTRY FORM**

| ID | 1 |
|----|---|
| FORENAME | John |
| SURNAME | Stevens |
| DEPT | Finance |

A user-friendly data entry form is used to add new records and amend existing records.

| ID | Forename | Surname | Dept |
|----|----------|---------|------|
| 1 | John | Stevens | Finance |
| 2 | Michael | Lee | Marketing |
| 3 | Sally | Atkinson | Finance |
| 4 | Harinda | Singh | Hum Res |
| 5 | Shima | Begum | Finance |
| 6 | Helen | Doods | Marketing |
| 7 | Duane | Courcy | Hum Res |
| 8 | Tony | Yip | Ops |
| 9 | Julia | Wallace | Ops |

The table is populated with records which can then be interrogated.

**DEPARTMENT REPORT QUERY**

DEPARTMENT — Finance

A form is used to set the parameters of a query. In this case the user wants to extract the names of all those who work in the finance department.

| ID | Forename | Surname | Dept |
|----|----------|---------|------|
| 1 | John | Stevens | Finance |
| 3 | Sally | Atkinson | Finance |
| 5 | Shima | Begum | Finance |

The query is run and selects only those records that match the criteria. In this case those records where 'finance' is the entry in the 'dept' column.

**Department personnel report**

Dept: Finance

| ID | Forename | Surname |
|----|----------|---------|
| 1 | John | Stevens |
| 3 | Sally | Atkinson |
| 5 | Shima | Begum |

A report can now be created based on the information returned by the query. The report can be stored and recreated using different data as and when required.

## Who uses databases?

A wide variety of individuals and organisations use databases; below are just a few examples:

Police forces keep databases of crimes and criminals. This is used to aid detection and analyse patterns of criminality, policing levels, etc.

Schools use databases to keep records of pupils, their assessment data, the timetable they follow, etc.

**DATABASES**

Hospitals maintain databases of patients, doctors, treatments, etc. This is used to administer consultations, admissions, etc.

Businesses of all sizes maintain databases to keep track of sales, stock purchases, etc. and to analyse their performance.

# Flat-file systems

## What is a flat-file system?

A flat-file system refers to a database where all the data is held in a single table or file. Below is an example of a flat-file database that might be used by an electrician to keep a record of work completed.

| Job No. | Customer | Contact No. | Address | Estimate | Completion | Amount paid |
|---------|----------|-------------|---------|----------|------------|-------------|
| A113 | Mr K Jones | 0309 224567 | 23 High St, Sutton SM1 8YG | £330.75 | 12/01/02 | £335.00 |
| A114 | Mrs R Tennet | 0309 556213 | 14 Eastfield Rd Wallington WA4 5RT | £240.00 | 15/01/02 | £230.00 |
| A115 | Mr P Suliman | 0309 872136 | 4 Jones Aveune Sutton SM6 7TY | £195.00 | 25/01/02 | £210.50 |
| A116 | Mr P Suliman | 0309 872136 | 4 Jones Aveune Sutton SM6 7TY | £500.00 | 15/02/02 | £560.50 |

Even though this is a relatively simple system with limited data, some of the problems inherent in flat-file systems are already evident:

**Data redundancy** — This is an important concept in database design. It refers to the unnecessary duplication of data. In the table above, data will be repeated each time the electrician does another job for the same customer. The unnecessary duplication of the customer's details constitutes data redundancy.

**Data integrity** — The integrity of data is its correctness, i.e. the extent to which it truthfully represents the original source information. One of the problems of maintaining integrity arises when updating occurs. In the example above, if Mr Suliman changes his phone number, it must be updated in every record where his name occurs. If it were left undone in one record, the data associated with Mr Suliman would no longer be wholly correct.

## Flat-file systems in organisations

In the early days of computers, organisations would store data in separate files, each file related to a functional area of the organisation. The data held in such systems was manipulated and interrogated using software called 'file management systems'. This is shown in the diagram below.

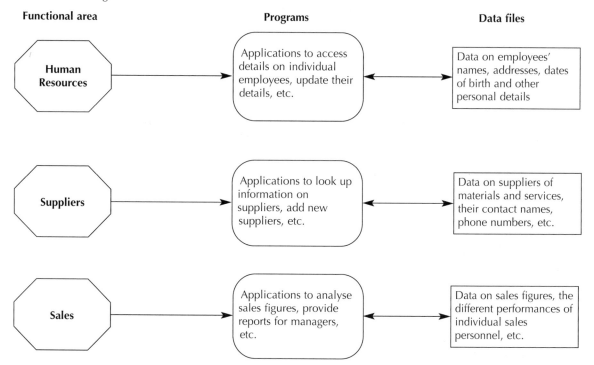

| Functional area | Programs | Data files |
|---|---|---|
| **Human Resources** | Applications to access details on individual employees, update their details, etc. | Data on employees' names, addresses, dates of birth and other personal details |
| **Suppliers** | Applications to look up information on suppliers, add new suppliers, etc. | Data on suppliers of materials and services, their contact names, phone numbers, etc. |
| **Sales** | Applications to analyse sales figures, provide reports for managers, etc. | Data on sales figures, the different performances of individual sales personnel, etc. |

In such a system, problems related to data integrity and data redundancy are multiplied many times over. It is likely, for example, that data related to individual products would be stored both in the 'Sales' data files and the 'Suppliers' data files. Such data would be held more than once – leading to data redundancy. The integrity of such data would also be under threat. If the details of a product were changed in the 'Suppliers' file, procedures would be needed to ensure that it was updated in any other data files where it occurred. Such procedures would be difficult to maintain.

Another factor has to be taken into account when separate but overlapping data files are used – that of data consistency.

**Data consistency** — When data is held in more than one file it should be stored in a consistent form. In the example above, there would be data on sales personnel in both the 'Sales' file and the 'Human Resources' file. If in one file the date of birth was held as a text data type (e.g. 21 September 1960) and in the other as a time/date data type (e.g. 21/09/60) the data would be incompatible.

# Relational databases

## What is a relational database?

Relational databases were first developed in the 1970s by Edgar Codd as a way, initially, of providing a more flexible system for responding to spontaneous requests for management information. As they developed it was found that they also helped to solve many of the problems associated with data redundancy, data integrity and data consistency associated with flat-file systems. The key difference between relational databases and flat-file systems lies in the creation of separate tables that are related to each other. The diagram below uses the example of the electrician's data file.

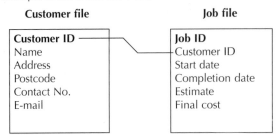

All the data associated with the customer is now held in one file and all the data associated with each job is held another file. In order to create a connection between the two sets of data, a relationship must be created by using two **key fields.**

**Primary key**   A key field is a unique identifier, usually some type of code number. The primary key is the start point of a relationship and will only occur once in that file. In this case each record in the customer file will describe the attributes of one customer and one customer only. That customer will be uniquely identified by the customer ID field.

**Foreign key**   The foreign key is the destination point of the relationship. It remains a unique identifier as regards the customer, but may occur more than once in the Job file, i.e. because the customer may have more than one job completed by the electrician.

The records might now look like this:

| Customer ID | Customer | Contact No. | Address | E-mail |
|---|---|---|---|---|
| **KJ2245** | Mr K Jones | 0309 224567 | 23 High St, Sutton SM1 8YG | Kjones@serveme.co.uk |
| **RT5562** | Mrs R Tennet | 0309 556213 | 14 Eastfield Rd Wallington WA4 5RT | – |
| **PS8721** | Mr P Suliman | 0309 872136 | 4 Jones Avenue Sutton SM6 7TY | Psulxx@onserve.co.uk |

| Job No. | Customer ID | Start Date | Estimate | Completion date | Final cost |
|---|---|---|---|---|---|
| A113 | KJ2245 | 05/01/02 | £330.75 | 12/01/02 | £335.00 |
| A114 | RT5562 | 13/01/02 | £240.00 | 15/01/02 | £230.00 |
| A115 | PS8721 | 20/01/02 | £195.00 | 25/01/02 | £210.50 |
| A116 | PS8721 | 10/02/02 | £500.00 | 15/02/02 | £560.50 |

As you can see, the Customer ID field acts as the **primary key** in the Customer file and the **foreign key** in the Job file, thus enabling a relationship between the two tables.

## What are the advantages of a relational database over a flat-file system?

| | |
|---|---|
| **Data integrity** | There is no need to change data in more than one table. If a customer's details require updating this only needs to happen once, i.e. in the Customer file. All references to that customer in any other file (i.e. via the primary key) will automatically reflect the update. |
| **Data redundancy** | In a well-designed relational database there should be no 'repeating attributes', i.e. no piece of data should be unnecessarily repeated. |
| **Data consistency** | Because the attributes of any one entity (e.g. a job, a customer) are contained within one file, there is no risk of the same attribute being stored in a different format in a different file. |
| **Flexibility** | A relational database can be queried with greater flexibility than a flat-file system. Data drawn from different files can be combined in a variety of ways, producing better-quality information. |
| **Greater efficiency** | Data only has to be inputted once and this saves on time and human resources. The memory space required is also less and this saves on computing resources. |

# Properties of data held in a database

A database is generally made up of data organised into tables.

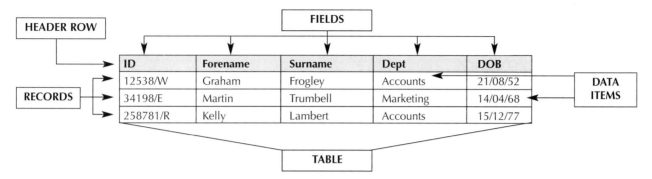

When a database is being created it is important to define what properties each data item will have, i.e. how it will be stored. This is undertaken at the design stage and involves setting field properties. The field properties will determine how each item in that field will be stored.

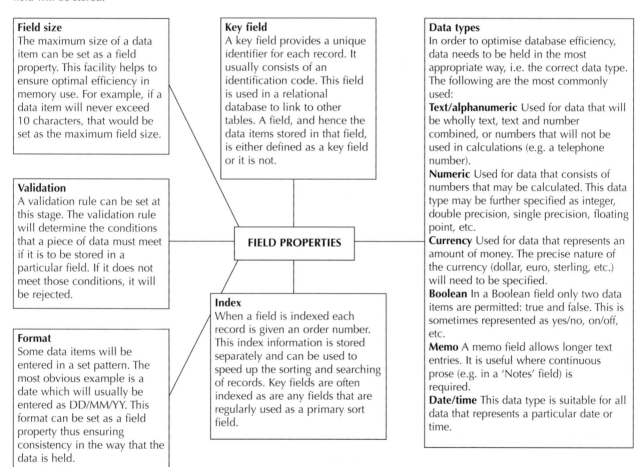

**Field size**
The maximum size of a data item can be set as a field property. This facility helps to ensure optimal efficiency in memory use. For example, if a data item will never exceed 10 characters, that would be set as the maximum field size.

**Validation**
A validation rule can be set at this stage. The validation rule will determine the conditions that a piece of data must meet if it is to be stored in a particular field. If it does not meet those conditions, it will be rejected.

**Format**
Some data items will be entered in a set pattern. The most obvious example is a date which will usually be entered as DD/MM/YY. This format can be set as a field property thus ensuring consistency in the way that the data is held.

**Key field**
A key field provides a unique identifier for each record. It usually consists of an identification code. This field is used in a relational database to link to other tables. A field, and hence the data items stored in that field, is either defined as a key field or it is not.

**FIELD PROPERTIES**

**Index**
When a field is indexed each record is given an order number. This index information is stored separately and can be used to speed up the sorting and searching of records. Key fields are often indexed as are any fields that are regularly used as a primary sort field.

**Data types**
In order to optimise database efficiency, data needs to be held in the most appropriate way, i.e. the correct data type. The following are the most commonly used:
**Text/alphanumeric** Used for data that will be wholly text, text and number combined, or numbers that will not be used in calculations (e.g. a telephone number).
**Numeric** Used for data that consists of numbers that may be calculated. This data type may be further specified as integer, double precision, single precision, floating point, etc.
**Currency** Used for data that represents an amount of money. The precise nature of the currency (dollar, euro, sterling, etc.) will need to be specified.
**Boolean** In a Boolean field only two data items are permitted: true and false. This is sometimes represented as yes/no, on/off, etc.
**Memo** A memo field allows longer text entries. It is useful where continuous prose (e.g. in a 'Notes' field) is required.
**Date/time** This data type is suitable for all data that represents a particular date or time.

### Example – the properties of two data items

| Data Item: 12/09/86 | |
|---|---|
| Field name | Date_of_Birth |
| Field description | Employee's birth date |
| Index | No |
| Key field | No |
| Validation | Must be <([Now]) |
| Data type | Date/time |
| Format | DD/MM/YY |
| Field size | 8 characters |

| Data Item: North West | |
|---|---|
| Field name | Region |
| Field description | Define employee's base region |
| Index | No |
| Key field | No |
| Validation | Must be drawn from Region table |
| Data type | Text |
| Format | - |
| Field size | 25 |

# Different methods of file organisation

## SEQUENTIAL ORGANISATION

A file that organises data sequentially stores records according to a predefined sequence. The sequence of records may be determined simply by the order in which they were written to the file or a key field may be used to sequence them. In the example below the records have been put in sequence according to the primary key, i.e. the stock number.

| Stock No. | Cat. | Name | Stock |
| --- | --- | --- | --- |
| 123705 | Electric | 2 gang switch plate – brass | 43 |
| 133456 | Electric | 3 gang switch plate – brass | 56 |
| 145221 | Electric | 2 gang socket – brass | 27 |
| 145332 | Cable | 2 core 50m | 76 |
| 158724 | Cable | 2 core 100m | 51 |
| 167322 | Cable | 3 core 10m | 44 |

Sequential processing is the simplest method of file organisation and the one that requires the fewest memory resources. In order to access a particular record, one must also read all the other records that physically precede the searched-for record. Also, whenever new records are added, existing records are amended or unwanted records deleted, the whole file must be rewritten to maintain the sequence.

For these reasons sequential organisation is not suitable for situations where a specific record is being sought. Finding a record in a sequentially organised file is analogous to finding a music track on a cassette tape: one has to work through all the songs that precede the desired one.

It is, however, very effective for batch processing programs, i.e. where *all* of the records in a file will be subject to the same processing activity. In the above example, sequential organisation would be appropriate if a batch program were run at the end of each day to update stock levels.

## DIRECT ORGANISATION

A file based on direct organisation stores records at a designated 'address' on the storage medium. This address is calculated using a technique called 'hashing'. Hashing entails applying a mathematical algorithm to a unique numerical field (usually the key field) to create an address for each record.

| Stock No. |
| --- |
| 123705 |
| 133456 |
| 145221 |
| 145332 |
| 158724 |
| 167322 |

**Apply hash function**

| Address |
| --- |
| 43 |
| 67 |
| 21 |
| 17 |
| 15 |
| 66 |

The algorithm makes a calculation based on the numerical composition of the field, e.g. by adding the numbers together, multiplying the result by a set number and then dividing that result by the sum of the last two digits. This system can also be applied to text-based fields, i.e. by first converting the characters to their ASCII code equivalents.

One problem with this approach is that, however sophisticated the algorithm, it may produce the same result for two different records. This is referred to as a 'hash collision'. Another program may then be used to store records located to the same address in an overflow table.

Direct organisation (sometimes called 'random organisation') files are most efficient when programs have to search for individual records. Searching for a particular record in a direct organisation file is analogous to finding a track on a CD when you know what the track number is.

## INDEXED SEQUENTIAL ORGANISATION

A file that uses an indexed sequential system of organisation orders the records according to a key field, but additionally creates an index file that can be used to increase the efficiency of searches. An index file can be created using any field in the record. In practice, the field that is chosen is one that will regularly be used for setting search criteria.

In the example below a separate index file has been created for Cat. (i.e. category of product). This is a field that may be used as a search or sort field. When a particular stock item needs to be located, the index file is read first. After the category the item belongs to has been located, the number of records that must be searched is diminished, thus speeding up the search.

### Stock file

| Stock No. | Cat. | Name | Stock |
| --- | --- | --- | --- |
| 123705 | Electric | 2 gang switch plate – brass | 43 |
| 133456 | Electric | 3 gang switch plate – brass | 56 |
| 145221 | Electric | 2 gang socket – brass | 27 |
| 145332 | Cable | 2 core 50m | 76 |
| 158724 | Cable | 2 core 100m | 51 |
| 167322 | Cable | 3 core 10m | 44 |

### Index file

| Cable | 145332 |
| --- | --- |
| Cable | 158724 |
| Cable | 167322 |
| Electric | 123705 |
| Electric | 133456 |
| Electric | 145221 |

Indexing significantly speeds up the process of locating individual records, but it does require more memory resources, especially if index files are maintained on several fields. Another problem with indexing is that when records need to be added or deleted the index files also require updating. This can slow down processes.

# Querying databases: 1

The prime function of a database is to store data in an organised way so that users can interrogate and manipulate that data. There may be many reasons why users may wish to undertake this process, e.g. identifying a group of records that share specified qualities; calculating totals based on the information held in records; updating the details of a specified record or group of records; viewing data in different combinations and formats, etc. Databases usually allow users to define and store their own queries. The nature of the query will depend on the task it has to perform. Below are some examples of different querying techniques.

## A select query – single criteria

A select query extracts a sub-set of data from a table or more than one linked tables. Criteria are used to establish which records will be extracted.

**TABLE**

| Product_ID | Prod_Name | Cost_price | In_Stock |
|---|---|---|---|
| CA/34/99 | 20m Cable | £12.65 | 21 |
| CA/56/98 | Cable Ties | £4.50 | 6 |
| CO/73/99 | Connectors | £2.35 | 5 |
| SW/86/98 | Switches | £4.67 | 17 |
| FC/54/99 | Fine Cable | £16.78 | 9 |

**QUERY**

| | Product_ID | Prod_Name | Cost_price | In_Stock |
|---|---|---|---|---|
| Criteria | | | | <8 |
| Sort | | Ascending | | |

**RESULT**

| Product_ID | Prod_Type | Cost_price | In_Stock |
|---|---|---|---|
| CA/56/98 | Cable Ties | £4.50 | 6 |
| CO/73/99 | Connectors | £2.35 | 5 |

## A select query – multiple criteria

Sometimes it is necessary to set more than one criteria. Boolean operators (e.g. 'AND', 'OR', etc.) can be used to make the selection criteria more specific.

**TABLE**

| Product_ID | Prod_Name | Cost_price | In_Stock |
|---|---|---|---|
| CA/34/99 | 20m Cable | £12.65 | 21 |
| CA/56/98 | Cable Ties | £4.50 | 6 |
| CO/73/99 | Connectors | £2.35 | 5 |
| SW/86/98 | Switches | £4.67 | 17 |
| FC/54/99 | Fine Cable | £16.78 | 9 |

**QUERY**

| | Product_ID | Prod_Name | Cost_price | In_Stock |
|---|---|---|---|---|
| Criteria | | | >£4.00 | <20 |
| Sort | | | Ascending | |

**RESULT**

| Product_ID | Prod_Type | Cost_price | In_Stock |
|---|---|---|---|
| CA/56/98 | Cable Ties | £4.50 | 6 |
| SW/86/98 | Switches | £4.67 | 17 |
| FC/54/99 | Fine Cable | £16.78 | 9 |

## An update query

An update query can be used to change data in a table. This function is especially useful when block updates, e.g. a price change, need to be made.

**TABLE**

| Product_ID | Prod_Name | Cost_price | In_Stock |
|---|---|---|---|
| CA/34/99 | 20m Cable | £12.65 | 21 |
| CA/56/98 | Cable Ties | £4.50 | 6 |
| CO/73/99 | Connectors | £2.35 | 5 |
| SW/86/98 | Switches | £4.67 | 17 |
| FC/54/99 | Fine Cable | £16.78 | 9 |

**QUERY**

| | Product_ID | Prod_Name | Cost_price | In_Stock |
|---|---|---|---|---|
| Update to | | | £13.15 | |
| Criteria | | = "20m Cable" | | |

**RESULT**

| Product_ID | Prod_Type | Cost_price | In_Stock |
|---|---|---|---|
| CA/34/99 | 20m Cable | £13.15 | 21 |
| CA/56/98 | Cable Ties | £4.50 | 6 |
| CO/73/99 | Connectors | £2.35 | 5 |
| SW/86/98 | Switches | £4.67 | 17 |
| FC/54/99 | Fine Cable | £16.78 | 9 |

## A query with calculated totals

Queries can be used to make calculations based on the data held in tables. In addition to the formula used here, queries can show averages, sums, counts, etc.

**TABLE**

| Product_ID | Prod_Name | Cost_price | In_Stock |
|---|---|---|---|
| CA/34/99 | 20m Cable | £12.65 | 21 |
| CA/56/98 | Cable Ties | £4.50 | 6 |
| CO/73/99 | Connectors | £2.35 | 5 |
| SW/86/98 | Switches | £4.67 | 17 |
| FC/54/99 | Fine Cable | £16.78 | 9 |

**QUERY**

| Product_ID | | |
|---|---|---|
| | = Cost_price*In_Stock | |

**RESULT**

| Product_ID | Value of stock |
|---|---|
| CA/34/99 | £265.65 |
| CA/56/98 | £27.00 |
| CO/73/99 | £11.75 |
| SW/86/98 | £79.39 |
| FC/54/99 | £151.02 |

# Querying databases: 2

## What is SQL?

Database applications usually provide users with a user-friendly means of constructing queries, whereby the user can specify the parameters of the query, the data they wish to interrogate, and the form they would like the results presented in. This approach works well at a basic level but can be restrictive when the needs are more complex. For example, a developer may be trying to create an application that draws on data held in different databases, running on different platforms. She will need to write her code in such a way as to communicate with a range of database formats. In order to meet this need a set of 'query languages' has emerged. These languages give users a common platform from which to interrogate and manipulate data held in different databases. The most widely used of these languages is Structured Query Language (SQL).

SQL is not as easy to use as database programs that provide user-friendly interfaces for the construction of queries. It is a complex computer language with its own vocabulary, grammar and syntax, all of which need to be learnt if it is to be used effectively. It can also be time-consuming to write out extensive SQL code. There are, however, programs that help the user write SQL code and its flexibility and robustness make it a boon for developers. It can deal with complex, multi-faceted relational database queries and is now widely accepted as a standard for interrogating and manipulating data.

## SQL example 1

| TABLE (PRODUCTS) | | | |
|---|---|---|---|
| Product_ID | Prod_Name | Cost_price | In_Stock |
| CA/34/99 | 20m Cable | £12.65 | 21 |
| CA/56/98 | Cable Ties | £4.50 | 6 |
| CO/73/99 | Connectors | £2.35 | 5 |
| SW/86/98 | Switches | £4.67 | 17 |
| FC/54/99 | Fine Cable | £16.78 | 9 |

| SQL STATEMENT |
|---|
| SELECT Product_ID, Prod_Name, Cost_Price, In_Stock |
| FROM Products |
| WHERE Products.In_Stock < 8 |
| ORDER BY Prod_Type |

| RESULT | | | |
|---|---|---|---|
| Product_ID | Prod_Type | Cost_price | In_Stock |
| CA/56/98 | Cable Ties | £4.50 | 6 |
| CO/73/99 | Connectors | £2.35 | 5 |

In this example the 'SELECT' clause of the code indicates which fields should be displayed in the result, the 'FROM' clause indicates the table where the data resides, the 'WHERE' clause defines the criteria that will be used to define the extracted data and the 'ORDER BY' clause determines how the result will be sorted.

## SQL example 2

| TABLE (PRODUCTS) | | | |
|---|---|---|---|
| Product_ID | Prod_Name | Cost_price | In_Stock |
| CA/34/99 | 20m Cable | £12.65 | 21 |
| CA/56/98 | Cable Ties | £4.50 | 6 |
| CO/73/99 | Connectors | £2.35 | 5 |
| SW/86/98 | Switches | £4.67 | 17 |
| FC/54/99 | Fine Cable | £16.78 | 9 |

| SQL STATEMENT |
|---|
| UPDATE Products |
| SET Products.Cost_price = "£13.15" |
| WHERE Products.Product_Name = "20m Cable" |

| RESULT | | | |
|---|---|---|---|
| Product_ID | Prod_Name | Cost_price | In_Stock |
| CA/34/99 | 20m Cable | £13.15 | 21 |
| CA/56/98 | Cable Ties | £4.50 | 6 |
| CO/73/99 | Connectors | £2.35 | 5 |
| SW/86/98 | Switches | £4.67 | 17 |
| FC/54/99 | Fine Cable | £16.78 | 9 |

In this example the 'UPDATE' clause indicates the name of the table in which the data items to be updated reside, the 'SET' clause indicates the field to be updated, and the 'WHERE' clause defines the criteria that must be met if the records are to be updated.

# Using queries to create reports

One of the prime functions of a database is to provide reports for the user. These reports, which can be presented on-screen but are more often printed as hard copy, provide information in an appropriate format for the user. The precise nature of the report's format will depend on the use to which the user is going to put the information. For example, a distribution manager may want a simple printout of drivers' phone numbers, whereas as a senior manager might want a monthly summary of sales figures in graphical form. The format will be determined by the use.

## How a query can be used to create a report

A video store keeps its data in a relational database. It has tables for data on Customers, Video, Loans, Suppliers and Miscellaneous Sales. The tables are related to each other using key fields. Below are extracts from the customer file and the loan file.

**CUSTOMER FILE**

| Customer_ ID | Name | Surname | Address | Town | Code |
|---|---|---|---|---|---|
| 12/578/AF | Miss K Stevens | Stevens | 12 The Grove, | Newton | NW3 7YT |
| 12/987/PH | Mr T Koways | Kowaya | 34 West Street | Newton | NW3 8YH |
| 12/960/LK | Mr F Greene | Greene | 14 High Road | Forsham | FS4 9RE |
| 13/97/LH | Mrs D Patel | Patel | 3 Grand Drive | Newton | NW3 8TT |
| 13/652/PF | Mr L Wai Lun | Wai Lun | 12 Wick Ave | Forsham | FS4 3ES |
| 13/041/UG | Miss F Rogers | Rogers | 15 Smiley Street | Newton | NW4 6RS |
| 12/749/SA | Mr J Nunn | Nunn | 11 Lode Cres | Yale | NW6 5GT |

**LOAN FILE**

| Loan_ID | Video_Id | Customer_ID | Date_out | Date_Back | Paid |
|---|---|---|---|---|---|
| 1 | 128/AC | 12/578/AF | 12/01/02 | 13/01/02 | £3.50 |
| 2 | 134/RO | 12/960/LK | 12/01/02 | 13/01/02 | £3.50 |
| 3 | 453/AC | 12/578/AF | 12/01/02 | 13/01/02 | £3.50 |
| 4 | 774/HO | 13/652/PF | 12/01/02 | 13/01/02 | £2.00 |
| 5 | 325/CO | 12/749/SA | 12/01/02 | 13/01/02 | £3.50 |
| 6 | 467/CO | 13/652/PF | 12/01/02 | 13/01/02 | £3.50 |
| 7 | 552/AC | 12/578/AF | 12/01/02 | 13/01/02 | £2.00 |

The video store owner want to offer his best customers 'Gold Card' status and so he needs to produce a report that will tell him who his best customers are. He uses a user-friendly interface to create the query.

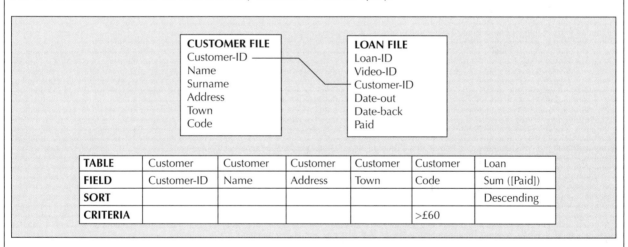

This query has selected the fields that will need to be shown in the report, determined the order in which it will be sorted (i.e. with the customer who has spent the most money shown first) and set the criteria that will be used to extract the data from the tables (i.e. only those customers whose total loans exceed £60 will be included). The two tables that will be needed are linked together (i.e. related) by the Customer_ID key field. A report can now be generated which uses the above query as its data source.

### GOLD CARD CUSTOMER REPORT

*Quarter: January 1st – March 31st*

| Name | Address | Town | Code | Total value of loans during last quarter |
|---|---|---|---|---|
| Miss K Stevens | 12 The Grove, | Newton | NW3 7YT | £90 |
| Mr T Koways | 34 West Street | Newton | NW3 8YH | £86 |
| Mr F Greene | 14 High Road | Forsham | FS4 9RE | £78.50 |
| Mrs D Patel | 3 Grand Drive | Newton | NW3 8TT | £65.00 |

# Entity relationship modelling

Before a database can be designed and implemented, it is necessary to model the underlying data elements. There are various methods for doing this, one of which is entity relationship modelling. Three key concepts involved in this process are:

**Entity**        An entity is a person/object/event/concept on which data can be held. In a hospital database the following would all be entities: patient, nurse, treatment, ward, bed, appointment, test, etc.

**Attribute**     Each entity has a series of attributes. These describe different properties of the entity. Using the above example, the attributes of a patient would include age, weight, home address, dietary needs, etc.

**Relationship**  In a relational database, entities will relate to each other in some way. For a example a doctor will treat a number of patients, a nurse may be attached to a particular ward, etc.

Entity relationship modelling involves the creation of diagrams that show which entities will need to exist in the database and how they will need to relate to each other.

In the example below the database is for a veterinary surgery. The following entities might be identified: patient, vet, owner, room, appointment, treatment, nurse and test. The diagram should indicate how these entities relate to each other.

Another aspect of the diagram will be the *types* of relationship that exist between the entities. There are three types of entities:

**One-to-one**    In this example each vet is allocated one room. It is only possible to have one vet attached to one room at any time.

**One-to-many**   In this example a vet makes a number of appointments – i.e. one vet, many appointments.

**Many-to-many**  In this example one animal/patient may see more than one vet and one vet may see any number of animals.

In databases, many-to-many relationships cause difficulties so they are usually joined together via another entity, using two one-to-many relationships. In this example, one vet will make a number of appointments and one patient may make many appointments.

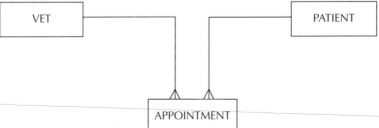

In this way a diagrammatic model is built up. It identifies all the entities that will be contained in the database and an indication of the way in which they relate to each other. This then provides a sound basis for designing the resulting database.

# Normalisation: 1

## What is normalisation?

Normalisation is a formal procedure undertaken during the design stage of database development. It entails creating a robust and valid database structure through a process of 'atomisation', i.e. breaking down the tables into the smallest possible units. Normalisation then involves the creation of a logical structure of related tables in which data will be stored. If completed effectively, it will help in the creation of an efficient, flexible, easy-to-query database. The ideal structure will ensure data consistency and data integrity, and eradicate the unnecessary repetition of data, i.e. data redundancy.

Normalisation is a staged process, usually consisting of a first, second and third normal form. At each stage the structural design is improved. The following illustrates how this process would be undertaken. It is not meant to represent a full data model and there are many other attributes one would expect to see in a database of this kind.

## First normal form

**Rule**   *A table is in first normal form when it contains no repeating attributes or groups of attributes.*

| Student_ID | Forename | Surname | Course_ID | Course_title | Lecturer_ID | Lecturer_name |
|---|---|---|---|---|---|---|
| 24500/V1 | James | Sawyer | PY/12AS<br>IT/12AS<br>MA/12AS | Psychology<br>Information Technology<br>Mathematics | AG<br>PHG<br>BD | Mr Gardner<br>Miss Graham<br>Dr Duckham |
| 34567/V1 | Lisa | Terry | CH/12AS<br>IT/12AS<br>PH/12AS | Chemistry<br>Information Technology<br>Physics | DD<br>PHG<br>VC | Mr Davenport<br>Miss Graham<br>Mrs Cadwell |
| 54783/V1 | David | Brown | MS/12AS<br>EN/12AS<br>HI/12AS | Media Studies<br>English<br>History | LP<br>KN<br>JF | Mr Peterson<br>Miss Nichols<br>Mr Forrest |
| 671200/V1 | Steven | Moody | PY/12AS<br>BI/12AS<br>GE/12AS | Psychology<br>Biology<br>Geography | AG<br>AM<br>LS | Mr Gardner<br>Miss Munir<br>Mr Stone |
| 439456/v1 | David | Powell | IT/12AS<br>FR/12AS<br>GR/12AS | Information Technology<br>French<br>German | PHG<br>ABL<br>GJ | Miss Graham<br>Mme Bailey<br>Mr Jemson |

In this table there are repeating attributes of the 'Course' entity, i.e. the course details are repeated for each student. In its present state then this data table would not satisfy the rule for the first normal form. It is therefore categorised as un-normalised. In its current form this set of data would not be able to function effectively as a database. In particular, problems would be caused when the user wished to update records, add new records or delete records no longer needed.

In order to move this data into the first normal form, it is necessary to split the table into two entities: student and course.

| Student_ID | Forename | Surname | Course_ID |
|---|---|---|---|
| 24500/V1 | James | Sawyer | PY/12AS |
| 24500/V1 | James | Sawyer | IT/12AS |
| 24500/V1 | James | Sawyer | MA/12AS |
| 34567/V1 | Lisa | Terry | CH/12AS |
| 34567/V1 | Lisa | Terry | IT/12AS |
| 34567/V1 | Lisa | Terry | PH/12AS |
| 54783/V1 | David | Brown | EN/12AS |
| 54783/V1 | David | Brown | HI/12AS |
| 54783/V1 | David | Brown | MS/12AS |
| 671200/V1 | Steven | Moody | BI/12AS |
| 671200/V1 | Steven | Moody | GE/12AS |
| 671200/V1 | Steven | Moody | PY/12AS |
| 439456/v1 | David | Powell | IT/12AS |
| 439456/v1 | David | Powell | FR/12AS |
| 439456/v1 | David | Powell | GR/12AS |

| Course_ID | Course_title | Lecturer_ID | Lecturer_name |
|---|---|---|---|
| PY/12AS | Psychology | AG | Mr Gardner |
| CH/12AS | Chemistry | DD | Mr Davenport |
| MS/12AS | Media Studies | LP | Mr Peterson |
| IT/12AS | Information Tech | PHG | Miss Graham |
| MA/12AS | Mathematics | BD | Dr Duckham |
| PH/12AS | Physics | VC | Mrs Cadwell |
| EN/12AS | English | KN | Miss Nichols |
| HI/12AS | History | JF | Mr Forrest |
| BI/12AS | Biology | AM | Miss Munir |
| GE/12AS | Geography | LS | Mr Stone |
| GR/12AS | German | DJ | Mr Jemson |
| FR/12AS | French | ABL | Mme Bailey |

This data is now in the first normal form because there are no repeating attributes or groups of attributes. There is, however, data redundancy: the students' names are being repeated unnecessarily. This will be dealt with in the move to the second normal form.

# Normalisation: 2

## Second normal form

**Rule**  *In the second normal form there will be no partial key dependencies.*

In this case the columns 'Forename' and 'Surname' are dependent on the Student_ID field, i.e. each entry in the Student_ID column is unique and there is a student name uniquely dependent on it. However, Forename and Surname are not uniquely dependent on the 'Course_ID' field, i.e. any number of student 'Forenames' and 'Surnames' may be linked to an entry in this column. There is, therefore, partial dependency.

The solution to this is one often used in relational databases: separating two entities in a many-to-many relationship by inserting a third entity. In this case many students can take many courses but to leave the tables in this form would not work well in a relational database, so they are linked by a third table called 'Enrolment'.

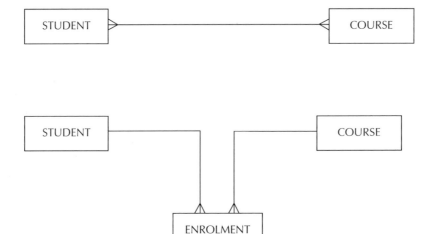

This would result in the following table structures:

**STUDENT**

| Student_ID | Forename | Surname |
|---|---|---|
| 24500/V1 | James | Sawyer |
| 34567/V1 | Lisa | Terry |
| 54783/V1 | David | Brown |
| 671200/V1 | Steven | Moody |
| 439456/v1 | David | Powell |

**COURSE**

| Course_ID | Course_title | Lecturer_ID | Lecturer_name |
|---|---|---|---|
| PY/12AS | Psychology | AG | Mr Gardner |
| CH/12AS | Chemistry | DD | Mr Davenport |
| MS/12AS | Media Studies | LP | Mr Peterson |
| IT/12AS | Information Tech | PHG | Miss Graham |
| MA/12AS | Mathematics | BD | Dr Duckham |
| PH/12AS | Physics | VC | Mrs Cadwell |
| EN/12AS | English | KN | Miss Nichols |
| HI/12AS | History | JF | Mr Forrest |
| BI/12AS | Biology | AM | Miss Munir |
| GE/12AS | Geography | LS | Mr Stone |
| GR/12AS | German | DJ | Mr Jemson |
| FR/12AS | French | ABL | Mme Bailey |

**ENROLMENT**

| Student_ID | Course_ID |
|---|---|
| 24500/V1 | PY/12AS |
| 24500/V1 | IT/12AS |
| 24500/V1 | MA/12AS |
| 34567/V1 | CH/12AS |
| 34567/V1 | IT/12AS |
| 34567/V1 | PH/12AS |
| 54783/V1 | EN/12AS |
| 54783/V1 | HI/12AS |
| 54783/V1 | MS/12AS |
| 671200/V1 | BI/12AS |
| 671200/V1 | GE/12AS |
| 671200/V1 | PY/12AS |
| 439456/v1 | IT/12AS |
| 439456/v1 | GR/12AS |
| 439456/v1 | FR/12AS |

The database structure is now in the second normal form because there are no partial key dependencies.

# Normalisation: 3

## Third normal form

**Rule**  *In the third normal form there are no non-key dependencies.*

After a disposal of any partial key dependencies in the second normal form, the last task in the normalisation process is to eradicate any non-key dependencies. In this case the 'Lecturer_name' field is dependent on the 'Lecturer_ID' field and not the 'Course_ID', as is the case with the second normal form. It is therefore necessary to create a new table called LECTURER. This will contain the unique 'Lecturer_ID' field and the 'Lecturer_Name' which is dependent on it.

**STUDENT**

| Student_ID | Forename | Surname |
|------------|----------|---------|
| 24500/V1 | James | Sawyer |
| 34567/V1 | Lisa | Terry |
| 54783/V1 | David | Brown |
| 671200/V1 | Steven | Moody |
| 439456/v1 | David | Powell |

**COURSE**

| Course_ID | Course_title | Lecturer_ID |
|-----------|--------------|-------------|
| PY/12AS | Psychology | AG |
| CH/12AS | Chemistry | DD |
| MS/12AS | Media Studies | LP |
| IT/12AS | Information Tech | PHG |
| MA/12AS | Mathematics | BD |
| PH/12AS | Physics | VC |
| EN/12AS | English | KN |
| HI/12AS | History | JF |
| BI/12AS | Biology | AM |
| GE/12AS | Geography | LS |
| GR/12AS | German | DJ |
| FR/12AS | French | ABL |

**LECTURER**

| Lecturer_ID | Lecturer_name |
|-------------|---------------|
| AG | Mr Gardner |
| DD | Mr Davenport |
| LP | Mr Peterson |
| PHG | Miss Graham |
| BD | Dr Duckham |
| VC | Mrs Cadwell |
| KN | Miss Nichols |
| JF | Mr Forrest |
| AM | Miss Munir |
| LS | Mr Stone |
| DJ | Mr Jemson |
| ABL | Mme Bailey |

**ENROLMENT**

| Student_ID | Course_ID |
|------------|-----------|
| 24500/V1 | PY/12AS |
| 24500/V1 | IT/12AS |
| 24500/V1 | MA/12AS |
| 34567/V1 | CH/12AS |
| 34567/V1 | IT/12AS |
| 34567/V1 | PH/12AS |
| 54783/V1 | EN/12AS |
| 54783/V1 | HI/12AS |
| 54783/V1 | MS/12AS |
| 671200/V1 | BI/12AS |
| 671200/V1 | GE/12AS |
| 671200/V1 | PY/12AS |
| 439456/v1 | IT/12AS |
| 439456/v1 | GR/12AS |
| 439456/v1 | FR/12AS |

The tables are now in the third normal form. This now provides the logical basis for a database structure.

## Database notation

When the normalisation process is being documented a conventional form of notation is used. In this form, the above example – in the third normal form – would be written out like this:

STUDENT (<u>Student_ID</u>, Forename, Surname)
COURSE (<u>Course_ID</u>, Course_Title, Lecturer_ID)
ENROLMENT (<u>Student_ID</u>, <u>Course_ID</u>)
LECTURER (<u>Lecturer_ID</u>, Lecturer_Name)

It should be noted that the entity is written in capital letters, the attributes are placed inside the brackets and separated by commas, and the key fields are underlined.

# Organisational database strategy

## Database reources that an organisation might use

| Data warehouse | Data warehousing involves storing data that is produced by Transaction Processing Systems. Data held in data warehouses can be 'mined' to discover patterns of association, sequences, groupings, etc. This can be of value to the organisation. |
|---|---|
| Company database | Company databases will contain a wide range of information that relates to the core activities of the organisation. The nature of the organisation will determine the precise nature of the data, but typically it will consist of a combination of operational data (e.g. sales, purchases, stock levels, etc.) and other data that the organisation needs to run its business (e.g. client details, suppliers, employees, etc). |
| Proprietary databases | Proprietary databases are collections of data related to a particular business area, e.g. detailed reports on global purchasing trends. Organisations develop them so that they can market them commercially. Other organisations with an interest in that business area then pay to have access to them. |

## Using databases

Data held in various databases can be combined and interrogated in different ways. The resulting information can be used by the organisation for different purposes, including:

| Strategic planning | The senior management of an organisation must make plans for its future. Data mining can indicate trends that will help it determine the optimal areas of development. |
|---|---|
| Self monitoring | Operational data held in company databases can be used by the organisation to monitor its own performance and to relate it to the performance of competitors. |
| Communication | Databases will contain details of customers, clients, suppliers, employees, etc. These can be used to facilitate efficient communication, e.g. using a mail merge facility. |
| Decision-making | Decision support systems draw upon data held in company and proprietary databases in order to aid the decision-making process. |
| Environment monitoring | It is essential that a business remains informed about changes in the environment in which it operates. Failure to do so might mean that competitors gain market advantage. |
| Legislative compliance | Organisations must ensure that they comply with legislation, especially – in this context – data protection legislation. Secure and well-organised databases make this easier to manage. |

## Factors determining a database strategy

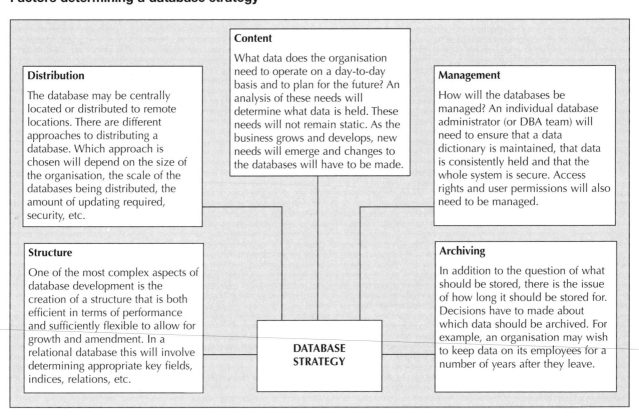

**Content**

What data does the organisation need to operate on a day-to-day basis and to plan for the future? An analysis of these needs will determine what data is held. These needs will not remain static. As the business grows and develops, new needs will emerge and changes to the databases will have to be made.

**Distribution**

The database may be centrally located or distributed to remote locations. There are different approaches to distributing a database. Which approach is chosen will depend on the size of the organisation, the scale of the databases being distributed, the amount of updating required, security, etc.

**Management**

How will the databases be managed? An individual database administrator (or DBA team) will need to ensure that a data dictionary is maintained, that data is consistently held and that the whole system is secure. Access rights and user permissions will also need to be managed.

**Structure**

One of the most complex aspects of database development is the creation of a structure that is both efficient in terms of performance and sufficiently flexible to allow for growth and amendment. In a relational database this will involve determining appropriate key fields, indices, relations, etc.

**Archiving**

In addition to the question of what should be stored, there is the issue of how long it should be stored for. Decisions have to made about which data should be archived. For example, an organisation may wish to keep data on its employees for a number of years after they leave.

**DATABASE STRATEGY**

# Database management systems: 1

### What is a database management system?

A database management system (DBMS) is a method for managing the interface between the data that an organisation stores and the programs that it uses to access that data. Typically, an organisation will store its data in a series of connected data files, e.g. a relational database. Various users will then need to access this database in order to perform a variety of functions on it, e.g. updating, querying, appending, etc. These different users will not all need to access the same data files. For example, a user in human resources may need to access only the 'Employee' and 'Wages' files whereas someone working in the warehouse department may need access to the data held in the 'Stock' and 'Orders' files. A DBMS manages these different needs in an organised and efficient manner.

### How does a DBMS work?

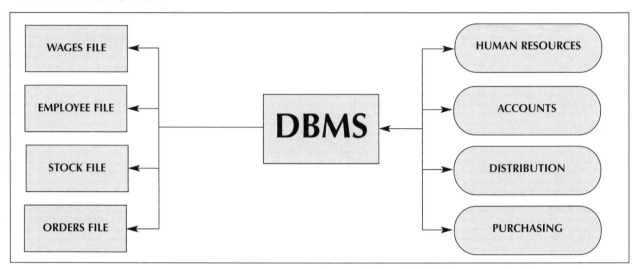

### Functions of a DBMS

*The DBMS should:*

- Allow a variety of users to perform standard database procedures: creating new files, updating existing records, deleting unnecessary records, extracting sub-sets of data, producing reports, etc.
- Ensure that data is securely held and its integrity is protected. Part of the security strategy should include organised back-up and recovery procedures.
- Create and maintain an up-to-date data dictionary. A data dictionary is a stored record of all the different elements of a database – i.e. names of tables and fields, data types used, relationships between different tables, validation rules, etc.
- Organise appropriate user access procedures. It may be necessary to restrict which data files users have access to and what actions they can perform on the data – i.e. some users may have read/write access, other may have read-only access.

### Advantages and Disadvantages of a DBMS

| Advantages | Disadvantages |
|---|---|
| • There is a greater degree of data standardisation within the organisation. Users are obliged to use the same data definitions and work within the confines of the data dictionary. <br>• Security is improved because the database is centrally located and access to it can be controlled. <br>• Data is independent from the programs that interact with it. This means that new programs can be created without developers having to worry about creating or amending underlying data structures. <br>• It is an economical use of organisational resources. The data only has to be stored once. It can then be accessed by the different functional areas of the organisation. This creates savings in terms of hardware and memory requirements. | • The creation and maintenance of a large scale DBMS will be costly. It is likely to require expensive hardware, considerable memory resources and high-specification processing devices. Cost may also be incurred acquiring the necessary staff expertise. <br>• Security procedures have to be detailed and extensive if an organisation's data resources are all centrally located. The organisation is more vulnerable to a disastrous data loss and so will need a well-maintained disaster recovery policy. <br>• Database management systems are complex products. In developing associated programs, developers will need to understand all of their workings. The training and additional time that this might involve will add to development costs. |

# Database management systems: 2

### The client–server approach

Many organisations take advantage of client–server technology to optimise the efficiency of their database management system. The users have client software on their machines and the network server runs DBMS server software. When a user wishes to query the database, the request is sent to the server. The server selects, sorts and returns the requisite records to the client. The user can then use the returned information as they wish. An example of this process is shown below:

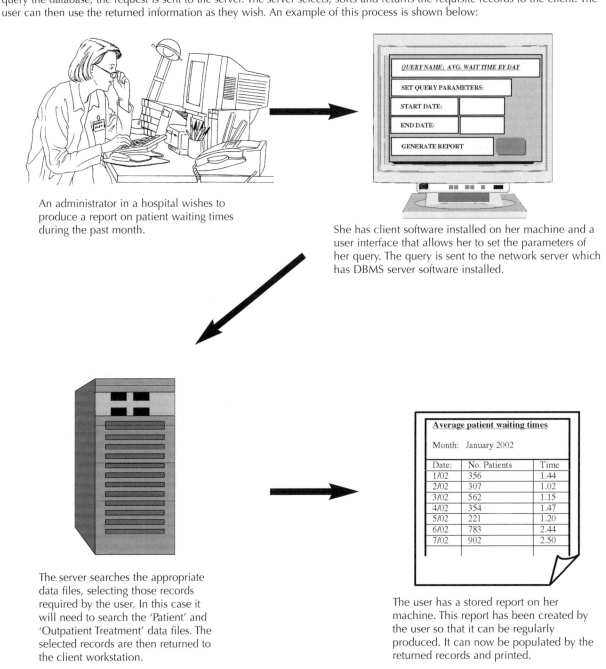

An administrator in a hospital wishes to produce a report on patient waiting times during the past month.

She has client software installed on her machine and a user interface that allows her to set the parameters of her query. The query is sent to the network server which has DBMS server software installed.

The server searches the appropriate data files, selecting those records required by the user. In this case it will need to search the 'Patient' and 'Outpatient Treatment' data files. The selected records are then returned to the client workstation.

The user has a stored report on her machine. This report has been created by the user so that it can be regularly produced. It can now be populated by the returned records and printed.

### The advantages and disadvantages of a client–server approach

✓ A large number of users can gain access to a centrally located database. This is more cost-effective than installing the same database on all users' machines.
✓ When a query is run only the required data is returned, this cuts down on network traffic and so improves performance.
✓ Centralised database management enhances security and helps to optimise data integrity and data consistency.
✓ Clients can be authorised not just to view data but also to update, amend and delete records. This increases flexibility.
✗ Initial purchasing and maintenance costs are higher.
✗ It is more complicated – and therefore more costly – to produce applications that are client–server-enabled.
✗ There is reliance on one main server with all the attendant dangers this implies.
✗ A large volume of data requests may overwhelm the network and slow down communications. For this reason, many organisations have developed distributed databases (see page 71).

# The role of a database administrator

A database administrator (DBA) is an individual within an organisation who has overall responsibility for overseeing the organisation's data resources. Depending on the size of the organisation, that person may lead a team, delegating various responsibilities as necessary. The responsibilities characteristically associated with the role are set out below.

## Training

The DBA is responsible for ensuring that all relevant personnel understand the way the database works. This training will need to be appropriately targeted for users at different levels. Senior managers, for example, will need to know what information requests can reasonably be made. Users at an operational level may need to learn how to run simple queries or update existing data files.

## Security

The DBA must ensure that the database is secure from all the usual internal and external threats. Data integrity must be maintained, e.g. through the use of validation programs. This work may involve liaising with other individuals/teams who have an overall organisational responsibility for security. It will also involve the development of an effective back-up and recovery strategy. There will also need to be a database focus to the organisation's disaster recovery procedure.

## Maintenance

Maintenance work can take various forms, including:

- ensuring that any changes to data structures – e.g. the creation of a new table – are compatible with the overall database architecture;
- dealing with problems encountered by users, and making necessary corrections to the database;
- managing the implications for the database of any general changes to the ICT infrastructure.

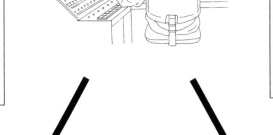

## Access and authorisation

A DBMS will involve a number of different users accessing different parts of the database. It is the responsibility of the DBA to ensure that users only access those aspects of the system that they need to. It may also be necessary to give different users different rights in regard to the actions they can perform, e.g. setting read-only, read/write access. A DBA may also take responsibility for maintaining a password system.

## Liaison with other departments

The DBA will need to liaise with various individuals whose work might impact upon the database. One critical aspect of this liaison is the communication with program developers. In a database management system, where programs and data are independent of each other, it is critical that developers understand the structure of the database. Liaison will occur at various stages of the development life cycle, ensuring that programs read from and write to the database effectively.

## Performance monitoring

How well the database operates will have a significant effect on the overall functioning of an organisation's ICT systems. The DBA should monitor the effectiveness of the database, perhaps using benchmark tests to investigate how efficiently it is performing critical tasks, e.g. how long it takes to run a particular query. Following such monitoring, it may be necessary to amend the structure of the database in order to improve its efficiency.

# Database security

In addition to all the established ICT security issues, there are specific issues associated with data integrity that those responsible for database management need to be aware of. A relational database contains a number of different tables linked by key fields. One property that a link between tables might have is 'referential integrity'. This means that when a user modifies the data in one table, linked data in other tables may also be affected.

In the example below, the user has deleted a customer from the Customer file. In the related Orders table, all of the orders made by the customer are also deleted. This may be exactly what is required but, equally, the organisation may want to use all the data in the Orders table for its own analysis, regardless of whether or not a customer is on its lists.

| Customer_ID | Name | Surname | Address | Town | Code |
|---|---|---|---|---|---|
| 12/578/AF | Miss K Stevens | Stevens | 12 The Grove, | Newton | NW3 7YT |
| 12/987/PH | Mr T Koways | Kowaya | 34 West Street | Newton | NW3 8YH |
| 12/960/LK | Mr F Greene | Greene | 14 High Road | Forsham | FS4 9RE |
| 13/97/LH | Mrs D Patel | Patel | 3 Grand Drive | Newton | NW3 8TT |
| 13/652/PF | Mr L Wai Lun | Wai Lun | 12 Wick Ave | Forsham | FS4 3ES |
| 13/041/UG | Miss F Rogers | Rogers | 15 Smiley Street | Newton | NW4 6RS |
| 12/749/SA | Mr J Nunn | Nunn | 11 Lode Cres | Yale | NW6 5GT |

**RUN DELETE**

Deleting this record will result in associated records in linked tables being deleted.

( Proceed )   ( Cancel )

| Order_No. | Customer_ID | Value | Date | Staff_code |
|---|---|---|---|---|
| 3345 | 12/578/AF | 120.65 | 14/02/02 | TL |
| 3346 | 13/97/LH | 335.75 | 14/02/02 | TL |
| 3347 | 13/652/PF | 1234.50 | 15/02/02 | SA |
| 3348 | 12/578/AF | 367.00 | 16/02/02 | DF |
| 3349 | 13/652/PF | 639.00 | 16/02/02 | FD |

## Establishing user/group permissions

It is the responsibility of the database administrator (DBA) to ensure that different users have only the access they need to perform their tasks. Accidental data loss, such as was illustrated in the example above, should not occur if user access is properly controlled. Each user should have an account that establishes which tables she can have access to and what processes she is permitted to perform. In a large organisation it may be more efficient to divide users into groups, allocate individuals to the groups and set permissions in relation to the groups. Additional security can be provided by obliging users to use a password system and by coding in warning messages before certain actions (e.g. deleting a record) are performed.

Below is an example of the way in which permissions may be set for an individual user.

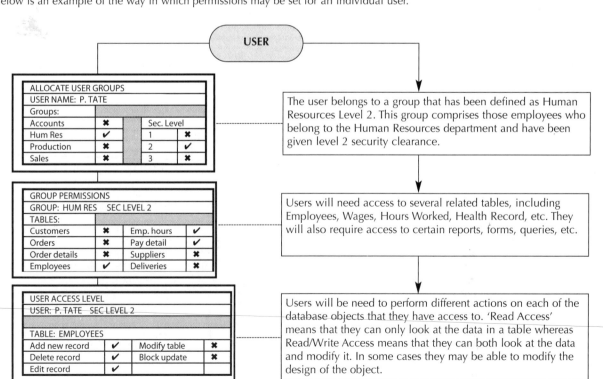

USER

| ALLOCATE USER GROUPS | | | | |
|---|---|---|---|---|
| USER NAME: P. TATE | | | | |
| Groups: | | | | |
| Accounts | ✗ | | Sec. Level | |
| Hum Res | ✔ | | 1 | ✗ |
| Production | ✗ | | 2 | ✔ |
| Sales | ✗ | | 3 | ✗ |

The user belongs to a group that has been defined as Human Resources Level 2. This group comprises those employees who belong to the Human Resources department and have been given level 2 security clearance.

| GROUP PERMISSIONS | | | | |
|---|---|---|---|---|
| GROUP: HUM RES   SEC LEVEL 2 | | | | |
| TABLES: | | | | |
| Customers | ✗ | Emp. hours | ✔ | |
| Orders | ✗ | Pay detail | ✔ | |
| Order details | ✗ | Suppliers | ✗ | |
| Employees | ✔ | Deliveries | ✗ | |

Users will need access to several related tables, including Employees, Wages, Hours Worked, Health Record, etc. They will also require access to certain reports, forms, queries, etc.

| USER ACCESS LEVEL | | | | |
|---|---|---|---|---|
| USER: P. TATE   SEC LEVEL 2 | | | | |
| | | | | |
| TABLE: EMPLOYEES | | | | |
| Add new record | ✔ | Modify table | ✗ | |
| Delete record | ✔ | Block update | ✗ | |
| Edit record | ✔ | | | |

Users will be need to perform different actions on each of the database objects that they have access to. 'Read Access' means that they can only look at the data in a table whereas Read/Write Access means that they can both look at the data and modify it. In some cases they may be able to modify the design of the object.

# Distributed databases

## What is a distributed database?

Organisations often have systems that rely on databases that must be accessible by users working in functionally diverse and geographically remote areas. One method of providing this service is to have one large database, stored on a mainframe computer and accessed via a wide area network. There are, however, drawbacks to such an approach:
- there is over-reliance on a single storage location which could crash and put the whole system out of commission;
- query processing may not be efficient, especially when many demands are being made at the same time;
- it may not be the most efficient use of the organisation's computing resources.

Declining processing costs and improved network communications have enabled the development of an alternative approach based on the distribution of databases across a number of different locations. This approach is referred to as a distributed database system.

## Four approaches to distributing a database

### Partitioned database

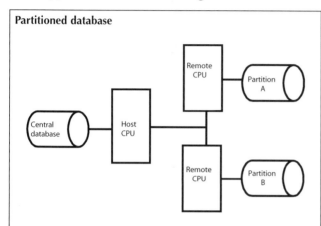

The remote databases download the portion of the database that they require for their local needs. Changes are made at a local level. The central database is then updated, usually via an overnight batch process.

### Duplicate database

The whole database is replicated and downloaded to each remote location. In a similar way to the partitioned system, changes made at a local level are justified with the central database later.

### Central index

The central index holds key indexing data, e.g. customer's name and ID number. The full data file is held and kept updated at a local level. Users can query the central database. The index is then used to direct the user to the location of the complete data file.

### Network query

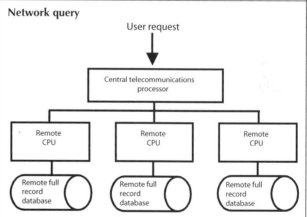

The central processor operates as a kind of search engine, querying all the remote databases, before returning the data from whichever location it is held in. All databases are stored and updated at a local level.

## Advantages and disadvantages of distributed databases

| Advantages | Disadvantages |
|---|---|
| • There is a reduction in risk of a central failure putting the whole organisation out of action.<br>• It is a more efficient use of an organisation's processing and storage resources.<br>• There is increased speed of response to local queries and less chance of excess data traffic jamming the system. | • Depending on the system used, there is an increased possibility of data integrity being compromised, i.e. as a result of running two versions of the database in parallel.<br>• As a consequence of the decentralised nature of the system, there is a greater security risk.<br>• There is a greater dependence on high-quality communications systems. |

# Computer networks

## What is a network?

A computer network describes any situation in which two or more computers are linked together via some form of communications medium for the purpose of exchanging data or sharing resources. Almost all organisational computing now takes place in a networked environment. Non-networked use of computers – i.e. a stand-alone environment – is still the norm in domestic situations, although one could argue that the Internet connection used by most domestic users transforms them into network users. Very small businesses and businesses where independent working is the norm, e.g. some design studios, may operate on a stand-alone basis.

## Two categories of network

One way of categorising networks is by considering their scale. Using this approach two major categories have emerged:

**Local Area Networks (LANs)**   An LAN is a network that is confined to a small geographical area, usually one building or closely connected group of buildings, e.g. a university campus. The predominant mode of communication is physical cabling, usually a combination of fibre optic and copper cabling, although there is growing use of wireless devices in LAN environments. Another defining feature of an LAN is that all of the network resources are owned and managed by the organisation that uses them.

**Wide Area Networks (WANs)**   A WAN is a network that spreads across a large geographical area, connecting LANs via a wide range of communications media. In addition to physical cabling, wireless and satellite technologies may be used to complete a network that may be literally world-wide. Working in a WAN environment will involve using network resources owned and managed by a wide range of organisations. WANs can be further sub-divided into public WANs (the Internet is, in effect, a public WAN) and private WANs, i.e. a secure network owned and managed by one organisation.

## Advantages and disadvantages of networked environments

| Advantages | Disadvantages |
|---|---|
| • Data can be pooled and therefore accessed by a wide range of users. This is especially valuable when access to a shared database is necessary. Instead of each user having a copy of the database on their machine, they can use client–server software to read-from and write-to the centrally stored database. This helps to ensure data integrity.<br>• Hardware resources such as printers and scanners can be shared. This is a more cost-effective solution than providing each user with their own set of peripheral devices.<br>• Software resources can be shared. Instead of buying a copy of the software for each user, one version can be bought and accessed by each user in the network. It will be necessary to purchase licenses to ensure that the shared use of the software is legitimate.<br>• Security is centralised and so improved. The network manager can control access by setting access rights and user permissions and by auditing computer use. Centrally located virus-checking software can be used to check all files on the network. It is easier to control access to Internet sites and to determine users' abilities to download files.<br>• Back-up procedures are easier to complete if centrally located and managed. Instead of each user being responsible for backing up their data, the network manager will take responsibility for running regular back-ups and recoveries. | • Setting up a network is more costly than running a group of stand-alone computers. In addition to the workstations, a central server – usually a more powerful computer – is required, as is communication media (e.g. cabling) and devices such as hubs, connectors, repeaters, bridges, etc.<br>• Networks are particularly vulnerable to viruses. If one machine is 'infected', it is easier for this infection to spread than would be the case in a stand-alone environment.<br>• Network management requires a degree of specialist knowledge and this will mean employing a network manager for this purpose.<br>• Networks are vulnerable to crashes. If a stand-alone computer 'goes down', only that machine is affected, whereas when a network crashes the whole system can be put out of commission.<br>• Networks require more maintenance. Put simply, there are more things that can go wrong with a network: cables can break, network files can become corrupted, the system can become 'jammed' due to excess data traffic. This often means employing people to complete this maintenance. |

# Hardware elements of a network: 1

## Physical cabling

**Twisted pair copper cabling**   As the name suggests this cabling consists of a pair of braided copper cables. They are braided to help protect them from electromagnetic interference. They can be either shielded or unshielded; the shielded version has an extra layer of insulation to prevent interference. Unshielded twisted pair cabling is the cheapest cabling option and is relatively easy to install. It has a lower capacity than fibre optic or coaxial cabling and has a maximum distance of 100 metres between network points.

**Fibre optic cabling**   A fibre optic cable consists of three elements: a core (a glass or plastic fibre); cladding (glass or plastic coating with a different composition to that of the core); the jacket (the outer protective layers, usually made of a plastic material, designed to protect the core and the cladding). Fibre optic cabling is expensive to buy and complicated to install. It is, however, the fastest physical medium and can send data across vast distances without the need for intermittent connections.

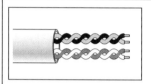

**Coaxial cabling**   Coaxial cabling has a single copper wire at its core. This is surrounded by a plastic insulation casing and a further layer of braided copper insulation. Finally, there is a plastic jacket to offer further protection. Coaxial cable is priced between twisted pair and fire optic cabling. It offers faster data communication than twisted pair but is slower than fibre optic. It can be difficult to install in a building as the cable is rather rigid and inflexible. It is suitable for medium distances, typically 500 m.

## Connection devices

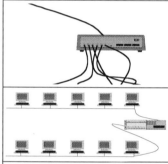

**Hub**   A hub is a device for connecting a number of terminals to a network connection in a 'star' configuration. For example, one network line comes into an 8-point hub. Each of the eight sockets in the hub can then be used to connect a terminal (or a peripheral device such as a printer) to the network. Hubs can be used in connection with each other: an output from one hub can lead to another hub which, in turn, can connect a further set of terminals.

**Bridge**   A bridge is a device that connects two different LANs. The incoming data from one LAN is stored in a buffer memory and then, when the second LAN is ready to receive it, the data is communicated. For a bridge to work effectively, the two LANs must run on the same platform but the buffer memory means that they can be running at different speeds.

**Gateway**   A gateway is a device that enables LANs to communicate with WANs. LANs may be operating on different, incompatible platforms. Gateways use conversion software to ensure that data transmission protocols are compatible and that dissimilar LANs can connect to WANs. Gateway devices have been critical in ensuring the success of the Internet.

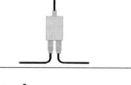

**Router**   A router is a device which helps to determine the optimum route for a packet of data across a network. It has been especially valuable in the development of the Internet, preventing 'traffic jams' of data communication. Routers can be dynamic or non-dynamic. A non-dynamic router sets an optimum route through a section of network and sends the data packet in that direction. A dynamic router monitors data traffic and can redefine the optimum route in response to that traffic.

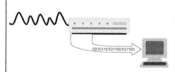

**Connector**   The RJ-45 connector is used with twisted pair cabling and connects to the back of the network card through the back of the computer. It will be familiar as a standard telephone connection. The BNC T-connector is a metal connector that is used with coaxial cable. One end plugs into the external end of a network card and the other two sockets provide a connection for other elements of the network.

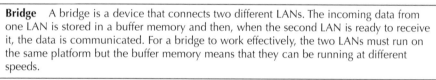

**Modem**   Modem is short for modulator/demodulator. A modem is designed to translate analogue signals to digital signals. Although there is a general trend towards all data communication being digital, there are still many occasions when data needs to be converted from analogue to digital format. Some Internet connections, for example, use a standard telephone line (i.e. analogue) connection. In order for a computer to process the incoming data traffic, the signal must be converted from analogue to digital.

# Hardware elements of a network: 2

### Network interface card

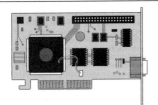

The network interface card (NIC) is a printed circuit board that plugs into one of the expansion slots of the computer's motherboard. It converts the data that is stored in the computer into a form that is suitable for transmission along the network. The type of NIC that is needed will vary according to what type of network is in operation. The most common type is the Ethernet card.

### Uninterruptible power supply

An uninterruptible power supply (UPS) is not an essential part of a network but is certainly a highly desirable one. If a power failure occurs when the main server is in the middle of a critical job, it may lead to a disastrous loss of data. A UPS helps to protect against this. A UPS consists of four essential components: a device that monitors the incoming electrical supply, checking for fluctuations in voltage; a back-up source of power, usually a battery of some kind; a means of switching from mains supply to battery supply if there is a power failure; a means of communicating to the server – and thus the network administrator – that there is a problem.

### Firewalls

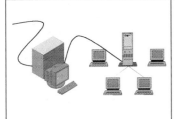

Any network that connects to the outside world, e.g. via the Internet, needs to protect itself against unwarranted intrusion. 'Firewall' is a generic term that describes a combination of hardware devices and software programs that act as a network filter, monitoring all incoming messages and determining whether the originator of the message should have access to the network they are protecting. They are, in effect, computerised security guards, authenticating and validating the credentials of visitors. Where security is critical, firewalls are often established in their own small network. This mini-network – sometimes referred to as a sandbox or DMZ (demilitarised zone) – lies between the internal network and external connections.

### Servers

Strictly speaking, a server is any computer that runs server software. In practice, because computers acting as servers have to perform tasks that client computers don't, they are designed specifically to fulfil a server role. Servers, then, are powerful computers that are designed to fulfil a specific purpose, i.e. to share their resources in a networked environment. The key features of a server are set out below:

#### Powerful processing capabilities

CPUs found in servers run faster than those in PCs. This is because they have more data to process, specifically more data to locate on the hard drive and transfer to the network connection. In many servers more than one CPU is provided, thus enhancing processing capabilities.

#### Built-in network cards and hubs

Unlike most PCs, servers have their own built-in network cards, allowing them to connect to other network components. Many also have a built-in hub. This is a switching device that helps to manage the flow of data traffic around the network.

#### Redundant hard drives

Hard-drive redundancy refers to the practice of automatically backing-up data on to more than one hard drive. This type of set-up (referred to as RAID: Redundant Arrays of Inexpensive Discs) operates in different ways. One method (referred to as RAID 1) entails disc mirroring or duplexing. All data is written identically to two different drives. If one drive fails – or the connection to the drive is lost – the other drive kicks in, allowing continuous data access.

#### Fault tolerance

If an individual network workstation crashes, it is a problem for the user but is unlikely to lead to massive loss of data or significant computer 'downtime'. This is not the case with the server. Therefore, servers have more built-in 'fault tolerant systems' to protect them against crashes. These may include 'redundant' data storage, back-up power supply and even back-up motherboards.

# Software elements of a network

## Network operating systems

A network operating system provides many of the same functions for a network as an operating system does for a stand-alone PC. It manages resources, allocates memory, communicates with input and output devices, schedules tasks and provides a user interface. The key differences are in terms of scale (there is far more of this work to do on a network) and priority (a desktop OS is designed to optimise the performance of whatever application a user is using; a network OS is designed to balance the needs of all those users who are logged on to the network at any one time).

As with desktop OS's, there are different proprietary brands to choose from. The three best known are: Microsoft Windows NT (to date, this system has evolved into Windows 2000 Advanced Server), Novell Netware, and Unix. They all have their strengths and weaknesses and often the decision to choose any one of them will depend on compatibility with existing systems and the preference and experience of the network administrator.

## Network management software

The network administrator will routinely need to perform network maintenance tasks and application software can make these tasks more manageable. In some cases, the software required to perform the task will have been 'bundled' with the network OS; in other cases, it will need to be acquired and installed as an add-in. Below are the some of the tasks that a network administrator would use software to perform:

### SETTING UP ACCOUNTS

The network administrator has to ensure that each user has his own network account. The account will specify which applications he can access, what levels of access he has to different data, how much disc space he has to store files, etc. The network account system will also define user names, passwords and user permissions. In some cases users of a similar kind are categorised into workgroups, e.g. 'student' and 'teacher' on a school network.

### ACCOUNTING LOG

Network software can automatically maintain an accounting log that records various details about the use of the network. Details recorded by such a system will include: user name, workstation used, log-on and log-off times, applications used, files opened/amended/deleted, errors and crashes, etc. This information can be used for a variety of purposes including security checks and analysis of errors/crashes.

### REMOTE MANAGEMENT

Remote management is a valuable tool for supporting users working on a network. In the event of a significant problem or recurring error, it allows the network administrator to take control temporarily of a user's workstation. Once in control the problem can be identified and (hopefully) solved. The user can also be advised on what to do to avoid similar problems in the future. It is especially valuable when the network is spread across a number of remote sites.

NETWORK MANAGEMENT SOFTWARE

### HARDWARE/SOFTWARE INSTALLATION

It is the task of the network administrator to ensure that all new software and hardware installed on the system is compatible with existing systems. Installation-enabling software speeds up this process, facilitating the distribution of software to local hard drives where necessary. Software-metering programs can be used to monitor software usage, checking for illicit installation and ensuring the organisation is not in breach of any licensing agreements.

### CONFIGURATION MANAGEMENT

One of the challenges of network management is to maintain a balance between the need for centralisation and the needs and preferences of individual users. Configuration management programs enable the network administrator to monitor the way in which individual workstations are configured (i.e. what applications are available, the appearance of the desk-top, etc). This can help prevent users down-loading potentially harmful software for personal use.

### AUDITING

Auditing, i.e. the systematic examination of resource usage, may be undertaken for a number of reasons, e.g. concern about the downloading of illicit material, monitoring of network performance, unusual patterns of data access, etc. An automated accounting log may well provide the base data for such an audit, but software will also be needed to interrogate this data meaningfully and present information in a form that is useful for the person conducting the audit.

# Network topologies

A topology is a way of describing the <u>physical</u> layout of a group of networked computers. It describes the various elements of the network (server, PC's, printers, etc.) and the connections between them. The three main topologies are described below:

---

### Star network

There is a central computer – called a hub – that connects all the nodes of the network. All data communications between workstations/servers/printers go through this central hub.

| Advantages | Disadvantages |
|---|---|
| • Because each computer is independent of the others, if one breaks down, the others can continue to function.<br>• Different workstations may need to send different volumes of data across the network. The Star set up allows for different capacity communication links to be established, related to the different needs of the workstations. | • There is a good deal of dependency on the hub working effectively. If this component fails, the whole system may be put out of action.<br>• Both the hardware and software required for the effective running of a Star network are expensive to set up. |

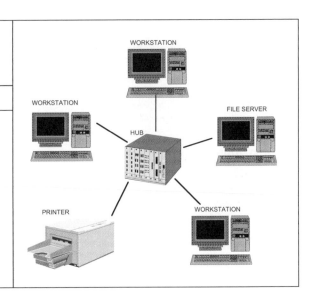

---

### Bus network

In a bus topology, the different nodes are all connected to a single communication path. Data is transmitted in any direction along a central cable. Using this system workstations can communicate with each other, with servers and with peripheral devices.

| Advantages | Disadvantages |
|---|---|
| • Compared to other topologies, a bus network is the least expensive and the easiest to set up.<br>• If one workstation malfunctions, it does not affect the rest of the network.<br>• It is easy to install additional devices. | • The system is dependent on the correct functioning of the main cabling. If this malfunctions, the whole network will go down.<br>• If the cable does fail, the point of failure is difficult to isolate.<br>• The performance of the network will be detrimentally affected by heavy data traffic. |

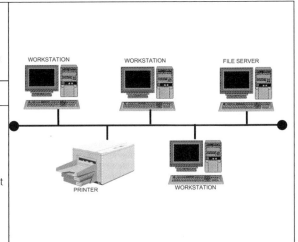

---

### Ring network

This topology usually consists of a collection of workstations and peripheral devices linked together in a circular configuration. There is no central host computer in a ring network, though one node may control overall access to the network.

| Advantages | Disadvantages |
|---|---|
| • The system is not dependent on a central computer.<br>• Using fibre optic links, good transmission speeds can be achieved over a wide area.<br>• This system works effectively when processing is distributed across a number of remote sites. | • The effective running of the system is dependent on one communication link. If this malfunctions, the whole system goes down.<br>• If one node malfunctions, it can have a negative effect on the whole system. |

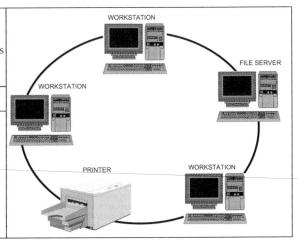

# Logical topologies

The physical topologies (layouts) of networks are described on page 76. In addition, one can define a network in terms of its logical topology. Whereas the physical topology defines the physical arrangement of servers, workstations, cabling, printers, etc. the logical topology defines the way in which data is transmitted around the network. There are two predominant logical topologies: ethernet and token ring.

### Ethernet

Networks transmit data using a packet-switching system. A block of data – a word-processed file, for example – is divided into standard-sized chunks (i.e. packets). These packets are then given a destination address, a sender's address, a means of checking whether the transmission has been error-free (e.g. a check sum) and instructions for the reassembly of the original file (since these packets may not arrive in the same order that they were sent).

Ethernet is an approach to packet-switching data transmission that was first developed in 1973 by Robert Metcalfe. It is based on a protocol called 'Carrier Sense Multiple Access/Collision Detection' (CSMA/CD). According to this protocol, all computers logged on to a network share a segment of the network called a 'collision domain'. Each computer monitors this 'collision domain' and determines whether there is 'free run' available to transmit data. If there is, that computer sends its packet(s) of data. If another computer sends its packet(s) at the same time, a 'collision' occurs. The computers on the network acknowledge the collision and wait a random time before sending their packets of data again. Even in a small network segment, collisions are inevitable. This is not as damaging as it sounds. The time that a computer has to wait for a free run can often be measured in nanoseconds, although it is true that the more network traffic there is, the slower the network will run. There are different varieties of ethernet, each being suitable for different physical topologies and cabling media.

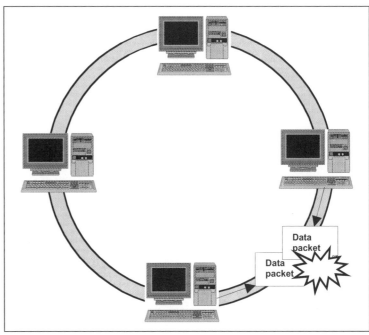

### Token ring

The token ring system also operates on packet-switching principles. When the network is switched on, a special data packet – called a 'token' – circulates the network. When an individual workstation has a data packet to transmit it waits until the token is available. It then takes control of the token, and transmits its data. When it has finished transmitting, it releases the token, thus making it available to any other workstation on the network that is waiting to transmit. A token ring system is a robust system that works well with both twisted pair and fibre optic cabling. It is a lot more costly than ethernet, more difficult to set up and harder to troubleshoot. Consequently, it is not suitable for all organisational set-ups.

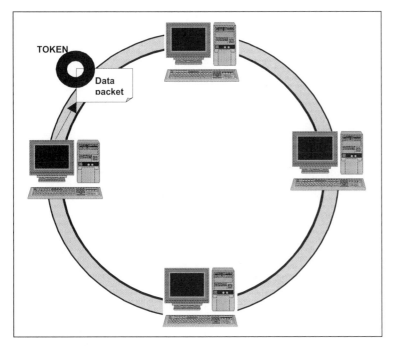

# Creating a networked system

A network is a collection of ICT components linked together in order to facilitate the sharing of resources and/or transmission of data. Part of the work of an ICT department is the creation of new network systems or the expansion/development of existing systems. In undertaking this process, a number of key decisions will have to be made about what software, hardware and communication technologies will be employed and in what configuration. The main decision areas involved are described below. These decisions will be informed by several factors that must be taken into account. These are described on the following page.

## Decisions that have to be made

### TOPOLOGIES

There are three main topologies to choose from: ring, bus and star. Each of these have strengths and weaknesses and will be more suited to some contexts than others. Most networks are not restricted to one of these topologies but are rather combination of different topologies. These are known as 'hybrid networks'.

### SERVERS

There are several different servers that might be used in a network, including: file servers, database servers, web servers, application servers, etc. One or more of these servers may be combined in one machine held in one location or they may be distributed on different machines around the system.

### DISTRIBUTION

Increasingly organisations distribute processing and/or databases around their network. Decisions will have to be made as to where the processing will take place, i.e. whether it will be centrally located or distributed to remote locations. There are also different approaches to distribution (e.g. duplication, partition, etc.).

### NETWORK STRATEGY

There are three main network strategies: terminal (i.e. mainframe plus dumb terminals); peer-to-peer and client–server. The decision will be based largely on a consideration of network size and primary usage. If a client–server strategy is chosen, a decision will have to be made about whether 'thin' or 'fat' clients are used, i.e. whether or not the workstations require a stand-alone capacity.

**DECISIONS**

### SHARED RESOURCES

In addition to workstations and servers, a network will also allow access to resources that can be shared by network users. Printers are the most obvious example of a resource of this kind. Decisions will have to be made about which resources are required, where they will be located, which users will have access to them, how the 'queuing' system will operate, etc.

### COMMUNICATION MEDIA

There are decisions that will have to be made about whether to use cable-based or wireless communication media. If cabling is chosen, there will be further decisions to be made about what type of cabling to be used where, e.g. UTP, coaxial, fibre optic, etc. This decision is constrained by both cost and the physical layout of the area being networked.

### NETWORK OPERATING SYSTEM

Network operating systems (NOS) control and centrally manage the activities of computer resources on a network. This work includes the management of user access, data transmission, file sharing, network accounting, etc. There are various proprietary systems that are available, including Windows NT and Novell.

### STORAGE NEEDS

Decisions will have to be made about the storage capacity of the system, considering questions such as:
- What data will need to be stored and for how long?
- How many applications will need to be stored and who will need access to them?
- What back-up/duplication facilities are required?
- What will happen to data that needs to be archived, etc?

# Creating a network architecture

## Factors informing the decisions

### COST

Whether developing a computer network from scratch or developing an existing system, the individual(s) responsible will have a limited budget to work within, i.e. budgetary constraints will determine what can and cannot be purchased. Fibre optic cabling, for example, offers faster transmission times than other media, but costs significantly more. It is important to take into account not only the initial capital outlay but also the ongoing maintenance costs, e.g. wireless systems can offer greater flexibility but are more costly to maintain than a conventionally wired system.

### SCALE

The size of a network can vary in scale from a small room, containing half a dozen PCs and a printer, to a global network, consisting of a huge number of network elements. The network may be a small, self-contained LAN, connecting the users on one site, or a combination of LANs based in different geographical locations connected in a WAN. Even where a small-scale network is being developed, the physical geography of the area being covered by the network will need to be factored into any decisions, e.g. some communications media are limited by the distance they can cover.

### USAGE

A key question to ask is: How will this system be used? Are users going to require access to a wide range of applications? Are they going to store a large number of data files? Where will the majority of processing be done? The nature of the usage will determine the nature of the network in a number of different ways. For example, if users are required to complete a significant amount of processing, their workstations will need to be sufficiently equipped, whereas if the majority of processing is completed by a central mainframe, individual workstations will require fewer resources.

**FACTORS**

### EXISTING SYSTEMS

Although there are occasions when networks are set up from scratch, it is more often the case that networks have to be built as extensions of existing systems. For example, a company may open a new office and establish a network system for that office. That network will have to connect to the rest of the company's network. The platform that this existing network uses will have certain defining features, including: the communications media it uses, its geographical location, the network operating system it employs, etc. These all constitute constraints that the new system will have to work within.

### PERFORMANCE

There are various ways in which a network's performance may be measured: speed of processing, reliability, user friendliness, capacity, etc. Different organisations – and, indeed, different functional areas within an organisation – will prioritise different performance criteria. For example, a company whose core operation involves real-time processing may be primarily concerned with speed of processing, whereas an organisation with a large multi-user environment and a small maintenance team may be more concerned with robustness.

### SECURITY

There are a number of security issues that need to be taken into account when setting up a network and these will vary according to the organisation concerned. For example, a business organisation may be primarily concerned with outsiders accessing and compromising their business critical systems, whereas a college may be more concerned with students downloading illicit material from the Internet. Different security emphases will lead to different decisions being made about how the system should be set up to minimise areas of vulnerability.

# Managing a network

### Why does a network need to be managed?

Even the simplest of networks needs to be managed by an individual (a network manager) or team of individuals. Almost all organisations that use computing resources do so in a networked environment. These organisations rely heavily on the effective operation of the network. Even minor network problems, e.g. a slowing down of the system due to data traffic, can lead to operational inefficiency and user frustration. Major network crashes can be disastrous and lead to a loss of business. It is therefore essential that networks run well and that users can access the parts of the network they are authorised to use whenever they wish.

There is another critical aspect of networks that needs managing and that is security. The strength of networks, i.e. their ability to allow easy communication between remotely located users, is also their weakness, i.e. they allow access to the 'wrong' people. A good example of network vulnerability is virus spreading. If an individual user infects a stand-alone machine with a virus, the problem remains isolated. In a network environment, the virus uses the existing connections to spread itself to all connected machines.

### The main requirements of network management

**ACCOUNTING**

For a variety of reasons it is important to maintain a check on who uses the network, when they use it, and what they use it for. Each user has an account and accounting software keeps a log of the occasions when that user has logged on to the network, how long they were logged on for, what applications they loaded, what files they amended, etc. The network manager may be required to check this accounting log for a specific security enquiry or it may be used for a general audit of network usage.

**SECURITY**

This aspect includes:
- User access: setting access rights and user permissions for all network users.
- Password system: this is most effective when it is centrally organised and systematic, i.e. *not* individuals using their own passwords.
- Firewalls: these provide a 'gate-keeping' facility to check the legitimacy of extra-network communication.
- Back-ups: the network manager must ensure that there is a reliable back-up system in place.
- Physical security of stations.

**MAINTENANCE**

A network manager needs to:
- Ensure that faults in the system are reported, preferably in a systematic manner, i.e. via a fault log, and that there is a maintenance programme to deal with these faults.
- Take responsibility for the installation of new software and hardware, ensuring that there are no compatibility problems.
- Ensure that upgrades to the system are well managed with the minimum of disruption to normal operations.

**NETWORK MANAGEMENT**

**TRAINING**

All users must understand:
- how to use the network
- the file/directory structure of the network
- what network 'rights' they have
- what the log-in procedure is
- the importance of security
- what constitutes responsible and legitimate usage of the network.

There should therefore be a well-structured induction program for new staff and regular training sessions and information-giving procedures for established staff.

**USER INTERFACE**

Using a network means interacting with a specific user interface. This will be noticeable in three ways:
- When the user logs in they will need to go through a password protected interface in order to gain access to network resources.
- The user's account will determine which applications they have access to. This in turn will help define the appearance of their desktop.
- When using applications, access rights will determine what actions users can and cannot perform.

**PERFORMANCE MONITORING**

The network manager needs to keep a check on how efficiently the network is running. Software can be installed which will help in this process. It is particularly important to monitor how different levels of data traffic affect the speed of access/processing. Following analysis, it may be possible to isolate areas of the network that need to be upgraded or replaced because they are inadequate to the needs of the system and are slowing it down.

# Protecting a network

## Threats to a network

It is the paradox of networks that their greatest virtue is also their chief weakness. They allow users to connect to each other and beyond that, via the Internet, to an unbounded global network. This confers enormous benefits in terms of the sharing of resources, the efficient transfer of files and data, and access to remote sources of data. The same connectedness, however, also creates a point of vulnerability. The network is, to a determined hacker, the equivalent of a window to a burglar: a possible point of entry. Whether the network is the equivalent of a cracked window in a rotten frame or triple-glazed security glass in a fixed metal frame will depend on the security measures that the organisation employs.

The security threats that network administrators need to be aware of fall into three broad categories:

**Non-malicious attacks** The aim of the intruder is simply to break through the network's defences just to prove that they can. It is, as far as the hacker is concerned, a type of game where their skill is pitted against the security resources of the system. These attacks can, none the less, create a great deal of damage.

**Malicious attacks** For whatever reason, the intruder wishes the organisation ill. They want to cause as much damage as they can to the ICT systems. They may achieve this by causing crashes, introducing viruses or corrupting data.

**Criminal activity** The prime aim of the intruder is not to cause damage but to commit a criminal act, e.g. by altering data for financial gain or by stealing information that has commercial value.

## Defending the network

### FIREWALLS

A firewall is a security device designed to protect a network from intrusion via the Internet connection. It may consist of a dedicated computer running firewall software or a specific piece of hardware that looks very much like a router. Whatever form it takes, its primary function is to authenticate incoming messages and verify the legitimacy of users trying to enter the network via an Internet connection.

A typical firewall set-up comprises a separate network (sometimes referred to as a 'sandbox') that sits between the internal network and the connection to the Internet. The firewall then checks incoming packets of data against rules of authentication (which can be determined by the network administrator). Any data packet that fails the authentication test can then be discarded. Firewalls allow the network administrator to determine what data should and should not be let through.

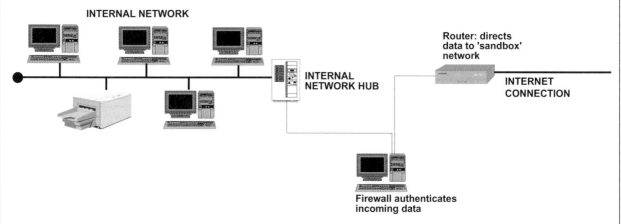

### PROXY SERVERS

A proxy server is a device that stops potential intruders from identifying the Internet Protocol (IP) address of an individual user making an Internet request. All requests go first to a proxy server, the server notes the IP address of the user making the request, then sends the request out to the Internet. When the file is returned, it goes first to the proxy server. The proxy server then sends it to the user that made the request. This means that the only IP address that has been made accessible is that of the proxy server. The IP address of the proxy server is not much use to a hacker, whereas an individual's IP address is.

# Wireless networking

### The need for wireless networks

Traditional wired networks make an assumption about the way that people work: that they will only need to access network resources from static locations. There are, however, many areas of work where people need to be mobile *and* access a network. Some doctors, for example, visit their patients in a wide range of locations. Data on these patients may well be held on a networked database. It would clearly be advantageous for the doctor to access this information at the point of contact with the patient and to be able to update the same database following the examination. There are workers in other environments who would benefit from the same technology: sales staff who travel around the country, emergency and breakdown personnel, delivery drivers, etc. The advent of wireless networks offers a solution to this problem.

Wireless networking may be used as part of a LAN, e.g. a mobile bar code reader being used in a warehouse stock control system, or as part of a WAN or Virtual Private Network, e.g. a delivery driver using a hand-held device to confirm deliveries and update a central database.

### What wireless networking entails

Wireless systems transmit data by using radio waves or infrared light. They consist of devices with radio transmission capabilities and radio receivers able to capture the signals from such devices. The receivers are attached (usually via cable, thus ensuring that wireless networks are not wholly wire-less) to individual computers or network servers. A simple model of wireless data transmission is shown below.

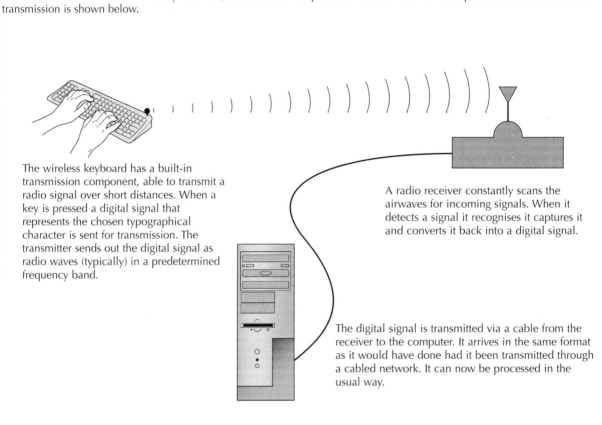

The wireless keyboard has a built-in transmission component, able to transmit a radio signal over short distances. When a key is pressed a digital signal that represents the chosen typographical character is sent for transmission. The transmitter sends out the digital signal as radio waves (typically) in a predetermined frequency band.

A radio receiver constantly scans the airwaves for incoming signals. When it detects a signal it recognises it captures it and converts it back into a digital signal.

The digital signal is transmitted via a cable from the receiver to the computer. It arrives in the same format as it would have done had it been transmitted through a cabled network. It can now be processed in the usual way.

### Problems with wireless networking

Wireless networking technologies are still in early stages of development and there are at the moment a number of problems associated with their implementation.

- There is a gradual move towards standardisation of wireless devices, with two standards Bluetooth and IEEE 802.11 currently dominant. In order for wireless networking to develop fully, manufacturers of input/output devices, computers, transmitters, and receivers need to agree on a broadly implemented, common standard. There is a trend towards this but it has not, as yet, been achieved.
- At the moment, the cost of wireless networking exceeds that of traditional, cabled networks. It is , therefore, only cost-effective for organisations that would benefit materially from greater mobility and flexibility.
- Transmission speeds are slower than cabled networks and there can be problems if there is too much competing radio traffic in one building.
- There are new security issues that need to be dealt with. Viruses can be spread through wireless networks and the technology exists for radio frequencies to be monitored and the data transmitted across these networks to be captured by unauthorised individuals. There are encryption technologies available – e.g. Wired Equivalent Privacy – but these have been shown to be vulnerable to intrusion.

# Standards and protocols

During the period when computers were first being developed for the mass market, manufacturers gave little thought to the need for compatibility between different systems. The new computer industry did not have a regulatory body imposing authoritative standards on it, and so each company operated according to its own rules. Before long, however, it became clear that some form of standardisation would be necessary. Organisations did not necessarily buy all of their hardware and software from one manufacturer but they did need all the different components of their systems to work together. Standards therefore began to emerge in two distinct ways: *de facto* standards and *de jure* standards.

### DE FACTO STANDARDS

*De facto* means 'in effect' and describes the way that some standards have emerged gradually through the market domination of a particular product or set of products. The clearest example of this in the world of ICT is the domination of the PC operating systems market by Microsoft's Windows products. The Windows standard is so dominant that other companies coming into the market are obliged to adhere to it or risk rendering their products unsaleable. *De facto* standards are not laid down in law but companies have to take them into account when developing new products.

### DE JURE STANDARDS

*De jure* means 'by law' and describes the way in which some standards are imposed by a group that has some form of authority. *De jure* standards can be defined by groups such as the International Standards Organisation (ISO), the International Electrotechnical Commission (IEC) and the American National Standards Institute (ANSI). National and transnational government organisations may also become involved in determining standards. In computing, the majority of standards are voluntary. Manufacturers tend to comply with them rather than risk producing incompatible products.

## Standards – good or bad?

It may seem, at first sight, that standards in ICT are eminently desirable. Users, after all, want to be able to transfer data and connect devices without worrying all the time about compatibility. On the other hand, the existence of standards can be seen as a conservative force that limits innovation. It is a balancing act that manufacturers and consumers need to be aware of.

**Standards ensure that users can connect devices to each other, transfer data easily, purchase software from different vendors, etc. They make possible the development of public Wide Area Networks like the Internet.**

**Standards stifle innovation. The dominance of the market by one manufacturer, and the creation of standards that perpetuate this dominance, prevents new businesses producing innovative products.**

## Protocols

Protocols are sets of rules that are agreed to by a group of people involved in a co-operative enterprise. In ICT terms it refers to agreements made by manufacturers to abide by a set of rules that have been defined by industry bodies such as the International Standards Organisation. Many of the key protocols in ICT relate to the way in which data is transmitted across networks. They include:

**TCP/IP**    Transmission Control Protocol/Internet Protocol. TCP/IP is the glue that holds the Internet together. Without an agreement about how data will be broken up into packets for transmission (TCP) and how those packets will be addressed (IP), the various elements of the Internet would not be able to communicate with each other. In fact, TCP/IP encompasses a suite of protocols, all of which play a part in making transmission across the Internet possible. They include Routing Information Protocol (RIP), Simple Mail Transport Protocol (SMTP) and Post Office Protocol (POP).

**OSI**    Open System Interconnection. OSI is not strictly speaking a protocol. Rather, it is a model for how data should move around a network. It effectively operates like a protocol, i.e. by providing an agreed approach to network architecture that is adopted by manufacturers.

**FTP**    File Transfer Protocol. FTP defines the way in which files can be downloaded from the Internet. If a user wants to download graphics, audio files, software, etc. from an Internet site, FTP facilitates this.

# Open system interconnection

## What is open system interconnection?

Open System Interconnection (OSI) is a standard model for describing network architecture and, in particular, the way in which computers on a network communicate with each other. It is a conceptual model rather than an actual description of what takes place when one device on a network sends data to another. It was developed by the International Standards Committee as a way of creating greater commonality of approach among different commercial manufacturers and operators. Each of the layers described below has protocols associated with it. So, for example, Transmission Control Protocol (TCP) maps on to the Transport Layer and Internet Protocol (IP) maps on to the Network Layer.

## How OSI works

|  |  |
|---|---|
| APPLICATION LAYER | The highest level in the OSI, this defines the way in which applications interact with the user. As the top layer, it provides a gateway through which all the other layers are accessed. |
| PRESENTATION LAYER | This layer defines the way in which data is represented. It deals with the translation of data that arrives via the network in a different format to the one used by the host computer. For example, displaying UNIX style data on an MS-DOS interface. |
| SESSION LAYER | The sharing of a connection between networked computers is referred to as a session. The session layer handles events such as synchronisation of data transmission, permission requests, etc. This layer also sets boundaries (or brackets) to define the start and finish of the message. |
| TRANSPORT LAYER | The transport layer is concerned with ensuring the data arrives at the destination computer(s) correctly. This may involve subdividing the data into segments, adding check sums to trap transmission errors, determining the optimum size for each segment, etc. |
| NETWORK LAYER | The network layer is primarily concerned with the movement of the data across the network. This involves defining segments of data as appropriately sized packets, addressing the packets, etc. It also defines the use of routers, switches, etc. to create an optimum route for the data. |
| DATA LINK LAYER | The data link layer supervises the actual transmission of data, confirming checksums and creating duplicates of data packets. The data link layer holds the duplicate packet until the point on the route confirms that it has received a correct copy. |
| PHYSICAL LAYER | The physical layer is concerned with the physical aspects of network transmission, the cabling, network cards, wireless devices, etc. It specifies how the data will actually travel along these media, what translation will need to happen, etc. |

APPLICATION LAYER

PRESENTATION LAYER

SESSION LAYER

TRANSPORT LAYER

NETWORK LAYER

DATA LINK LAYER

PHYSICAL LAYER

# Development trends in communications technology

There are many, diverse trends in the development of information and communications technology. One key trend, a trend driven by commercial demand, can be summarised as follows:

**Faster access to a wider range of content, including sound and video files, using compact, mobile devices.**

In practice this means the development of wireless devices, such as mobile phones and Personal Data Assistants (PDAs), with the capacity to connect to wide area networks (such as the Internet). These devices need to be able to receive and send data and output downloaded content, including video and sound files. In short the aim is to develop something as small and flexible as a mobile phone with the computing capabilities of a desktop PC.

## Some key developments in mobile Internet access

| | |
|---|---|
| **WAP** | WAP stands for Wireless Application Protocol and refers to a set of industry standards that allow mobile devices to access the Internet. The first attempt to provide mobile Internet access used this technology and led to the development of WAP-enabled phones. This first attempt was largely a failed one because the range of available websites was small and the download times slow. |
| **GPRS** | General Packet Radio Service is a wireless technology that depends on packet switching rather than circuit switching (as WAP phone technology did). It offers an always-on system that downloads data via the Internet in the same way as a wired computer, i.e. through the transmission of addressed data packets. Mobile systems based on GPRS systems are known as 2.5g. The 'g' stands for generation, i.e. the phones are between the second generation of mobile phones (which made the move from analogue to digital technology) and third generation (see below). |
| **3G** | Third-generation phones use a combination of technologies to offer an always-on, broadband service. 3G does not just refer to mobile phones but to a whole range of multi-function mobile devices that can provide a range of communication services. |
| **i-mode** | Japan has been the test bed for mobile computing. The i-mode phones (and their 3G successors) developed by the company NTT DoCoMo have revolutionised the way in which people access the Internet in Japan. Consumers are offered a wide range of services, both leisure-oriented (e.g. online games, horoscopes) and business-oriented (e.g. mobile banking). The service is fast and broadband equivalent. To date there are 31 million users, i.e. almost one quarter of the population. |

## Some issues in communications development

*There are a number of issues associated with the development of fast, broadband, mobile access. These include:*

- The number of incompatible transmission standards. Unlike the Internet, there is no global wireless network. American wireless operators use three competing standards and only one of these is compatible with the leading European transmission standard.
- The current download speed is still too slow for users who are used to the more or less instant access offered by wired, digital networks. Improved compression techniques are helping to make access faster, but there is still some way to go.
- Consumers need to be convinced that they will be able to access applications that will be of use to them. The failure of WAP phones was due, in part, to the lack of availability of useful websites. The development of i-mode and its enormous take-up in Japan shows that the market is there if the service can be provided.
- Mobile devices use a lot of components that are dedicated to performing one function. More recently, they have been given limited programmability, but this is defined at the point of manufacture. The consequence of this, is that as standards change and new applications come online, users have to change their equipment and manufacturers run the risk of being left holding stocks of unwanted devices.
- The telecom companies have spent many millions (£22 billion in the UK alone) paying for radio spectrum access. These companies are now heavily indebted and, if there isn't consumer take-up soon, they will face financial collapse.
- Despite reassurances from both government agencies and telecom companies, there are still fears about the health risks associated with the extensive use of mobile devices. These health fears have been increased by reports of 'cancer clusters' near radio transmission masts. This fear is something the telecom companies will need to tackle: they are estimating that they will need to build 100 000 more transmission masts to deliver 3G services in the UK.

# Different platforms

In making decisions about the purchase of hardware and software, organisations need to have a clear strategy. They cannot acquire elements of their ICT infrastructure in an *ad hoc* manner, with no regard for the interoperability of these different elements. Components of the infrastructure must be able to communicate with each other. This is referred to as 'connectivity' and failure to achieve it will create problems for the organisation's information systems.

A particular combination of software and hardware elements is referred to as a 'platform'. A platform is a combination of hardware devices, operating systems and applications. One of the best known platforms is 'Wintel', the combination of Microsoft's Windows OS and the Intel family of processors. Other platforms include Unix, Linux and MacOS.

There are also older, mainframe systems, called 'legacy systems'. These may include:

- IBM mainframes running their own proprietary operating systems
- Digital VAX systems running VMS
- UNISYS mainframe systems.

These systems may have been designed to do a specific task for the organisation, transaction processing for example, and though they may have been in existence for some time they still perform business critical tasks.

## Making decisions

In making decisions about hardware/software acquisitions the organisation will need to think about the following questions:

- What platforms are currently in place?
- What platforms do they see themselves working on in the future?
- What is the interoperability of these platforms? Does the purchase of a particular piece of hardware limit the OS/applications that they can use?
- What account must be taken of legacy systems that cannot be replaced and must be able to connect to new systems?

## Solving connectivity problems

It is usual for large organisations to have cross-platform ICT infrastructures. A retail business may have a Wintel platform for its office work, a Linux OS for online transaction processing and a Unix mainframe for daily batch processing. There are different ways in which the problems of cross-platform incompatibility can be addressed:

### Emulation

Emulation is the process whereby a device that belongs to one platform behaves *as if* it is on another platform, i.e. it emulates it. Emulation software may be used in a situation where the user wishes to use an application that normally works on one platform (its native platform) on a platform it is not usually compatible with (a non-native platform). As the user loads and uses the application, the emulation software translates the coded instructions into a format that the non-native OS will understand. The user is able to use the application as if it is operating on a native machine. Emulation can help to solve some connectivity problems but the price is often a slow-down in processing speeds, as the translation process takes additional time.

### Enterprise application integration (EAI)

These are proprietary tools that allow the different components of an organisation's ICT infrastructure to 'talk' to each other. These systems employ a range of methodologies to integrate different applications with databases and legacy systems. They are expensive to purchase and their complexity makes them difficult to maintain.

### Web services

Web-based technologies form a new approach to developing inter-operability. They are based on an agreed set of standards that are used to move data around the World Wide Web, chief of which is XML. XML stands for Extensible Mark-up Language. It was originally designed to create a common information format for exchanging data on the internet and is 'related' to the HTML format that is used to create web pages. The use of common formats allows applications running on different platforms to communicate with each other. At the time of writing, this is a new technology that seems to hold much promise. It has not as yet, however, proved itself in the market place and many organisations do not have the expertise to implement it.

# Distributed computing on the Internet

## What is distributed computing?

The idea behind distributed computing is a simple one. Most desktop PCs have more processing power than they need and certainly more than is actually used at any one time. There are at least 300 million computers linked to the Internet and – it has been suggested – up to 90% of their processing power is currently being wasted. If it were possible to harness this spare processing capacity and put it to use, a new generation of networked 'supercomputers' could be created that could undertake the type of work currently undertaken by fixed-location supercomputers. The idea of creating transient peer-to-peer networks first became widely known through file-sharing services such as Napster and Gnutella. These were used for the – sometimes illegal – sharing of music and video files. The potential of such an approach appealed to organisations – both commercial and non-commercial – that had large-scale processing needs that would normally entail the purchasing of a supercomputer.

Distributed computing works like this: the organisation installs client software on a number of networked computers. The network in question can be an organisational one or a public one, i.e. the Internet. The organisation then distributes part of a processing task to each of the computers. The client software uses the computer's spare capacity to undertake the processing whenever it can, i.e. any time when the computer is not completing the user's own processing. Some organisations achieve this through installing a screen-saver on the target computer. Whenever the screen-saver is activated the code is run to initiate the processing task.

Some commentators have seen this approach as a significant development in computing technology. They foresee the development of 'grid computing', whereby processing power is distributed across millions of computers and organisations and individuals purchase processing power as and when they need it. This may well provide a future model for computing but there are still a number of hurdles, primarily concerns about the reliability of individual PCs and the security implications.

## Some examples of distributed computing in action

### POPULAR POWER

This company launched its application by helping to facilitate non-profit-making medical research into the development of an influenza vaccine. The investigation of vaccines is an iterative process, i.e. the same process has to be run through over and over again with minor variations and the results computed and compared. The project, which was run under the aegis of the World Health Organisation's National Influenza Laboratory in Rotterdam, entailed the creation of simulations of the human immune system and the recording of effects on this system of simulated vaccines. With more than 10 000 clients running the software, the project has processed millions of virtual experiments and developed new thinking on creating a suitable vaccine.

### SETI

SETI was one of the first projects of this kind. Based at the University of California, it is a project designed to analyse radio signals from outer space in order to determine whether or not they contain any patterns that might be indicative of intelligent extra-terrestrial life. The data comes from radio telescopes. This data is then divided into different 'data chunks' that represent different frequencies and 'segments' of outer space. These chunks can then be distributed to individual users that have downloaded the program. If the program detects a pattern in the signal, the main SETI site is informed. At the time of writing there are almost 4 million users world wide who have downloaded the SETI program.

### COMPUTE AGAINST CANCER

A company called Paradon has developed a distributed computing application called 'Compute against Cancer'. An 'umbrella' project that included an exploration of the side effects of chemotherapy and the behaviour of cancerous cells, one of its programs involved the comparison of protein sequences in an attempt to understand the development of malignant cells. The client computers would process some of the publicly available data on protein sequences and return their findings to the project organisers.

### FightAIDS

The Scripps Research Institute sends out small blocks of data for analysis. The main focus of the research is to analyse the effect of different drugs on various HIV virus mutations. The overall aim of the project is to develop, if not a cure for AIDS, new ways of treating it. In common with many other projects of this kind, once the software has been downloaded the user doesn't need to do anything else.

# The Internet: introduction

## What is the Internet?

The Internet is, in effect, a very large network of computers. It might better be described as a network of networks. It works by allowing individuals to connect to a worldwide network so that they can communicate with any other computer user in the world who has the same facility. This essentially simple concept, which has developed during the past few decades, has had a revolutionary impact in many areas of human interaction.

- People are able to communicate more easily with people who live far away from them. The Internet has made such communication cheaper, more instantaneous and more flexible, allowing the user to send not just text but also still images, video images and sound.
- Virtual communities have been created whereby people sharing areas of interest can exchange opinions and information. This has had an enormously beneficial effect on those working in specialised fields whose colleagues may be based in locations on the other side of the world.
- Individuals who, because they live in remote locations or because they suffer from a disability that renders them house-bound, can feel more connected to the rest of the world and can avail themselves of services that were previously unavailable to them.
- Business organisations that have branches in different locations can improve the level of communication, collaboration and sharing of information between branches.
- At the moment the Internet is (relatively) unregulated. This has led to it being a place where individuals and organisations can express opinions and publish materials that are not usually granted expression in the mainstream media or are explicitly banned, e.g. under a repressive regime that forbids anti-government views. This has had both beneficial effects (allowing people living under dictatorships to communicate with the outside world) and more problematic effects (the availability of previously banned hard-core pornography).
- It has facilitated the creation of new businesses and has transformed the way in which established organisations conduct their business. As with any change in business methods, this has created losers as well as winners.

## Moral, social and ethical issues associated with the Internet

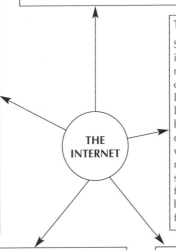

### Censorship

The Internet is transnational in its scope and not centrally owned or controlled, making it virtually impossible to police. Consequently, material which would be illegal if published in 'hard copy' format, is easily accessible on the Internet. The clearest example of this is hard-core pornography. This leads some people to argue that the Internet should be censored. While many agree with the need to prevent the publication of offensive material, e.g. paedophiliac imagery, others argue that the introduction of censorship will undermine the freedom of expression that, at the moment, the Internet facilitates. There are also issues about who does the censoring and what form of centralised control might be needed to impose censorship.

### Accuracy of information

Many people use the Internet as a source of information. There is no guarantee, however, that the information that they find is accurate. An example of this can be found among the many websites that offer medical advice. The advice given on some sites has been shown to be erroneous and there is a danger that some people will accept this advice at face value. It could be argued, of course, that this is equally true of other media, e.g. newspapers and magazines, but the unregulated nature of the Internet can make the publication of inaccurate information a particular issue.

### The effects on community

Some argue that the Internet has increased valuable interactions between individuals as a result of its new modes of communication. Additionally, it is argued that communities previously separated by geographical location are now able to form connections and this has led to a greater awareness of other cultures. There is, however, a counter-argument. Some have suggested that computer usage is essentially a solitary activity and that valuable forms of social interaction are declining as a result of its increase. An example of this would be shopping on the Internet. If people increasingly shop from home using the Internet, local shops will go out of business and their capacity to act as a site of interaction for a local community will be lost.

### Privacy

The technology involved in the Internet means that it is a fairly straightforward matter to intercept and view Internet communications. This leads some to argue that communication on the Internet should be protected by privacy laws and that one's e-mails should be as confidential as one's conventional mail. Others argue that, because the Internet has been used to assist in the commission of criminal acts, industrial espionage and terrorist attacks, law enforcement agencies should have the power to intercept and view electronic correspondence. This issue has come to the fore in the debate over encryption: should individuals/organisations have the right to encrypt their data without providing the security services with the key?

### Ownership and control

The ideal of many of those involved in creating the Internet was that it would be a virtual location for the free exchange of knowledge, opinions and ideas. While this still holds true to some extent, the Internet has also become a profoundly commercialised space where different corporations struggle to increase their market share. There are people who fear that the Internet will go the way of other media, i.e. it will become dominated by a small number of organisations who will effectively determine its content. Others argue that the Internet is big enough to allow both large-scale commercial and small-scale independent concerns to coexist. They further argue that without commercial investment the Internet will not be able to sustain itself.

# Uses of the Internet

## Communication

Electronic mail has become a widely used mode of communication within a very short space of time. Its relative immediacy makes it more popular than conventional mail for communicating urgent messages, it is cheaper than the telephone and more flexible than a fax (being able, for example, to carry file attachments such as photographs and even video clips). Its chief weakness is its reliance on both sender and recipient having access to suitable software and hardware. But, as the growth of Internet cafés and street terminals demonstrates, even this restriction need not diminish its growing popularity amongst people of all ages and backgrounds. It is seen as a valuable business tool. Businesses value its ability to copy a piece of correspondence to any number of people selected from an electronic address book. For many people 'checking one's e-mails' has become an established part of office life. In fact, in some instances, this has proved counter-productive, with many hours being spent opening, reading and responding to e-mails. This has been exacerbated by the 'spam' phenomenon, i.e. where people receive unsolicited e-mail, usually from companies trying to sell them something.

## Publishing information

One of the most noteworthy benefits of the Internet has been the way it has provided opportunities for individuals and small organisations to create their own websites. In recent years the software and hardware required to create a website has become widely accessible and relatively easy to use. Individuals with relatively little experience of computers have found themselves able to create websites that have proved more popular than those of large, commercial concerns. This has meant that people with minority interests have been able to publish information about those interests and so make contact with people around the world. In this sense, the Internet has been a democratising force. It is a space which, at the moment, is not dominated by controlling interests, and so offers a platform to groups and individuals who might otherwise be denied a voice. There is, however, a negative consequence of this openness: the presence of sites run by paedophile groups, race-hate organisations, terrorist sympathisers, etc.

## Making files available

Organisations sometimes need to make document files, data or software available to other parties. The Internet is a simple way of achieving this. The file in question is stored on a special server called a file transfer protocol (FTP) server. Specified users can then contact this server and download the files that they need. Some of FTP sites are private and require an ID and password before they can be accessed, others (anonymous FTP sites) are freely accessible. FTP is often used by software companies who want to distribute their products online. They may wish to make free trial products available or distribute upgrades or anti-virus 'patches'.

## Sharing ideas

The 'Newsgroups' Internet application is perhaps the element of the Internet that is most consistent in its purpose with the ideals of the Internet's originators. These are sites where people who share a common area of interest or expertise can exchange views, ideas and information. Newsgroups are organised into a hierarchical tree structure to make searching for the site of your choice easier. If, for example, you wanted to enter into an online discussion about a recent film, you could go first to the heading 'rec' (for recreation), from there you would go to the subgroup 'arts.cinema.name of film'. A newsgroup user can make comments of their own, respond to comments made by others and even create their own newsgroups. Some businesses have found that there are newsgroups about their products that are not always complimentary or accurate. In some cases the business has monitored the newsgroup so that it can effectively counter any negative publicity.

## Accessing information

The World Wide Web is a vast repository of information. Organisations and individuals have created websites containing information on just about every subject imaginable. In fact, increasingly, the difficulty lies not in accessing information but in locating the particular information that one needs. Some now argue that there is too much information on the Internet and that it is virtually impossible to isolate what you need from all the irrelevant material that is offered. This difficulty notwithstanding, the Internet continues to be the first port of call for many in their search for information. It can provide reasonably up-to-date information on the weather, travel conditions, the stock market, and breaking news stories. It can also be searched for archive information on recent news events, advice on everything from DIY to snake handling, current research in all major academic disciplines, the latest bargains from online stores, etc. Some commentators feel that this free access to information cannot last for ever. As has already been noted, information has value and the practice of charging for access to valued information has already begun on the Internet. For example, some financial research papers are only available to those users who pay a subscription to a commercial company.

# Accessing a website: 1

### Step 1: Requesting a website using a URL

One way of accessing a particular location on the Internet is to type the address of the site that you wish to visit into the address box of the web browser. This address is known as a Unique Resource Locator (URL) and is made up of different elements:

http: indicates that the site is located on the World Wide Web and that it uses hypertext markup language. Some URLs have the prefix 'ftp', indicating that the site is on a File Transfer Protocol server.

www: originally this was used to distinguish between sites that were on the World Wide Web and Internet files. It is now almost redundant and can be omitted from most addresses.

org. this part of the URL is called the Top Level Domain. .org is a generic TLD and refers to the type of organisation that the site belongs to. Other generic TLDs include .net, .com and .gov. There are also ccTLDs (country code TLDs). These indicate the country of origin of the site. ccTLDs include .uk (United Kingdom).de (Germany), and .es (Spain)

ADDRESS http://www.suttonlea.org/welcome.html

:// is a signal to the browser that what follows is the domain name. The rest of the domain name will be separated by full stops and, where necessary, slash marks.

suttonlea: this is the domain name, a unique combination of letters, numbers and punctuation marks that has been registered with an Internet registration company. It usually describes the owners or nature of the site. This domain name is that of Sutton Local Education Authority.

welcome.html: this refers to a specific page, in this case the welcome page, of the site. html (hyper text markup language) indicates that the page, in common with most files on the Web, has been coded using this language and so requires this file extension.

### Step 2: Accessing the Internet Protocol address

When the enter key is pressed or the 'Go' icon clicked upon, the address (**1**) is sent to the Internet Service Provider (ISP) (**2**) or Local Area Network (LAN) that is being used to connect to the Internet. The ISP or LAN connects to a device called a Domain Name Server (DNS) (**3**). The DNS is a collection of databases that stores all registered domain names. It contains the data to match the URL to an Internet Protocol (IP) address. Unlike the URL, the IP address is expressed wholly in numerical terms. So the IP for the above URL would be 23.45.168.98. This change is required because computers find it easier to use numerical identifiers whereas humans prefer text-based names. The DNS returns the IP, and this is used to direct the request through a series of routers (**4**) to the server where the website resides (**5**).

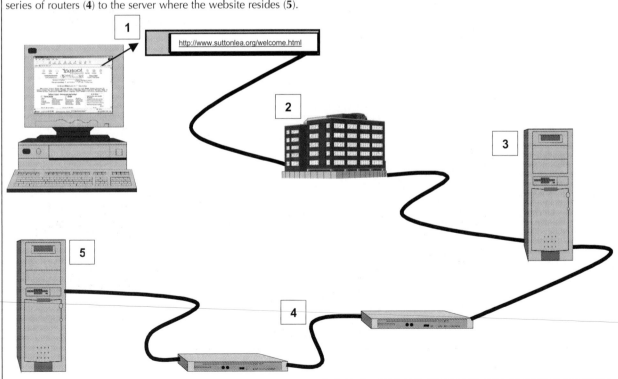

# Accessing a website: 2

### Step 3: Retrieving the web page from the web server

The server where the website is located receives the request (**1**). The server can tell where the request originated by looking at information contained in the request header. The server (**2**) sends a message back indicating: "Website found. Waiting for reply." Somewhere on the server the web page itself will be stored as an HTML text file (**3**). The code contained in this text file will define the content and appearance of the web page. It may contain references to URLs where graphics, video or sound files are stored. (**4**) The server will put the request in a queue. When it is in a position to respond, the server sends the HTML file to the requester's browser. (**5**) It also sends a message to those locations where other files (e.g. graphics) are stored to send the appropriate files to the same browser.

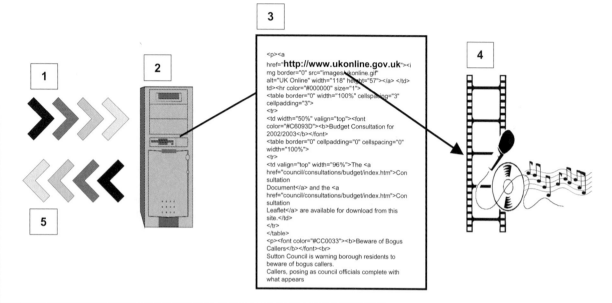

### Step 4: Opening the web page

As the different parts of the web page arrive (**1**) at the requester's PC or server, they have to be stored before being reassembled. They are therefore held in the computer's cache memory (**2**), a particular type of memory that temporarily holds required data. As the data is being collected, the browser begins putting the page together. It uses the HTML code as a guideline for this process (**3**). The different elements of the website arrive at different times – larger graphics/animation files arriving later than simple text. This is why the website visibly 'constructs' itself on the screen in stages. When the page is complete, the user is generally given a message to this effect, e.g. 'Done' (**4**).

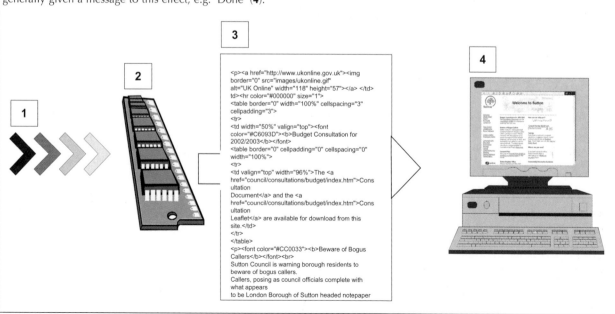

# Doing business on the World Wide Web

The Internet was not originally designed as a commercial enterprise. Its original aim was to provide an electronic means of sharing ideas and information. As it grew in popularity, however, commercial organisations quickly saw the business opportunities that it presented. They recognised that it allowed people to interact with each other in a different way, and in this difference lay the potential for creating new markets and reinvigorating old ones. Businesses began to use the Internet, and in particular the World Wide Web, in different ways:

- as a means of communicating information about the products and services they offer;
- as a 'virtual shop', allowing customers to purchase goods and services online;
- as a free service which makes money by allowing advertisers to use the site;
- as a subscription service, e.g. allowing subscribers access to valuable information such as might be contained in research papers;
- as an interactive site that encourages customers to give them feedback on their products.

## How interactive shopping works

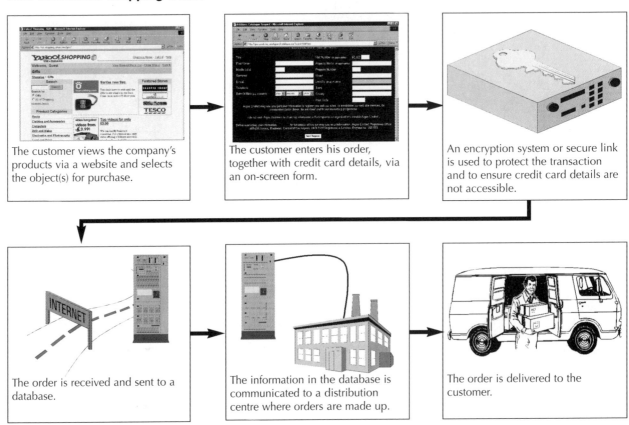

The customer views the company's products via a website and selects the object(s) for purchase.

The customer enters his order, together with credit card details, via an on-screen form.

An encryption system or secure link is used to protect the transaction and to ensure credit card details are not accessible.

The order is received and sent to a database.

The information in the database is communicated to a distribution centre where orders are made up.

The order is delivered to the customer.

| Advantages to the customer | Advantages to the business | Some difficulties |
|---|---|---|
| • Customers do not have to travel long distances to shops and struggle through crowds to make their purchases. <br> • It can be beneficial to those customers who are disabled or who, for some other reason, find it difficult to travel to shops. <br> • New, smaller, more specialised businesses present themselves on the web, thus widening the range of goods and services available. | • Overheads can be cut. A web-based business does not necessarily need a high street shop and staff to run it. Small, specialised concerns have therefore been able to establish themselves on the web with very little capital outlay. <br> • Many new businesses have been created via the Internet; some have been successful, some not. The overall effect, however, has been to invigorate the business environment by introducing healthy competition. | • Despite assurances by businesses that their sites are secure, many people are anxious about giving out their credit card details online. There have been sufficient examples of Internet-based credit card fraud to justify this fear. <br> • Anybody can set up an online business and some websites are not run in an honest and reliable manner. Customers have ordered and paid for goods that have never arrived. <br> • Shopping is not just a functional act. It is also a social activity. People go shopping to be with their friends and to enjoy the atmosphere of towns and cities. |

# E-mails

Electronic mail (e-mail) has been an extremely popular and successful aspect of the Internet. It is a means of sending written messages via the network of networks that comprises the Internet. E-mail is now an essential communication tool, used extensively for business and personal purposes.

## How e-mail works

Using e-mail client software the sender composes a message, addresses it to the recipient (using their e-mail address), and sends it. The sender may also choose to attach a document. E-mail software allows for the attachment of files in a variety of formats: images, spreadsheets, etc.

When the 'send' command is given, the software connects with the Internet Service Provider. The ISP has a mail server and, using a protocol called Simple Mail Transfer Protocol (SMTP), the message is transferred to this server. The server confirms to the sender that the message has been received.

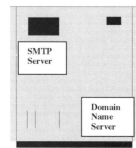

The e-mail server communicates with another piece of software – the domain name server – and this determines what path the message will take to reach its destination. The domain server looks at the destination part of the address and works out the most effective route through the Internet.

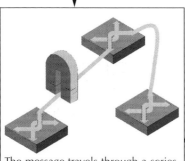

The message travels through a series of routers. Routers are devices which decide upon the optimum electronic route for the message to take, i.e. to reach its destination in the shortest time. To take account of different operating systems, the message may have to pass through gateways – i.e. devices that translate data when necessary.

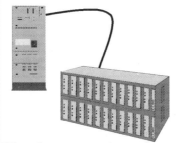

When the message arrives at the destination server, it passes the message to another server, called a Post Office Protocol (POP) server. The POP server is like a set of electronic pigeon holes. It stores messages in designated locations until they are ready to be collected.

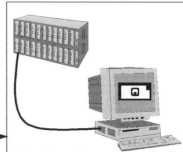

When the recipient wants to check their mail, their e-mail client software communicates with the ISP and checks the contents of their POP server 'pigeon hole'. If there are messages there, they are transmitted to the recipient's client software. They can then be opened and read.

## Advantages and disadvantages of e-mail

| Advantages | Disadvantages |
| --- | --- |
| • Messages can be sent across the world for the price of a local phone call.<br>• You can send not only simple text messages but also attached files in a variety of formats.<br>• You can use an address book to send the same message to several different people.<br>• The message will arrive much more quickly than conventional mail (though it is less instantaneous than a telephone message). | • You are reliant on the recipient having suitable hardware and software. Though e-mail is increasingly popular, it is still not universal.<br>• There are security and privacy issues. Confidential mail is travelling across a very public network.<br>• E-mail attachments have proved to be a security 'Achilles' heel', providing an entry point for destructive viruses. |

# Using search engines

According to the statistics there were over 32 million websites on the Internet in May 2002. A user who wishes to access one of these sites, can type in the domain address and be immediately connected. It is, however, more often the case that users do not wish to access a specific site. Rather, they wish to see what information is available on a particular topic. In this case they must use one of the several websites that run web-wide searches. These are known as 'search engines'. They allow the user to view a list of those websites that are most likely to contain the information they need.

## How a search engine works

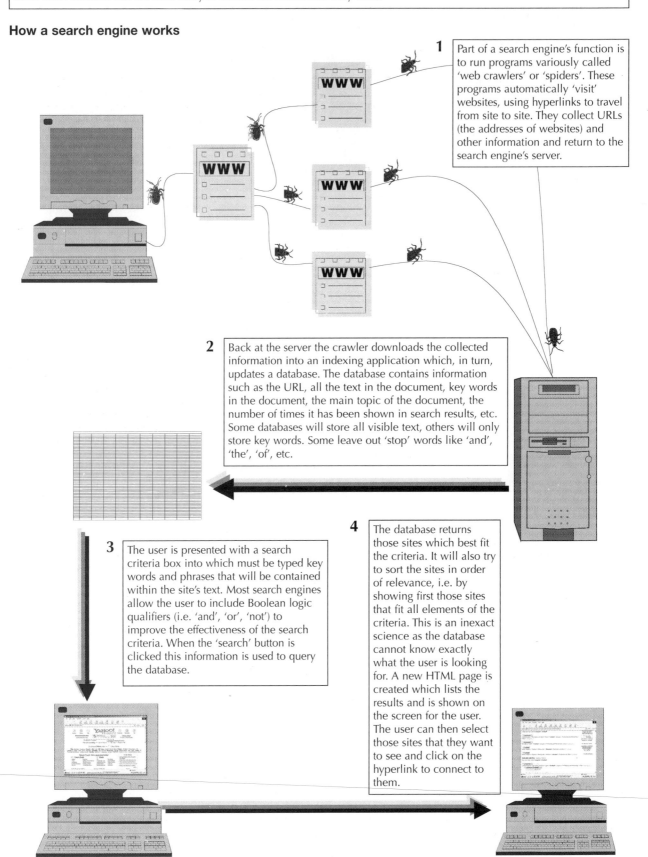

**1** Part of a search engine's function is to run programs variously called 'web crawlers' or 'spiders'. These programs automatically 'visit' websites, using hyperlinks to travel from site to site. They collect URLs (the addresses of websites) and other information and return to the search engine's server.

**2** Back at the server the crawler downloads the collected information into an indexing application which, in turn, updates a database. The database contains information such as the URL, all the text in the document, key words in the document, the main topic of the document, the number of times it has been shown in search results, etc. Some databases will store all visible text, others will only store key words. Some leave out 'stop' words like 'and', 'the', 'of', etc.

**3** The user is presented with a search criteria box into which must be typed key words and phrases that will be contained within the site's text. Most search engines allow the user to include Boolean logic qualifiers (i.e. 'and', 'or', 'not') to improve the effectiveness of the search criteria. When the 'search' button is clicked this information is used to query the database.

**4** The database returns those sites which best fit the criteria. It will also try to sort the sites in order of relevance, i.e. by showing first those sites that fit all elements of the criteria. This is an inexact science as the database cannot know exactly what the user is looking for. A new HTML page is created which lists the results and is shown on the screen for the user. The user can then select those sites that they want to see and click on the hyperlink to connect to them.

# Different ways of connecting to the Internet

| MEDIA | HOW IT WORKS | EVALUATION |
|---|---|---|
| Dial-up | The user's standard telephone line is used in combination with a modem. The modem, which may be located internally or externally, converts the analogue telephone signal into a digital signal that can be processed by the computer. | This is still the most commonly used approach to domestic Internet connection in both the UK and the USA, although it is not generally considered suitable for business organisations. It has the advantage of using existing telephone connections and it is relatively cheap. The main disadvantages are its slow transmission speeds, its inability to manage broadband access and the fact that, unless you have a dedicated second line, you cannot make telephone calls when on the Internet. |
| ISDN | ISDN stands for Integrated Services Digital Network. ISDN connections use existing telephone cables but require both the telecom provider and the user to have digital switching equipment installed. These terminal adaptors facilitate the transmission of digital data across existing connections. | ISDN is an improvement on dial-up, allowing both faster transmission speeds and greater bandwidth. Many versions also allow simultaneous transmissions over the same line, making it particularly useful for video conferencing. It is more expensive than dial-up, the telecom companies charging both an installation fee and a regular (usually monthly) tariff. It is also slower than DSL and cable and there have been problems about availability in some areas. |
| DSL | DSL stands for Digital Subscriber Line. Like ISDN this system uses existing telephone lines for transmission but sends and receives all data in a digital format. It requires the telecom provider to have digital switching equipment installed and the user to have a DSL modem. This modem enables end-to-end digital transmission. DSL comes in many flavours including ADSL (Asymmetric DSL) and HDSL (Higher-speed DSL). | DSL is faster than ISDN and many times faster than dial-up. It is an 'always-on' broadband connection that can be used simultaneously with normal telephone communications. Unlike cable, each user has a dedicated line. This means that (a) the connection is more secure and (b) transmission speeds are not affected by the number of subscribers using the service. It costs more than a dial-up service but competition is strong in this area and, at the moment, prices show a downward trend. One disadvantage is that the distance between the user and the telecom office will significantly affect the quality of the connection. For this reason, DSL is not viable in some remote locations. |
| Cable | The coaxial connection that is used in some areas to pipe television services into the home, coaxial cable, has broadband capacity and so is capable of simultaneously delivering television signals and data. The cable provider needs to have a high speed connection to the Internet and communication devices to service all the connected homes in one neighbourhood. The user has to have a cable modem to convert the incoming signal. | Cable is a broadband connection that can provide very high transmission rates. There are costs involved but the consumer may have already absorbed those costs as part of the TV access package. Cable does not tie up any other domestic communication services, i.e. one can surf the net, watch TV and be on the phone at the same time. The main disadvantage is that cable access has to be in place before the connection can take place. This will depend on the geographical area: some locations have well-developed cable infrastructures, other have little or no cable access. Because each neighbourhood – a neighbourhood may consist of up to 500 homes – has one dedicated node, an excess of traffic can cause the system to slow down significantly. |
| Wireless | Radio frequencies are used to transmit data from a local network station to a receiver on one's device. | The main growth in the use of wireless access is likely to be on mobile devices, in particular the 3G (third-generation) mobile phones and hand-held devices currently being developed. The promise is of fast, always-on Internet access, with users being able to download large files quickly and view/listen to them on their portable devices. This could prove to be the major ICT development of the next five years, though it is not without its problems, e.g. how will the telecom companies be able to make the provision of such access profitable? |

## The broadband issue

A broadband connection offers 'always-on' Internet access, with the capacity to download large files, e.g. video files, quickly and without loss of quality. At the time of writing only 1% of British households have broadband access although there is currently a marketing drive to increase this. The expectation in some quarters is that in the home of the future broadband connections will be the norm in the same way telephone connections are now. There is a growing demand for broadband but three issues are still affecting the take-up level:

- At the moment it is quite costly and the general user may feel there is insufficient benefit in the improved service to justify the cost.
- The telecom companies are having problems rolling out broadband access to all areas of the country. Some of these problems are logistic (e.g. proximity to a telephone exchange for rural areas) and some financial (e.g. the investment in improving communication infrastructure has to be able to show a return).
- Users have to be convinced that there are tangible benefits in acquiring broadband. At the moment many of the applications that are being used to sell the appeal of broadband (e.g. Internet-based games) are insufficiently attractive to consumers.

# Hypertext

## How did hypertext develop?

The term hypertext is usually associated with the World Wide Web and is taken to refer to the way in which clicking on a specially demarcated piece of text or image will link the user to another piece of information. On a typical web page there will be several hypertext links. These are usually in the form of words or short phrases that can be identified by the fact that they have a different colour typeface and because of the way the mouse cursor changes shape when it moves across them. Activating such a link may open a dialogue box with further information in, open a picture file or take the user to a new web page. The links are not necessarily between two pieces of text-based information: sound/graphics/video files may also be involved. Consequently, the term 'hypermedia' may also be used to describe this process.

In fact, the concept of hypertext predates the World Wide Web by over 40 years and has its own history. In 1945 Dr V. Bush outlined the idea of a mechanical store for different forms of information based on microfilm. He termed this idea Memex. The central principle was that the reader would be able to create their own pathways through the mass of information, linking ideas in an individualised way. Bush argued that such an approach is more consistent with the way our minds work than the strictly sequential approach of a book or a lecture. Our minds do not generally investigate ideas in a linear fashion. Rather, they jump around from topic to topic, going off at tangents and spending time exploring off-shoots of the central idea.

This idea was further elaborated on in the 1960s by Ted Nelson (who coined the term 'Hypertext') and Douglas Englebart (the inventor of the mouse), but didn't really take off until Apple Computers devised the Graphical User Interface and the HyperCard system, that operated on the hypertext principle. Those working on the development of the World Wide Web used the concept of hypertext as an organising principle for their new creation.

## How does hypertext work?

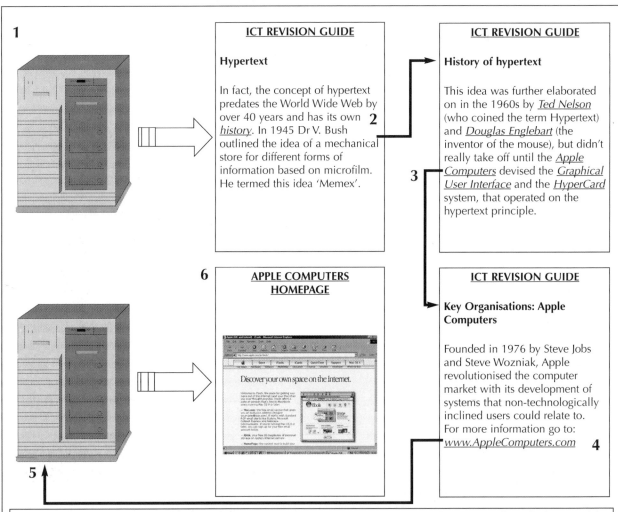

The first web page is requested from the web server (**1**). The user decides that he wants to know more about the history of the term 'hypertext'. and so he clicks on the hypertext 'history' (**2**). This action creates a request for a page from the server that contains the desired information. This is called a 'relative link'. The second page contains a number of hyperlinks, all of which would take the user to different pages containing more detailed information on that particular topic. The user chooses to find out more about 'Apple Computers' (**3**). A new page is requested and opened by the browser. This page offers a different kind of link, called an absolute link (**4**), that will make a request to a different web server, in this case the one storing the official website of the Apple Corporation (**5**). The appropriate page is opened by the user's web browser (**6**).

# Internet protocols

### Why does the Internet need protocols?

The Internet is a complex 'network of networks'. It consists of many systems located all over the world, all unified by a series of communication links. These systems will vary in many ways. For example, they will not all use the same operating system: some may be operating on a Windows platform, others on a Linux platform. In order for Internet traffic to move smoothly through this network, there needs to be an agreed set of rules – or protocols – for the transmission of data. All data traffic must conform to these protocols if the system is to work effectively. The most important of these protocols is TCP/IP

### What is TCP/IP?

TCP stands for Transmission Control Protocol and IP stands for Internet Protocol. The two terms almost always appear together because they form two complimentary halves of a system that ensures consistency in the transmission of data across the Internet.

The Internet is a packet-switching network. This means that when a piece of data is sent across the Internet it is first divided into 'packets', i.e. blocks of data comprising no more than 128 kb of data. These packets are then sent across the network, being directed on their journey by routers which determine the optimum path to their destination. At the destination machine the packets are reassembled in the correct order. TCP/IP ensure that this process is conducted according to set rules:

**TCP** creates the packets, adding a 'header' that contains information about how the data packets should be reassembled at the destination. A checksum is also added as a validation device.

**IP** labels each packet with a correct destination address. This address is the one used by routers to direct the packet to its destination.

### How does TCP/IP work?

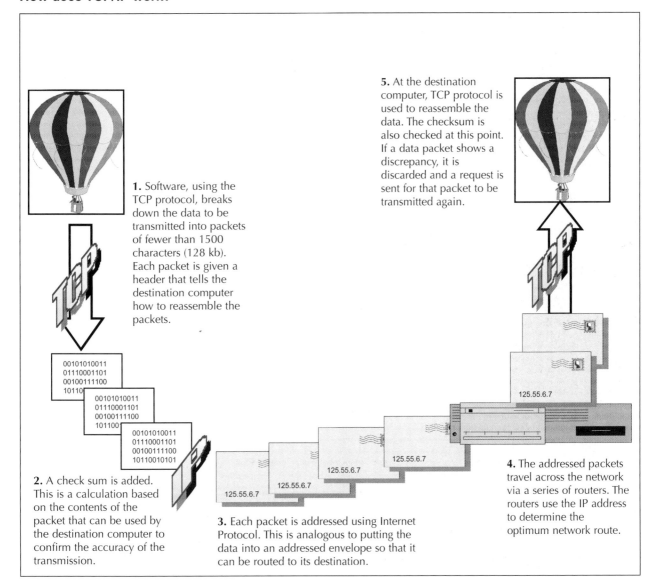

**1.** Software, using the TCP protocol, breaks down the data to be transmitted into packets of fewer than 1500 characters (128 kb). Each packet is given a header that tells the destination computer how to reassemble the packets.

**5.** At the destination computer, TCP protocol is used to reassemble the data. The checksum is also checked at this point. If a data packet shows a discrepancy, it is discarded and a request is sent for that packet to be transmitted again.

**2.** A check sum is added. This is a calculation based on the contents of the packet that can be used by the destination computer to confirm the accuracy of the transmission.

**3.** Each packet is addressed using Internet Protocol. This is analogous to putting the data into an addressed envelope so that it can be routed to its destination.

**4.** The addressed packets travel across the network via a series of routers. The routers use the IP address to determine the optimum network route.

# An Internet timeline

**1958** The 'Cold War' between the United States and the Soviet Union is at its height. The launch of the Soviet's Sputnik satellite in 1957 created a fear in the US administration that, technologically speaking, they were falling behind. President Eisenhower's response is to bring together a group of scientists and engineers under the heading of the Advanced Research Projects Agency (ARPA). Its original role is to advance the US space program but, when this role was taken over by NASA, ARPA reconstitutes itself as a sponsor of all manner of advanced scientific and engineering projects.

**1960** Paul Baran of the Rand corporation writes a series of papers for the US Defense Department. One of these papers proposed a distributed network that could break up messages into blocks – or packets – which would be transmitted via any available route on the network. The paper did discuss nuclear war. This led to the false rumour that the original aim of the Internet was to develop a military communications system capable of withstanding a nuclear attack.

**1960–1969** During this period various people at ARPA propose, design and develop a packet-switching means of communication. The aim of this network is primarily to allow those working on different ARPA sponsored projects to exchange ideas and information. The first connection was made on 1 October 1969.

**1969** The firm of BBN (Bolt, Beranek and Newman) constructs a network that becomes known as ARPANeT. ARPANeT links together various American universities and scientific/engineering laboratories.

**1971** Ray Tomlinson, an engineer at BBN, sends the first e-mail message over the ARPANeT which, by this time, connects 23 host computers in 12 US cities.

**1973** The ARPANeT continues to expand, making international connections to University College, London and the Norwegian Royal Radar Establishment.

**1974** Bob Kahn and Vint Cerf develop the idea of a 'network of networks' which would use the TCP/IP (Transmission Control Protocol/Internet Protocol) communication standard to connect different networks. ARPANeT now has a network consisting of 62 computers.

**1980** Tim Berners-Lee, a scientist working at the European Laboratory for Particle Physics (CERN) in Geneva, develops a means of connecting files stored in different locations through 'hyperlinks'.

**1980–1990** During this time different networks are developed along the ARPANeT model. The term 'Internet' becomes common currency during this time. In 1982 TCP/IP is adopted as the standard transmission protocol for Internet communications. In 1986 the National Science Foundation establishes 5 super computers linked by a 56 kbps 'backbone'.

**1983** The Internet becomes a reality when the ARPANeT is split into civilian and military sections.

**1990** Under the guidance of Tim Berners-Lee at CERN the World Wide Web, a linked, international network of websites, is launched. At this stage, the web can only be accessed via CERN. ARPANeT ceases to exist, having been supplanted by more sophisticated networks.

**1991** The World Wide Web becomes more generally available via the Internet. There are 600 000 Internet hosts.

**1994** Marc Andreessen who, the previous year, had developed 'Mosaic', a piece of web-browsing software that would allow users to search for and connect to different websites, launches Netscape. The Netscape Navigator 1.0 browser is launched. The number of Internet hosts is over 3 million.

**1995** The number of web hosts grows to over 4 million. It is no longer free to register domain names. Individuals and organisations will have to pay a fee for a two-year registration. The Java programming language is introduced by Sun Microsystems.

**1996** The Communications Decency Act is passed in America. This is the result of concern about the type of material that is available on the Internet. The number of Internet hosts now exceeds 9 million.

**1997** The one millionth domain name (bonnyview.com) is registered. The number of Internet hosts is in excess of 16 million.

**1999** The Computer Industry Almanac reports that there are 150 million Internet users world-wide.

**2000** The dot.com bubble bursts. Many of the Internet start-up companies that launched themselves in the 1990s crash. The NASDAQ index, which shows the value of technology stocks, plummets. The 10 millionth domain name is registered.

# Designing an effective human–computer interface (HCI)

## Factors to take into account when designing a user interface

| | |
|---|---|
| **Task** | The first question to ask in relation to interface design is: what is the program designed to do? The interface design should be consistent with the overall aims of the program. So, for example, if the program is a sophisticated business decision support system, designed for use by strategic management, the design elements should reflect this, e.g. muted colours, business-like graphics, minimum clutter, etc. Equally, if it is a program designed to help home users design their garden, the interface may be colourful and 'fun'. |
| **User expertise** | While it is not always possible to know in advance what level of expertise a program's users will have, designers can make a reasonable estimate of their likely skill level. If, for example, a business-specific accounts package is being designed, it is reasonable to assume that the users of such a package will be familiar with programs designed to manipulate numerical data. The most challenging interfaces in this regard are those for programs that might be used by everybody from complete novices to computer professionals, e.g. a generic spreadsheet package. |
| **User preference** | Some interfaces take into account the desire of users to create screen configurations that suit their particular needs. Such interfaces allow the user to configure some elements of the screen design in accordance with their own preferences. For example, the arrangement and selection of icons on a tool bar might be changed so that they are consistent with the functions that the user employs most frequently. |
| **Resources** | Graphical design elements need more memory resources than text-based ones. This can, in some cases, lead to a strain being put on resources and a concomitant diminishment of performance. This is particularly evident when a memory-heavy interface is loading up. With the increased memory and processing power of computers this is less of a problem than it used to be, but still something that some system designers may need to account for. |

## Elements of a well-designed user interface

**HELP**

The online help files should be well sign-posted, easily accessible and sensibly organised. The topics covered should relate to the questions a user is most likely to need answers to. The language used should be set at a suitable level for the general user. Other help may also be provided, e.g. pop-up screens with tips that appear when a certain action is performed.

**DIFFERENTIATION**

Users with different levels of experience may need to interact with the same interface. In such cases, the effective interface will offer differentiated approaches to interacting with the computer. For example, novice users generally prefer to use point-and-click icons and drop-down menus to issue commands to the computer, whereas experienced users are more likely to use keyboard short-cuts.

**CONSISTENCY**

Users will find it easier to learn how to use a new application if its interface is similar to others they have already worked on. The familiarity is reassuring and the amount of new learning that is required is cut down if interfaces are consistent in their design. This can be achieved through the use of conventional colour schemes, well-established menu items, e.g. cut/copy/paste, commonly used icons, etc.

**USER INTERFACE**

**CLARITY**

Most applications require the user to follow instructions that are communicated via the interface. These instructions must be clear and easy to understand. This is especially the case with error messages which, if unclear, can create anxiety in the nervous user. On-screen communication should also take into account the level of expertise of a possible user and pitch the language used at that level.

**LAYOUT**

The layout should be well organised and easy to follow – i.e. the user should know where to move on the screen in order to perform an action. The colour scheme should be 'easy on the eye' as the user may have to stare at the screen for many hours at a time. The screen should be free of 'clutter' with a good ratio of 'white space' to information.

**STRUCTURE**

The way in which the interface leads the user through the application should be logical. The user should be able to grasp quickly the 'geography' of the applications, e.g. how one screen relates to another. The interface should not take the user to a place that they are unfamiliar with and it should always offer a route back to a reassuring place – a home page, for example – if an error is made.

# Psychological factors in HCI design

## Psychological factors involved in designing effective user interfaces

If a computer interface is to be effective, it must be designed with the needs of the user in mind. Users come in all shapes and sizes: they have differing levels of expertise, different attitudes towards computers in general, and they use their computers for different reasons. Those responsible for designing interfaces must consider the various ways in which users will interact with their hardware/software, and design systems that will make those interactions positive experiences. Some of the specific psychological factors that should be taken into account are set out below.

### Reducing fear

For some users, computers are a source of fear. This fear, sometimes referred to as 'technophobia', may be summarised thus: ease with computers is increasingly expected by society in general and employers in particular; if a person is apprehensive about using computers, she will be disadvantaged at work and may even lose her job. To such users the computer represents a threat to their well-being, a threat that they don't feel equipped to cope with. The effective interface will take account of this fear, especially in the case of applications aimed at the general user, e.g. by offering an easy way of rectifying an erroneous action.

### Using existing cognitive structures

Cognitive structures are the (conceptual) mechanisms we use to make sense of the world and process new information. New information will be processed most easily if it fits smoothly into our current understanding of the world around us. Computer users are most likely to learn how to interact with a new program if its interface (a) is similar to what they have already experienced in other programs (b) is consistent with their general experience (e.g. 'escape' means the same in computer terminology as it does in real life) and (c) responds in a logical manner, e.g. moving the mouse in one direction elicits a similar, proportional movement by the screen pointer.

### Allowing personalisation

While it is desirable that a user interface should share common elements with other interfaces, users also like to be able to customise their screens. Through the process of customisation the user is exerting a degree of control over the computer and expressing their personal preferences in regard to the look and feel of the interface. This can make users feel less 'at the mercy' of their computers. Customisation may be at a relatively simple level, e.g. adjusting the configuration of screen colours, or at a more sophisticated level, e.g. creating personalised toolbars with custom-built commands.

### Avoiding information overload

Humans can only cope with so much information at one time. Experiments into the capacity of short-term memory have shown that it can hold only 7 ($\pm$2) pieces of information. Furthermore, that information is only held there for approximately 20 seconds. After that, it must be transferred to the long-term memory or it will disappear. The designers of user interfaces should therefore avoid bombarding the user with more information than they can cope with. Nor should the interface expect them to remember more items of information than can be stored in the short-term memory. This can be achieved through designing uncluttered screens, concise message boxes and menus that aren't too extensive.

### Minimising frustration

Frustration occurs when one wishes to achieve a certain objective and is prevented from doing so. A build-up of frustration leads to increased stress and, in the view of some psychologists, aggression. Many users experience frustration in relation to computers. The most common complaint is that the computer 'won't do what I want it to'. In other words, the interface is not providing a sufficiently transparent mechanism for the user to issue commands to the computer and receive information in return. The more that is at stake for the user, e.g. the shorter the time available in which to prepare for a critical meeting, the more pronounced the frustration.

# Physical factors in HCI design

When creating HCI systems, designers need to take into account the way in which the user will physically interact with the computer. The keyboard plus mouse input/screen output is the most typical model but there are others. When using computer game programs, for example, one might use a specialised input device such as a joystick, 'steering wheel' or generic game-playing device in order to make the most of the game's facilities. The challenge for designers is to create an HCI that is intuitive — i.e. the nature of the interactions closely resembles the interactions humans experience in the real world. The design process includes a consideration of the following factors:

| | |
|---|---|
| **Purpose** | The nature of the interface will be partially determined by the program it is designed for. If the program is a graphics package designed to allow the user to draw images directly on to the screen, an appropriate input device will need to be used – a stylus or light pen, for example. The way in which this device interacts with the program will need to built into the overall program design. |
| **User** | Some programs are designed for an individual user, some for a small group of users and some for the general user. The physical nature of the HCI may be able to take into account the needs of likely users. For example, an educational program designed to be used by young children could be designed with their needs in mind, e.g. use of bright colours, interactions with pointing devices that aren't too finely calibrated, simple commands in a large font, etc. |
| **Environment** | The general environment where a program will be used may also affect the way the interface is designed. For example, a CAM system designed for use in an industrial environment would need to be robust enough to deal with the rough handling it may receive and not be oversensitive to dirt or noise. |
| **Health and safety** | It is important that normal use of the system should not result in short-term discomfort or long-term injury for the user. Awareness of this issue has led designers to develop more ergonomic keyboards that lessen the chance of regular users developing repetitive strain injury. |
| **Users with disabilities** | Some programs are specifically designed for users with disabilities, e.g. a voice-activated system for those with visual impairments. Those responsible for designing HCI systems intended for use by the general public, an interactive museum information system for example, should take into account the needs of users with disabilities. |

## Different ways of interacting with computers

### Voice input

There are a number of systems that work on the basis of voice recognition. They can range in sophistication from simple command systems to voice activated text processing. Being able to 'talk' to computers directly is clearly a desirable facility, but there are a number of inherent difficulties involved, e.g. the changes in pronunciation created by regional accents.

### Graphics devices

Graphic designers, architects and others working in a similar field need to be able to interact with computers in a very specific way. For example, they may wish to 'draw' an image on the screen in the same way as they would if they were doing it on paper. Standard pointing devices are not always adequate for this. Light pens and digitising tablets are used in this context.

### Game-playing devices

The computer games market is highly competitive. One way in which manufacturers have sought to gain an advantage over their rivals is through the development of sophisticated interaction devices. The joystick and 'steering wheel' were examples of this but, increasingly, this market is dominated by multifunction, generic game-playing devices that can be used with a wide range of programs.

### Pointing devices

The mouse was first developed in 1963 but didn't come into general use until the introduction of the Apple Macintosh PC in 1984. It is now established as a standard means of communicating with a Graphical User Interface. The mouse is becoming more sophisticated with the introduction of wireless devices, programmable functions and motion-sensitive devices that can move a pointer in three dimensions.

### Touch screens

Touch screens allow the user to press parts of the screen to activate different functions. Simple systems may use pressure pads, more sophisticated ones have an infra-red matrix over the screen that identifies the point being touched. Such systems are often used in public places, such as shopping malls, to give information, or as input devices in retail outlets.

### Biometric systems

Biometric systems are those that can 'read' individuals' biological attributes, e.g. iris-recognition devices that can decode the unique configurations of the subject's eye. The most widespread use of such devices is in security systems, where they can be used to check the legitimacy of an individual seeking entrance to a room or building.

# The human–computer interface

At the computer–user interface the user tells the computer what to do and the computer delivers its response to the user. This interface consists of a particular combination of input and output devices. These may include input devices such as keyboards, sensors, joysticks, microphones, etc. and output devices such as monitors, speakers, etc. The interface not only describes the combination of devices but their precise configuration. For example, the most characteristic mode of computer/user interface is the keyboard/mouse/monitor set-up. But this does not adequately define the interface. It is also necessary to describe how the software used creates a particular screen configuration for the user to interact with.

## Command line interfaces

Command line interfaces were the first visual user interfaces to be employed and, despite their intrinsic limitations, are still regularly used. The most common example of usage is the MS-DOS interface which can be used to perform a number of system operations such as creating directories and deleting files. As can be seen from the screen shot below, the interface requires the user to type in coded commands which the computer then performs. This means that the user must learn the coded commands. For this reason, command line interfaces tend to be used mainly by technically oriented computer professionals (network managers, for example) rather than by ordinary users. For those users that have learned the commands, this approach can be an efficient method of communicating with the computer.

## Graphical user interfaces

The graphical user interface (GUI, pronounced 'gooey') is now the standard mode of computer–user interface for the keyboard/mouse/monitor set-up. GUIs have the following defining characteristics (usually referred to as the 'WIMP interface'):

**W**    The screen is organised into **windows**, i.e. overlapping frames that can be viewed singularly or in combination with other windows.

**I**    Graphical features are used as short-cuts for the user, i.e. instead of having to type in a command they can click on an image – or **icon** – that symbolises the action.

**M**    Menus are presented to the user so they can select a command from a predefined list. These menus may be presented as 'pop-up' screens or as 'pull-down' lists on a **menu** bar.

**P**    A **pointing device** is used to move around the screen, to locate where on the screen the user is working and to identify which command is to be issued.

There are clear advantages to this approach to computer–user interfacing:
• The user does not have to learn a specific computer language to communicate with the computer.
• The use of graphical images provides effective short-cuts that are particularly useful as a 'way in' for novice users.
• The mouse provides an 'intuitive' method of communicating instructions, i.e. our hand movements correspond precisely to the movements of the pointer on the screen.
• There is a reduction in ambiguous instructions – i.e. because menus offer a limited range of options the user has to choose a command that the computer will understand.

**One significant disadvantage should be noted: GUIs require more memory and processing resources to run effectively. The more sophisticated the GUI, the more this is the case.**

# The features of a sophisticated HCI

There are a number of defining characteristics of a sophisticated HCI, including:

**Online help**
Almost all software packages contain online help files. This means that users can access help without having to resort to books and manuals. The quality of these help files varies considerably and a sophisticated HCI will provide a comprehensive and appropriately targeted help facility. This may consist of a searchable index of topics, step-by-step 'how-to' guides, wizards for working through complex procedures, pop-up screens with tips for the user, etc. Highly sophisticated systems can 'learn' what sort of help the user needs most often and ensure that the availability of such help is prioritised.

**Differentiated interactions**
A sophisticated interface will allow different users to perform the same action in different ways, thus accounting for different levels of expertise and individual user preference. For example, a commonly performed action is 'cutting and pasting'. The interface may allow the user to perform the action via a menu item, a keyboard short-cut, clicking on icons or using a pop-up menu activated by clicking the right-hand mouse button.

**Multi-tasking**
Modern operating systems allow the user to multi-task, i.e. run several applications at the same time, switching easily between them. Interfaces will need to take this into account at the design stage, e.g. by providing minimise and maximise functions.

**Customisation**
Sophisticated systems often allow the user to customise the interface. This may involve changing the screen configuration (e.g. using different colours or font sizes), creating customised toolbars, developing personalised templates, etc.

The creation of a sophisticated HCI has implications for the resources required. These implications include:

**Processing resources**
The more sophisticated the interface, the more demands it will place on the central processing unit.

**Main memory**
Sophisticated HCIs require a large memory capacity to run, not least because they contain a considerable number of graphical objects.

**Backing storage**
An application with a sophisticated HCI will require more storage memory, whether this is on an applications server or a local hard drive.

**Development resources**
A sophisticated HCI will take more time to develop, may need more people to work on it and will require more testing. This will have a knock-on effect on development costs.

## Customising an interface

As has been stated, many applications allow the user to customise the interface to fit in with his particular needs. Some of the ways in which this might be achieved are set out below:

**Toolbars**

Toolbars generally sit at the top and sides of a screen and contain icons that can be clicked to perform actions. Which toolbars one has and which icons they contain can be determined by the user. In some cases the user can create their own functions, i.e. by using macros, and develop a customised toolbar to execute these functions.

**Menus**

Both drop-down and pop-up menus can be customised so that they only contain items the user knows that they will need. This helps to speed up menu use by reducing clutter.

**Font**

The font refers to the appearance of written text on the screen. The size of the font can be changed as can its colour and style. This may be just a matter of personal preference for the user, or it may reflect a more important need, e.g. a user suffering from a visual impairment may need text of a certain size and colour to be able to see it properly.

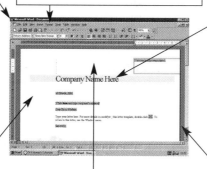

**Templates**

A template is an outline document that provides a generic framework for writing individual documents. If for example, a standard letter is regularly sent by an organisation, this can be set up as a template. When a letter needs to be produced, the template can be used to create the document. The user will just need to add in or amend individual details, e.g. the name of the addressee.

**Screen view**

The screen view can be changed to allow the user to see more or less of the document that they are working on. The screen shown, for example, allows the user to see the full width of the page, including margins.

**Screen colours**

The configuration of the screen colours may also be changed. The *de facto* standard for screen appearance uses grey, blue, black and white for different elements of the screen design. Research into visual perception has shown this to be an effective combination, but individual users may be happier with a different arrangement of colours.

# Speech recognition systems

## Speech recognition systems

The majority of communication between human beings entails people talking to each other. What we wish to communicate is contained in the meaning of the words we utter and qualified by our tone of voice and the secondary signalling of body language and facial expression. Creating a human–computer interface that mimics this intuitive mode of communication has proved to be an enormous challenge for the computer industry. The systems that have been developed to facilitate such interaction are still lacking in sophistication and are not yet in widespread use. The problem lies in the fundamental limitation of all computer systems: the need to reduce everything to digital data – i.e. a series of 0s and 1s – in order to process it. The human voice, with all its ambiguities and subtle nuances, has proved particularly resistant to this reduction. None the less there are software applications that allow users to speak directly to computing systems. These systems may be simple, e.g. voice-activated commands, or sophisticated, e.g. word-processing systems that translate the user's speech into text-based data, but they work in essentially the same way.

The user speaks into a microphone, ideally one able to filter out background noise. The quality of the microphone will be a key factor in determining the accuracy of the system. The first stage of the process is for the user to 'train' the software to recognise the particular properties of her voice. This usually involves reading a 'script' of commonly used sounds into the microphone. The computer then creates a database of vocal references to take account of regional pronunciations, individual vocal inflections, speech defects, etc.

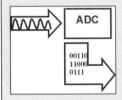

The speech generates an analogue signal which the computer needs to translate into a digital format in order to be able to process it. An analogue-to-digital converter samples the analogue signal every 10–20 milliseconds and assigns a digital value, thus creating a sequence of 0s and 1s that represent the pitch, volume, phoneme length of the vocal input. This data is then compressed to speed up transfer and processing and adjusted to take account of background noise, the properties of the microphone, etc.

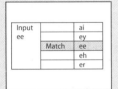

The software contains a database of known phonemes (sound units such as 'ee', 'aw' 'oh', etc.). The incoming data is compared with the binary values of the stored sounds and, using an acoustic probability method, the best match is found. Phoneme values are then combined and compared to a database, or lexicon, of known words, and a set of probable matches is found. The software then uses a 'natural language component' to reach a judgement about what the most likely choice is. This can then be displayed on the screen.

The screen displays the chosen word. The user may decide it is incorrect and effect a correction. In some cases the computer may be 'unsure' which choice to make. It will then query the user using a dialogue box to present the possible choices. The user may also choose to make corrections once the words have appeared on the screen. Some software has the capacity to 'learn' as it goes, i.e. it 'remembers' when mistakes have been made and factors them in to future decisions.

## Advantages and limitations

| Advantages | Limitations |
| --- | --- |
| • When working effectively, it is quicker and less monotonous than keyboard entry.<br>• It is hands-free which can be of value in some environments, e.g. an operating theatre.<br>• It can be used by users with disabilities, allowing them to communicate without having to use a keyboard. | • It is, at the moment, a developing technology and so many of its 'bugs' have yet to be ironed out.<br>• It finds it difficult to deal with homonyms (words that sound the same but have different meanings, e.g. 'there', 'their' and 'they're') of which there are many in the English language.<br>• Punctuation can be a problem: the user has to say 'comma', 'paragraph', etc. |

# The ICT professional: different roles

## Different roles

### Project manager

Project managers oversee the development of new ICT systems. They are responsible for a process that begins with identification of a problem and ends with the evaluation of an implemented solution. Having identified and defined a problem, they organise and analyse all the elements of the system (user needs, available resources, impact on existing systems, etc.) and design an appropriate solution. The design will specify the particular files and records to be used, the nature of the user interfaces, the sequence of processing, etc. They will then oversee the development of the system, the testing process and the implementation. Finally they will undertake a post-implementation evaluation of the system to determine which aspects of it have been successful and which have not.

**Key skills**

- Meticulous attention to detail
- Analytical mind
- Logical approach to problem solving
- Strong written and verbal communication skills
- An understanding of the interaction between business operations and technology

### Computer programmer

Computer programmers write the code that tells the computer how and when to perform the functions specified in the system design. They need an understanding of general programming structures and principles (e.g. iteration, conditional clauses) and a specialist knowledge of programming languages e.g. C++, Visual Basic. Their work involves:

**Coding:** writing step by step instructions in the appropriate language.
**Compiling:** putting the whole program together and converting it into binary code.
**Debugging:** testing the program, finding errors and correcting them.
**Maintenance:** amending the original code if errors occur after implementation.

**Key skills**

- A logical approach to problem solving
- Ability to concentrate on one task
- Ability to learn effectively
- Attention to detail

### Website administrator

Website administrators supervise and maintain an organisation's website. They are responsible for all aspects of the website, including: creating content or incorporating content provided by others, creating and amending the logical structure of the site, running the web server software, creating and updating graphic elements, evaluating the effectiveness of the site, etc.

**Key skills**

- Adaptability – ability to respond to changing circumstances
- Good design skills
- Technical knowledge of the Internet
- Strong verbal and written communication skills

### Database Administrator

Database Administrators (DBAs) take responsibility for different aspects of database maintenance. This may involve: providing support for existing databases, modifying the structure of databases as requirements change, overseeing the installation of new systems that write to or read from existing databases, providing staff training in database use, planning and designing new databases, ensuring the accuracy and security of data held within the database.

**Key skills**

- Awareness of legal requirements and need for accuracy
- Understanding of the relationship between different organisational systems
- Understanding of database principles (e.g. record structures, querying, etc.)
- Ability to analyse future needs
- Attention to detail

### Network administrator

Network administrators take responsibility for the security and administration of networks. Their work may involve: overseeing the installation of new hardware and ensuring its network compatibility, maintaining network hardware and ensuring that problems are fixed, setting up user accounts and passwords, ensuring that the network is secure and that users are using it legitimately, ensuring that there is an effective back-up system.

**Key skills**

- Strong technical knowledge
- Practical problem-solving skills
- Understanding of the overall technology needs of the organisation
- Good interpersonal skills

# The ICT professional: qualities required

In addition to the specific technical skills required by ICT professionals, there are personal qualities that it will be advantageous for them to possess. These qualities, which are described in more detail below, relate to the type of work ICT professionals are called upon to do.

**Problem-solving skills** ICT work often involves devising solutions to problems. A logical approach to problem-solving will therefore be a great asset. Effective problem-solving involves identifying the nature of the problem, designing and evaluating a range of possible solutions, and testing a chosen solution. This type of work is an essential component of systems development, computer programming and post-implementation user support.

**Communication skills** Effective communication is clear, accurate and appropriate for the intended audience. ICT professionals will need to be able to communicate effectively, both verbally and in writing. They will need to explain systems to users, provide documentation, give presentations, write/speak to clients, etc. The language and terminology they use must be pitched at an appropriate level for the person they are communicating with.

**Interpersonal skills** A good deal of ICT work involves team work and the effective ICT professional will be able to work well with others. Interpersonal skills include: the ability to listen to and empathise with the views of others, the capacity to resolve conflicts in a peaceable manner, a willingness to support others when they need it, etc. Without these skills, the behaviour of the individual may damage the productivity of the team.

**Initiative** Initiative is the ability to instigate new ideas and set projects and ideas in motion. The effective ICT professional will not wait to be instructed but will see new solutions to problems and the fresh potential of new technologies. This is an especially important quality in ICT managers who are constantly looking for new ways of using ICT to improve efficiency and enhance the success of the organisation.

**Learning skills** Everybody has the capacity to learn but some people are more effective than others. Effective learners can pick up new skills and assimilate new knowledge quickly and efficiently. This is an especially valuable skill in ICT. Technologies are changing rapidly and new products come on to the market with increasing regularity. It is therefore advantageous to be able quickly to acquire the requisite skills and knowledge in order to put these new technologies to use.

**Design skills** There are some areas of ICT where the ability to create well-designed, easy-to-access screens or reports is essential. Programmers who are developing user interfaces need such skills, as do web-designers and those responsible for the production of documentation. Stylish and ergonomic hardware devices will be attractive to buyers, and therefore people capable of producing such designs will always be in demand.

**Methodical approach** A methodical approach is characterised by planned, structured working and meticulous attention to detail. This is an especially important skill in computer programming. A single error in a line of code can create huge problems at the testing stage, problems that can set the project back weeks and result in additional costs. A methodical approach will help to minimise these errors.

**Organisational skills** ICT work involves planning, scheduling and resourcing projects. If an ICT project is to be successful, it has to be well-organised so that the resources required are available, the work is completed on time and everybody working on the project knows what they have to do. This skill is particularly important for those involved in project management.

# Employee code of conduct

### What is a code of conduct?

An employee code of conduct is an undertaking that an employee makes to abide by certain rules and work within specified guidelines. The code of conduct will explicitly set out what is expected of an employee, what will constitute an infringement of the policy and what the consequences of such an infringement will be. In relation to ICT, the code of conduct will focus on the manner in which the employee uses the organisation's information system resources. Depending on the nature of the organisation, the employee may be required formally to sign the code of conduct and accept it as part of their contractual obligation.

### Problems a code of conduct is designed to prevent

A significant number of problems that beset information systems have as their root cause the accidental or deliberate misuse of resources by employees. By obliging employees to abide by a code of conduct it is hoped that some of these problems can be avoided. These problems include:

- Introduction of viruses into the system – for example, by downloading illicit software from the Internet or carelessly opening an e-mail attachment.
- Distribution of material that is sexually offensive or likely to incite racial hatred. Infringements of this kind can leave the organisation vulnerable to legal action by employees who have been offended by the material.
- Extraction of data for illicit purposes. Activities such as this can make the organisation liable to prosecution under the terms of the Data Protection Act.
- Copying software for personal use or illicit sale, thus violating the terms of copyright laws and software licensing agreements.

### Contents of a code of conduct

**RESPONSIBILITIES**

This section will set out what responsibilities the employee has to the organisation. This may include: respecting the rights of other users; abiding by current legislation – e.g. Data Protection Act, compliance with current licensing agreements, protecting systems from damage, etc.

**PENALTIES FOR MISUSE**

This section will define what the penalties are for various infringements of the code of conduct. It is important that each employee knows what the consequences of violating the code will be. Penalties may range from an informal warning by a line manager to dismissal and prosecution.

**AUTHORISATION**

This section will define the employee's authority to access different parts of the information systems. It will also identify what authority is required for different actions – e.g. if the employee wishes to change a database structure. If actions are performed without authority, the code will have been infringed.

**SECURITY**

This section will set out the terms of the security policy as it applies to each employee. It might include the definition of rules concerning: use and disclosure of passwords, personal use of e-mail facilities, logging-on and logging-off procedures, routines for the transfer of information, etc.

# Telecommuting

Telecommuting occurs when a member of an organisation arranges to work at home rather than in the workplace. In some instances telecommuting – or teleworking – is a full-time arrangement; in other instances an employee may choose to work from home only at specific times. This arrangement has become increasingly achievable through the use of computers, the availability of Internet/intranet links and advances in communications technology – e.g. fax machines, e-mail, videoconferencing, etc.

## Conditions required for telecommuting to take place

- The organisation needs to be engaged in the kind of work that can be done at home. There are many examples of this, the most common being: data entry, secretarial work (e.g. copy-typing), design work, etc.
- The organisation needs to be able to trust the employee to work from home effectively, or have a means of monitoring them.
- There needs to be appropriate hardware/software provision. In addition to a computer, this usually involves an e-mail/Internet connection or a link to a company wide intranet.
- An appropriate home-working environment needs to be available, i.e. a space where the employee can work without interruption.

### Advantages for the employee

- **More flexible use of time** This can be particularly useful if the employee has other responsibilities, e.g. child-care, care for an elderly relative, etc.
- **Working in a known environment** Some people may prefer to work in a quiet, home environment rather than in a busy office.
- **No travelling involved** Some people live a considerable distance form their place of work. In such cases, telecommuting will cut down on time and money wasted on commuting.

### Disadvantages for the employee

- **Work is a social environment** Many people form social groups via their workplace and 1 in 3 people meet their future life partner at work. Telecommuting can lead to social isolation.
- **Some work requires interpersonal contact** Personal conversations form a vital part of the work process in any organisation. Direct, face-to-face interaction is sometimes the only way that information can be fully communicated.
- **Working at home is not always easy** There may be many interruptions and distractions, and this can make work difficult. Also the person may feel that their home now offers no escape from work.

### Advantages for the employer

- **Reduction of the need for office space** If employees don't need desk space, the need for large offices decreases. This can cut down on rental/purchase costs. There may be other associated costs which can also be cut: electricity bills, maintenance staff, etc.
- **Hiring staff on the basis of productivity** Some employers need to hire staff on a short-term basis to complete specific tasks, e.g. batch processing.
- **Greater productivity** Some employees, working in the right environment and away from the distractions of colleagues, can be more productive.

### Disadvantages for the employer

- **Difficulty in monitoring the productivity of employees** The employer may be concerned that insufficient work is being done and there may not be any easy way of monitoring this.
- **There are security issues** An Internet link is always a vulnerable point in a networked system. When it is linked to a domestic PC, this is even more the case.
- **There may be initial costs** Communications links may need to be set up and the employee may need a work-dedicated terminal.

# Videoconferencing

## How videoconferencing works

### 1 Videoconferencing room

The room will be set up like a standard meeting room, organised so that people can talk to each other and give presentations. Additionally there will be some specific pieces of technology that will permit video-conferencing to take place. There will be at least one large monitor/screen so that the people in the room can see participants who are in another location. There will be at least one microphone to pick up the voice signals of the people in the meeting and at least one camera to capture the visual images of the participants. If there is more than one camera/microphone there will also need to be some sort of mixing/controlling device.

### 2 Signal conversion

People speak and interact as they would do at a normal meeting. The camera(s)/microphone(s) pick up the signals in analogue form. These analogue signals will need to be converted to binary code before they can be transmitted. This is achieved through the use of a device – called a 'codec' – which can convert analogue to digital signals and vice versa. An additional step at this stage might be to combine the audio and video signals into one combined file format. An example of this is the .AVI (*audio video inter-leave*) format which combines the two types of signals and has the effect of compressing the data, making it easier to transmit.

### 3 Compression

Transmission will be more effective if the data can be compressed, i.e. made smaller without any significant loss of quality. There are various techniques that can be used for file compression. The method that is used will depend on the resources available (some are more costly than others) and how critical the quality of the image/sound is. A typical compression technique used by videoconferencing is 'lossy' compression. The lossy technique involves focusing on areas of high contrast and removing some pixels (units of visual data) from the image. Minor background variations are therefore sacrificed but, in most cases, this does not result in a significant loss of image quality.

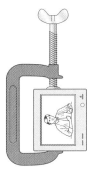

### 4 Transmission

Data is usually transmitted using an ISDN (integrated service digital network) line. ISDN transmits data in a digital rather than analogue form and supports simultaneous transmission of audio, video and computer data. This ensures that the video and audio data 'arrive' together. This makes it particularly useful for videoconferencing.

### 5 Destination

At the reception end the process is reversed. The data is decompressed where necessary, reconverted to an analogue signal and transmitted on the screen. The whole process is two-way so the capture/conversion/transmission procedure is repeated at the second location. In this way a live, two-way transmission environment is created.

| Advantages | Disadvantages |
|---|---|
| Many organisations have employees based in several countries. Bringing these people together for meetings on a regular basis is almost impossible. When meetings have to take place, it may involve expensive international travel with all the difficulties and costs that this involves. Videoconferencing allows for regular meetings between differently located individuals. It has the advantage over telephone conferencing that one can see the face of the person one is addressing. It can also be used in conjunction with the Internet to facilitate presentations. An individual in one location can create and run a presentation (using presentation software). People in the second location can then view this on a monitor that is logged on to a dedicated website. | The main disincentive to the use of videoconferencing is cost. It is expensive to set up, maintain and run. In order to justify this cost it must be cost-effective for an organisation. This is most likely to be the case when an organisation has key people in remote locations who need to speak to each other on a regular basis. Another potential weakness of the system is that subtle communications between people (i.e. through facial expressions, body language, whispered asides, etc.) can be lost because they are not picked up by the camera/microphone or are lost in the compression/transmission process. |

# Health and safety: 1

## Health and safety problems associated with ICT

### Repetitive Strain Injury

Repetitive Strain Injury (RSI) refers to a range of conditions affecting the neck, shoulders, arms and hands. RSIs result from forcing particular muscle groups to perform the same actions over and over again, e.g. working at a keyboard all day long. The most common type of computer-related RSI is Carpal Tunnel Syndrome. This is where the nerve that runs through the wrist is affected by the constant pressure of typing. Initially, this leads to wrist pain and numbness in the fingers. In extreme cases, the injury can make it impossible for the sufferer to pick up everyday objects.

### Eyestrain

Staring continuously at a brightly-lit screen all day can lead to eyestrain, the symptoms of which include headaches, blurred vision, dry and irritated eyes, etc. The effects of this are temporary and there is no evidence that computer use causes irreparable damage. None the less, eye strain can cause discomfort and make employees less efficient. It is therefore in an employer's best interests to ensure that working spaces are properly lit and display screens correctly adjusted.

### Stress

There is increasing evidence that working extensively in a computer-based environment can be stressful. While it was originally thought that computers would lighten people's workload, in many instances they have added to it. Computers have raised expectations about what is possible in the workplace and thus increased the demand placed on employees. In some workplaces, e.g. call centres, these expectations are made explicit, i.e. through continuous monitoring and logging of user interactions. Computers, however, remain fallible, breaking down at inopportune moments, 'losing' important documents, refusing to respond as expected, etc. The combination of increased demand and continued fallibility creates the conditions for stress, a psychological condition with physical symptoms.

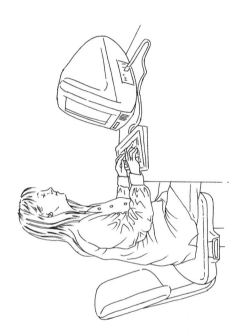

### ELF radiation

There is some debate about whether ICT workers are at risk from the effects of 'extremely low frequency radiation'. VDUs based on cathode ray tube technology emit non-ionizing electric and magnetic fields at low frequency. Whether or not these emissions have an effect on those exposed to them, is open to debate. There is research that suggests that long-term exposure may be hazardous to the health (especially of pregnant women), but the evidence is far from conclusive and most experts in this field do not believe the danger is significant.

### Dependency

The increasing sophistication of communications technology (remote access, the Internet, wireless transmission) has meant that people working with computers can do so from any location and at any time. The consequence of this, combined with the 'addictive' nature of some computer-based work, means that some people find it difficult to 'switch off', continuing their work while they commute and when they are at home. This inability to 'switch off' can lead to stress-related illnesses and other conditions associated with a lack of rest and relaxation.

# Health and safety: 2

## Complying with health and safety legislation

Health and Safety regulations provide legal guidelines for what constitutes a safe working environment. All organisations are legally required to comply with the requirements of such legislation. Failure to do so can lead to prosecution and/or legal action by employees who suffer from injuries or illnesses as a result of factors within their working environment. Most large organisations have a Health and Safety Officer who is responsible for monitoring working conditions and ensuring that anything that might be injurious to the well-being of employees is corrected. Organisations can also keep within the law by designing **ergonomic** work places. Ergonomics refers to the study of the relationship between people and their working environment. When an environment is described as being ergonomically effective, it means that it has been designed with the needs of people in mind.

## The ergonomic office

**General environmental factors** There are various environmental factors which, if left unchecked, can lead to problems. Air quality should be monitored and adequate ventilation provided. The temperature should be comfortable to work in: the recommended temperature is 20–23.5 °C in the winter and 23–26 °C in the summer. Noise levels should be monitored: an excess of loud, distracting noise can lead to stress.

**Monitors** VDUs should be positioned at a suitable height (eyesight naturally falls 20% below the horizon). They should be adjusted so that the user's neck is straight when they look at the screen. The monitor settings (e.g. brightness) should be at a level that is comfortable for the eyes. Anti-glare screen filters may be necessary.

**Timed breaks** In order to avoid both stress and some forms of RSI, it is necessary to take regular breaks. It is generally recommended that employees working at a computer screen should take 5–10 minute breaks every hour. They should ideally do something that involves standing up and moving around. This will give tired muscles a 'break'.

**Keyboard and mouse** The keyboard and mouse should ideally be slightly below elbow level and close to the body. The keyboard should be angled so that the user's wrists remain naturally straight. There are some ergonomically designed keyboards and mouse devices that have been designed to avoid problems associated with RSI. When the mouse is used for any length of time, the lower arms should be supported.

**Chair and posture** If an employee is seated for much of their working day, it is essential that their posture is good. Incorrect posture can lead to severe back problems. Chairs should be easily adjustable by the user whilst he is sitting in the chair. The backrest should be curved to fit the shape of the back and there should be padding for the lower back area. The user should be able to fit their legs comfortably under the desk. Angled footrests can also be used to improve the seating position.

**Light** Poor-quality lighting in an office environment can lead to eyestrain. Ideally there should be a good balance of natural and artificial light. The light should be strong enough for people to read documents but not too strong for working with a computer screen. There should not be direct sunlight on the screen.

**Hardware and software** Employee stress is a consequence of working with hardware and software that does not perform as it should. The hardware should be of a sufficient specification to do the job required of it, and minor technical problems should not be allowed to develop into major ones. Software should be designed to be user-friendly: the user should feel comfortable with the application and should not find themselves constantly encountering error messages and 'crashes'.

# Moral and ethical issues in ICT: 1

## What are ethics?

Ethics are moral principles that help to inform the decisions that individuals make. There are a number of professions where complex and far-reaching ethical decisions have to be made on a regular basis. The most obvious case is the medical profession: doctors have to decide whether to undertake a course of treatment that might mean the difference between life and death for the patient. In making this decision the doctor will be able to refer to her own set of moral principles, e.g. on whether euthanasia is morally justified. Additionally there are codified ethics that may be drawn upon, including:

**The law**  Law-making often starts with a moral principle (e.g. 'stealing is wrong') and codifies it as a law, the breaking of which incurs negative consequences.

**Codes of practice**  Many organisations develop codes of practice which, while not carrying the force of law, provide guidelines for employees to work within.

**Professional ethics**  Some professional bodies develop ethical principles that are relevant to the members of that profession. Although they do not carry the force of law, a breach of them may lead to expulsion from the professional body. The British Computer Society, for example, has developed a Code of Conduct for ICT professionals. It covers such areas as: The Public Interest, Duty to Employers and Clients, Duty to the Profession and Professional Competence, and Integrity.

ICT is not usually identified as an area where ethical issues are a priority. However, professionals working in ICT may well face a number of ethical issues related to the impact of their work, both on individuals and on society as a whole. ICT developments have had – and will continue to have – an enormous impact on society. Ethically speaking, ICT professionals have a responsibility to consider the consequences – positive and negative – of the technologies that they work to develop.

## Some ethical issues in ICT

### PRIVACY

ICT systems have enabled a wide range of private and public organisations to hold electronic data on vast numbers of individuals. Data subjects are not always aware of their rights under data protection legislation and not all organisations act ethically in regard to their use of data. Information that individuals may wish to keep private is not always securely held and can therefore be accessed by organisations and individuals who should not have access to it. Electronic monitoring systems, such as those that track e-mails, can be used – sometimes legitimately, sometimes not – to view individuals' personal messages.

### EMPLOYMENT PATTERNS

ICT has had an enormous impact on employment patterns and working practices. It would not be an exaggeration to state that ICT has transformed the workplace over the past 30 years. Some of this change has been beneficial to organisations and individuals but, while there have been obvious winners, there have been losers too. Some people have been de-skilled by the arrival of ICT and have found themselves out of work as a consequence. In other cases the nature of ICT-based work has created its own problems. Call centres, for example, which use computerised communication technology, have been referred to as 'the sweat shops of the 21st century'.

### EQUITY

It has been argued that the introduction of ICT has led to a divide both within and between societies. This divide has been characterised as one between 'information rich' and 'information poor'. As societies rely more and more on ICT, ownership of and access to the appropriate technologies increasingly determine which individuals/organisations/ societies succeed or fail. Since these technologies incur financial costs, those individuals/organisations/societies who already possess material wealth are in a stronger position to take advantage of them and, in so doing, increase their wealth, power and status still further. The materially less well off are excluded from the technological loop and thus the divide between the two groups widens.

### PROPERTY RIGHTS

The capabilities of ICT, and of the Internet in particular, have led to a number of problems associated with what is generally referred to as 'intellectual property'. The Internet was, in part, developed to facilitate the free exchange of ideas and research. Problems emerged, however, when the 'free access' principles of the world wide web were applied to such things as published text, music, video, software, etc. This has led to battles between those individuals and organisations who have ownership rights and those users who believe the Internet should not become another space that is owned and run by large corporations. This conflict of values is exemplified by the legal battles that have taken place between music publishers and file-sharing systems such as Napster.

# Moral and ethical issues in ICT: 2

## An approach to ethical decision-making

### IDENTIFY THE FACTS

An ethical dilemma is initiated when an individual is required to act in response to an event or an instruction. There is a dilemma because the individual feels uncomfortable with the required action as it conflicts with their principles of right and wrong. For example, an ICT professional may be asked to work on an application designed to help an organisation monitor employees' personal e-mail, and may feel that this conflicts with his notion that individuals have a right to privacy. In order to make an ethically sound decision, the individual first needs to apprise himself of all the relevant facts. In the example given, there would be a need to know who would be using the application, what purpose it would be put to, whether employees would know of its existence, etc. The individual must be in full possession of the facts before they can make an informed decision.

### DEFINE THE ETHICAL CONFLICT

Typically, an ethical conflict involves a choice between mutually exclusive courses of action, each of which is informed by a different set of values. Defining the ethical conflict requires the individual to identify the moral values that are in conflict. In the example given, the employees' right to privacy is in conflict with the organisation's right to protect itself from the damage caused by (for example) the circulation of false rumours. It may be, at this stage, that the ethical dilemma can be resolved by the emergence of a compromise solution that respects both sets of values. If for, example, the employees were aware that their e-mails were being monitored, they could choose a different means of communication for personal messages. Some ethical dilemmas, however, are not amenable to compromise solutions.

### TEST THE REQUIRED ACT AGAINST PERSONAL AND CODIFIED ETHICS

**The law**   If the required act is against the law, the dilemma may be solved. The ICT professional can, in this instance, justifiably claim an unwillingness to step outside the law. The law does not always provide a simple answer to ethical dilemmas: in some circumstances – i.e. where laws are unjust, an act that goes against the law may be the most ethical thing to do.

**Codes of practice**   Organisational or professional codes of practice may provide guidelines for action. The British Computer Society's Code of Conduct states that 'members shall avoid any actions that adversely affect (basic human) rights'. It could be argued that, in this case, the right to privacy in one's personal communications is a basic human right. Codes of practice do not, however, carry the weight of law and may be interpreted in different ways.

**Personal ethics**   Individuals live their lives according to a set of ethical principles. Those principles may be more or less flexible and more or less consistent with the general moral principles of a society. They provide individuals with guidelines for action. Some individuals have a relatively rigid moral code – inspired, for example, by religious precepts – and this will make ethical dilemmas easier to resolve: the action is either acceptable to them or it is not.

### DEFINE POSSIBLE COURSES OF ACTION AND THEIR CONSEQUENCES

If, after the required act has been tested against the above ethical codes, the dilemma still remains, the next stage is for the individual to set out the courses of action available. Each option will involve a different set of consequences. These positive/negative consequences can then be weighed against each other. In this example, the ICT professional can see that one option is to refuse to work on the system. The consequence of this may be that this contract is terminated and someone else is hired. This negative consequence has to be weighed against the consequences of a developing a system that diminishes his colleagues' right to privacy.

### APPLY ESTABLISHED ETHICAL PRINCIPLES

**The Golden Rule**   This can be stated as 'do unto others as you would have them do unto you'. The individual should put himself in the position of those likely to be affected by his actions. How would he feel were he in their position?

**Kant's Categorical Imperative** Immanuel Kant was a philosopher who proposed that one should, when making an ethical choice, ask oneself: 'If everyone in society acted in this way, could society survive?'. In other words, if an act is right for one person it should be right for all persons.

**The Utilitarian Principle**   This principle states that one should weigh all the consequences of different possible actions and select the one that results in the greatest good for the greatest number of people.

### DECISION

# Computer crime

## What is computer crime?

Computers have given workers in most fields new tools to work with, tools that have made their jobs easier and allowed them to do things that were not possible before. Unfortunately, this is as true for criminals as it is for doctors, teachers and designers. It is sometimes thought that 'computer crime' is a new phenomenon but, as the categories below demonstrate, it is more the case that computers have provided new ways to commit old crimes. The facilities provided by computers – their speed of processing, their capacity to connect to international communication networks, the way in which many of their processes are hidden – make them valuable to criminals whilst creating new challenges – and new opportunities – for law enforcement agencies.

## Categories of computer crime

### Unauthorised access

This is usually referred to as 'hacking' or 'cracking'. Hacking involves infiltrating a system to which the individual does not have authorised access. The purpose behind this infiltration varies according to the individual. Some hackers see their activities as a form of game-playing, i.e. where they are matching their computer skills against those of an adversary. The gaining of access is sufficient for them. Others are more destructive in their intentions. They target organisations that they are antagonistic towards and, having gained access, commit acts of 'electronic vandalism', e.g. amending critical data.

### Fraud

Developments in computerised systems have contributed to a growth in electronic transaction processing. This has led to a concomitant rise in computer-based fraud. Criminals have used computerised systems to steal people's credit identities. They then use those identities to make purchases or facilitate cash transfers. Another example of computer-based fraud is where individuals have gained unauthorised access to financial accounts and amended the details of those accounts to their advantage. There have also been examples of people setting up websites for companies that don't exist, and accepting people's credit card payments.

### Publication of illicit material

Material such as hard-core pornography cannot legally be published and sold in many countries. However, the Internet is transnational in its scope and so illicit material can be created in a country where it is legal and viewed in a country where it is not. It is not possible at the moment to police an international 'ownerless' system such as the Internet and, consequently, individuals can publish illicit material with impunity. Another example is the publication of material likely to incite racial hatred. Were material of this kind to be made available through a shop, the owner and publisher could be prosecuted. Such material is freely available on the web.

### Theft

Information stored on computerised systems has value. The code behind a piece of software, a database of consumer information, or the master copies of a new film can be sold for profit and criminals are therefore motivated to steal such items. In some cases this theft can be achieved through a conventional break in – i.e. the tapes or hard drives containing the data are physically removed. More often, however, the theft is achieved electronically. The system where the data/software/content is located is hacked into and the material electronically transferred to another site.

### Industrial espionage

Some organisations try to gain an advantage over their competitors by illicitly gaining access to information about the competitor's marketing strategy, latest research, expansion plans, etc. In the past this would have been achieved through breaking-in, illegal photographing of documents, insiders passing out information, etc. Now it can be achieved through hacking into organisational databases and viewing the information they contain. This process can be achieved more easily if the perpetrators have accomplices working within the organisation.

### Sabotage

For a variety of reasons an individual or individuals may wish to damage the effective functioning of an organisation. If they are able to gain access to that organisation's information systems, they can do a great deal of damage, both directly to the systems and indirectly by amending the way the systems operate. The motivation for such sabotage may be:

- personal – a grudge against an ex-employer;
- political – an attack on an organisation whose actions are disapproved of;
- economic – damaging the performance and reputation of a competitor.

## Computers and law enforcement

Just as criminals have taken advantage of the new opportunities offered by developments in ICT, so too have law enforcement agencies sought to improve their performance through the application of new technologies. There are numerous examples of where technological developments have aided law enforcement. These include:

- The use of centralised databases to store details of crimes and criminals. These databases can then be queried to aid investigation into ongoing cases.
- Improved communication between law enforcement agencies at both a national and international level. Information about crimes committed in one country can be accessed in other countries. This has become more and more necessary as criminals take advantage of the same technology to 'globalise' their operations.
- Use of computing systems for analysing DNA, fingerprints, voice samples, etc. The speed of processing has led to the increased use of forensic evidence as a means of detection and to assist in the securing of convictions.
- Use of specific computer-based technologies – surveillance cameras, speed cameras, alarm systems – to help prevent crime and catch those who break the law.

# Protecting systems

**Tape drive**

### Firewalls

ICT systems need to be in communication with the outside world. This often involves connection to publicly accessible communication systems. This creates an 'electronic gateway' that is difficult to police effectively. Firewalls have been developed to make this vulnerable area more secure. A firewall is a combination of hardware and software resources, designed to check the legitimacy of incoming messages and requests for service. Messages/requests whose source is questionable can be safely re-routed until the legitimacy of the communication can be verified.

### Access procedures

Access to networks should be protected by password systems. These vary in the degree of security they offer. Simple, user-defined passwords are not very secure: people tend to use predictable formulae for setting passwords, e.g. their birthdays. Some organisations use specially designed passwords that change daily according to a designated pattern. Security can be further enhanced by setting different access levels – e.g. a junior employee may have read-only access to a piece of data, whereas someone more senior may have read/write access to the same data. Employees should be able to access only those areas of the system that they have been cleared to work on.

### Encryption

Encryption may be used to make stored data more secure. Encryption involves taking a piece of data (cleartext) and translating it into a coded version of itself (ciphertext). Nobody can make sense of the data in its encrypted form: it will just appear as a collection of nonsense characters. In order to be able to make sense of it, the user must decrypt the ciphertext. This involves using a copy of the encryption key, i.e. a piece of software that translates cleartext into cipher text and back again. If an unauthorised individual managed to gain access to the data, it would be useless without access to the key.

### Physical security

It is necessary to protect the hardware from theft and unauthorised access. A number of measures can be employed:

- Security guards: responsible for permitting access to the building, logging visits, patrolling the site, challenging intruders, etc.
- Secure areas: some equipment (e.g. main servers) may be held in a secure area with limited access. Such an area may be locked, alarmed and monitored by security cameras.
- Biometric access devices: newer security systems are based on biometric readings of individual's fingerprints, voice, iris pattern, etc.

### Clerical procedures

The integrity of an organisation's data can be compromised by errors made at the point of data entry. In order to optimise data accuracy, there should be set procedures for data entry and a means to check the validity and – as far as possible – the accuracy of the data. This might involve batch-processing procedures, validation checks (e.g. range checks, presence checks, hash totals, etc.) and verification procedures, including double entry of data and confirmation of the accuracy of stored data with the original data source (e.g. confirming with a client that their address has been correctly entered). Security should be factored into the design of all procedures followed by users.

### Training

The most effective way of preventing employees unintentionally compromising the security of systems and data is to ensure they are well-trained. All employees whose work involves access to ICT systems should be aware of security issues. They should understand the importance of being security-conscious and know how to avoid the types of errors that lead to problems. For example, it is not possible to prevent a virus being sent to an organisation via an e-mail but, if staff are aware of the dangers of opening e-mails from unknown sources, the virus can be deactivated before it causes any damage. Security awareness can be reinforced through the use of posters, screen messages, etc.

### Backing-up

Security measures, however effectively employed, are never sufficient to prevent loss or corruption of data. It is impossible, for example, to account for the damage done by an unforeseen terrorist attack. The most effective security measure is, therefore, the existence of a well-organised, carefully executed back-up procedure. This allows for recovery from even a disastrous loss of data or system failure.

THREATS

# Viruses

### What is a virus?

A virus is a computer program that has been specifically designed to infiltrate a 'host' computer, to hide itself in that computer, and then, following a designated trigger event, perform actions that are, at best, an annoyance (e.g. an abusive screen message) and, at worst, catastrophically destructive (e.g. erasing all data on the hard drive). A virus is so called because, like its biological counterpart, it has the ability to replicate itself and spread to other 'hosts', infecting them as it does so. The first significant virus, known as 'Brain' appeared in 1986. It had the capacity to infect IBM PC's and was initially spread by students at the University of Delaware using floppy disks. Since then the number of viruses has grown exponentially and there are now many thousands of known examples. The media has tended to amplify the threat of viruses through its publicising of the effects of the most exotic examples ('Michaelangelo', 'Melissa', 'The Love Bug', etc.) The extent of the threat can, however, be overestimated. A combination of regularly updated anti-virus software and sensible computer usage will account for the threat posed by the overwhelming majority of viruses.

### Types of virus

**Boot sector viruses**

This type of virus is generally spread through the use of floppy discs. The boot sector is a location on the computer's hard drive that instructs the computer to load the operating system. If the boot sector is infected with a virus, this virus will become active each time the user 'boots up' (i.e. switches on) their computer. The virus can infect any floppy disc that is then placed in the drive. Thus the virus will be spread across many machines with floppy discs acting as carriers.

**File viruses**

A file virus attaches itself to an executable file (i.e. files with a .exe or .com file extension). It locates itself at the file's header. When the file is run, the virus replicates itself and spreads to other files. The virus can then begin its destructive work. The ExploreZip virus is a file virus that looks for Microsoft files and assigns a zero byte count to the file, thus ensuring its contents are wiped and unrecoverable.

**Macro viruses**

Increasingly the commonest form of virus, a macro virus, utilises the macro facility offered by Microsoft Office products. A macro is a simple program, which a user can write, to perform a specified set of actions. Generally speaking, any action that can be performed by the computer can be written in a macro. The virus is hidden in a simple file. Each time the file is opened it runs its hidden program. The macro might be programmed to wipe the contents of some or all of the user's files.

### How the Melissa virus worked

An e-mail is sent with a file attachment. The file attachment contains the virus which is triggered when the file is opened.

The virus now attaches itself to the user's file and runs a search on the contents of their e-mail address book. The virus then looks up the first fifty names in the address book.

The virus sends the original e-mail to all of the fifty people. Each time the attachment is opened, the process repeats itself. E-mail servers crash due to excess volume of traffic.

### Avoiding viruses

Simple measures can be taken to ensure that computers are not infected by viruses. These include:

• install and continually update anti-virus software;
• virus-check all floppy discs before using them;
• scan and check any software downloaded from the Internet;
• do not open e-mail attachments unless their origin is known;
• avoid any software (especially games) that might have been illegally copied (i.e. pirated versions);
• do not boot up from a floppy disc.

# Threats to data security

## Why is data security important?

As organisations become increasingly dependent on their information systems, it becomes more important for the organisation to protect those systems and the integrity of the data they contain. There are serious consequences of failing to do this adequately, including:

**Financial loss**          This results from having to replace systems, compensate customers, restore missing or compromised data, etc.

**Loss of reputation**      Businesses who fail to protect adequately clients' details, or their own confidential business information, will lose the trust of those who might have dealings with them.

**Legal consequences**      The Data Protection Act requires organisations to ensure that the data they store on individuals is securely held. Failure to do so can result in legal action by the Data Protection Commissioner or compensation claims by data subjects.

## Threats to data security

### Internal source – non-deliberate

An organisation's employees may accidentally compromise data security or integrity:

- simple clerical errors made during the inputting/processing stages may affect the accuracy of the data;
- files may be accidentally erased or corrupted through misuse;
- internally produced software applications may be flawed and may, consequently, damage data;
- e-mail attachments containing viruses may be accidentally opened and thus activated.

### Internal source – deliberate

Those responsible for ICT security need to be aware of the 'enemy within', i.e. employees with access to information systems who decide to act against the organisation. There are two main threats of this type:

- The disgruntled employee with a grudge against the company who may decide to use knowledge of the systems to cause damage.
- The employee who decides to defraud the organisation for financial gain, e.g. by creating non-existent orders and channelling the payments to themselves.

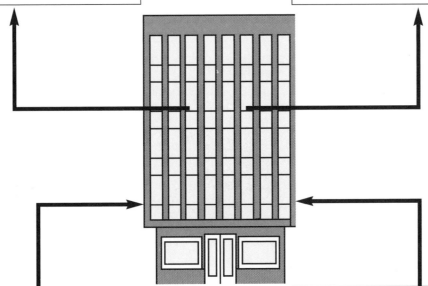

### External source – non-deliberate

The main threats of this type are 'disasters'. These may be natural (floods, extreme weather conditions, earthquakes, volcanoes, etc.) or human/mechanical (plane crashes, power cuts/surges, fires, building collapse, etc). Incidents like this have the potential to wipe out an organisation's information systems, destroying hardware and software and eradicating data. A less dramatic external, non-deliberate threat can occur when an organisation acquires software that has undiscovered 'bugs' in it. Such software can lead to data corruption or loss.

### External source – deliberate

Threats of this type can take many forms, including:

- criminals wishing to defraud the organisation by accessing and amending financial data;
- viruses with the potential to corrupt or wipe out data;
- industrial espionage, i.e. rival organisations accessing confidential information in order to gain competitive advantage;
- actual theft of hardware/software, i.e. through breaking in;
- terrorist attack, e.g. bombing, arson, systems attack.

# Corporate information security policy

## What is a corporate security policy?

- All organisations that store data have a legal obligation under the terms of the Data Protection Act to ensure that their data is secure and its integrity is protected. In addition to this statutory obligation, most organisations rely on their information systems to function effectively and cannot afford for those systems to be damaged, either accidentally or deliberately. In some instances, security of information is critical for a business and can mean the difference between success and bankruptcy.

- It is therefore important to ensure that all possible measures are taken to protect information systems from the threats that they are vulnerable to. These threats, and some of the protective measures that can be employed against them, are set out on pages 116–17.

- It is not, however, sufficient to employ these measures in a haphazard manner. Organisations that rely on their information systems must develop policies that define all aspects of corporate security. This policy should have the support of senior management and be clearly understood by all organisational members.

- If a security policy is to be successful, it must have high status within the organisation. All organisational members should be aware of its requirements and of the consequences of breaching it. One way of ensuring that the policy has the requisite importance is to make it the responsibility of a senior manager who has an organisation-wide remit to ensure its successful implementation.

## Factors to take into account when setting up a corporate security policy

### Prevention of misuse

The essential purpose of a security policy is to prevent the misuse of information systems. This means accounting for both accidental misuse (caused by incompetence, poorly designed systems, etc.) and deliberate misuse (caused by criminal activity, malicious damage, etc.)

### Detection

Computer systems are designed to hide their processes, so misuse can easily go undetected. One of the most powerful aids to a systematic approach to detection is the use of audit trails. Sophisticated software can be used to search file activities for irregularities.

### Investigation

Once an irregularity has been identified, it must be investigated thoroughly. The security manager will need to discover the cause of the breach and, if necessary, invoke disciplinary procedures. It will also be necessary to review security in the wake of any such breach.

### Procedures

Set procedures for accessing information should take into account the potential threats to systems. If followed, these procedures can contribute to system security. Systems can be designed so as to oblige users to follow set procedures, e.g. log-on procedures.

### Staff responsibilities

All staff should be aware of what their individual responsibilities are with regard to security. Managers should be aware of their responsibilities within the area that they manage. Senior managers should take an overview of security arrangements.

### Disciplinary procedures

If the policy is to have any force, there must be disciplinary consequences for breaches of security. All staff should be aware of these consequences. Disciplinary procedures should be clearly set out and should be in keeping with existing employment legislation.

## Creating an awareness of a security policy

It is not sufficient for a security policy to exist in documentary form. Its prescriptions must be embedded within the everyday practice of the organisation. The best defence an organisation has against threats to its information systems is a workforce that is security conscious. There are various ways of encouraging security awareness in employees, including:

| | |
|---|---|
| **Induction programmes** | When staff first join an organisation they are informed about all the security procedures that exist and what their own responsibilities will be. |
| **Security bulletins** | Employees are kept informed about changes to policy and specific security threats (e.g. a new virus) through printed and/or electronic bulletins. |
| **Training programmes** | Employees with specific areas of responsibility, e.g. department heads, may be sent on training courses to improve their awareness of security issues within their own area. |
| **Visible reminders** | Posters, on-screen messages, screen savers, etc. can all be used to reinforce the message that corporate security is important. |
| **Contractual obligation** | An element of an employee's contract of employment can be an undertaking to abide by the company's security policy. |

# The content of a corporate ICT security policy

## General aspects

- A security policy is a formal and official document that sets down the rules, procedures and responsibilities associated with the protection of information systems, the hardware and software used to run them and the data they contain.

- A typical policy would begin by setting out its aims, establishing its scope (i.e. who and what is covered by it) and defining the various responsibilities people within the organisation have.

- The rest of the document would cover in detail how different aspects of the policy should be implemented. Below are some of the areas that might be covered under different headings.

## Specific areas of implementation

### Personnel administration

The policy would:
- Set out procedures to be followed when new employees join the organisation, i.e. screening during the interview process, follow-up of references, checking police records, induction programmes, etc.
- Establish routines for the separation of duties and role rotation, thus avoiding a situation where one employee has sole access to certain parts of the system.
- Set out clearly established disciplinary procedures for breaches of security policy.
- Establish training programmes for employees in security procedures.
- Establish routines for distributing updated information on security issues to all employees, e.g. virus alerts.

### Operational procedures

The policy would:
- Define procedures and responsibilities for the systematic backing up of data and software. Where necessary, this would include the supervision of off-site storage.
- Define and establish responsibilities for the Disaster Recovery Programme, i.e. procedures to be followed in the case of a catastrophic system failure.
- Establish routines for auditing employee use of systems, including setting up software to run audit trails.
- Establish responsibility for maintaining awareness of current virus threats. Included in this would be the maintenance of virus protection software and rule definition regarding computer use, e.g. downloading files from the Internet.

**Security policy**

### Physical security

The policy would:
- Outline procedures for controlling access to the building, including the use of security guards, locked doors, signing in procedures, alarms, etc.
- Outline procedures for controlling access to specific rooms within the building, e.g. through swipe cards, iris recognition, etc.
- Define security status and physical access rights for different employees.
- Outline procedures for protecting hardware, e.g. through the use of locking devices, alarms, etc.
- Define and monitor a stock control system that would ensure that all items of equipment were accounted for.
- Establish procedures for maintaining document security, e.g. secure filing, document access restrictions, etc.

### System access

The policy would specify:
- Logging-on procedures, including use of passwords, different user access levels, call-back systems for remote access, etc.
- Define different access rights and user permissions for all employees, ensuring that access to critical information is restricted.
- Establish routines and responsibilities for maintaining network security, including procedures for remote access and the establishment of 'firewalls'.
- Define rules for personal use of systems, downloading information from the Internet, installing software, transferring data, use of floppy discs, etc.
- Establish procedures for encrypting data, including the use of private/public keys.

# Privacy

### Privacy issues

A distinction should be made between privacy and security. Security is primarily a concern for the organisation: How can it ensure that data and systems are protected from both internal and external infringements? Privacy is more a matter for individual users: How they can ensure that their personal information remains private? The coming of the Information Age has brought in its wake a number of new threats to personal privacy:

- The Internet is by no means a secure medium of communication, and yet individuals choose to divulge personal details on it, including financial information such as credit card numbers. There are many ways in which motivated individuals can gain access to insecure Internet transactions. At the criminal end of the spectrum, this includes individuals and (criminal) organisations who wish to steal credit card details and, in some cases, people's identities. At a less nefarious level, commercial companies may use 'cookies' to identify web-surfing behaviour.
- An inevitable consequence of the trend for commercial companies and public institutions to store personal records electronically is that one's personal details are likely to be held on a number of databases. The level of security applied to these databases varies widely, leaving open the possibility that such personal details may be accessed by individuals who should have no authority to do so.
- The use of the Internet, and e-mail facilities in particular, is widespread in places of work. In office environments employees are likely to spend a good deal of the time at a computer and research suggests that a significant proportion of that time will be spent sending personal e-mails and conducting personal business over the Internet. An increasing number of organisations use specialist applications to monitor both the web-surfing activities and the e-mail traffic of their employees. They can claim that they are justified in so doing because (a) time spent on personal business necessarily results in a loss of productivity and (b) they wish to protect themselves against the legally actionable offences of their employees, e.g. harassment suits that might result from the transmission of pornographic images. Employees, on the other hand, may feel that their privacy is under threat from such monitoring.
- National security organisations and law enforcement agencies have successfully argued that they are justified in monitoring electronic communications, including e-mails, because they are used in the commission of criminal acts and terrorist atrocities. There are a number of systems in operation that perform such monitoring, the best known of which are Carnivore, a monitoring system run by the FBI that filters Internet traffic looking for key words such as 'bomb', and Echelon, an internal data communications monitoring system run by a consortium of English-speaking countries. While most people would support measures taken against criminal and terrorist activity, there are many individuals and groups who believe that the individual's right to privacy is being undermined by the technological sophistication and secretive nature of such systems.

### Ways in which the individual user can preserve privacy

**ENCRYPTION**

Encryption programs convert one's text into (hopefully) indecipherable code. There is a wide variety of encryption programs available. The latest version of Windows has a simple encryption facility and programs such as Pretty Good Privacy (PGP) can be downloaded free from the Internet. Simple encryption systems are, of course, easily broken, but they do offer a measure of protection against unsophisticated 'data snoopers'.

**WEB BROWSERS**

All web-browsing software allows the user to define security settings. It is advisable to maintain the latest version of browser software, as security is an area that has improved with each successive version. The user should not just accept the default settings, but establish what each security level involves and define settings that are appropriate for the level of security they require.

**ANTI-VIRUS SOFTWARE**

Apart from the obvious threat that viruses pose to programs and data, they can also be used to invade privacy and capture data. The 'invader' deploys a 'worm' or 'Trojan Horse' to install a program called a 'keystroke logger' on the target computer. This program will remain hidden from the user and log every keystroke she makes. The resulting data can be retrieved by the hacker who can then 'read' everything that has been written via the keyboard.

**AWARENESS**

Being aware of threats to privacy will help one make informed decisions about what details to reveal via which medium. For example, if one is aware that employers have both the technological means and, in certain circumstances, the legal right to monitor one's personal e-mails, one may choose to be careful about how much one reveals during such communications.

**BASIC SECURITY**

Following some basic security procedures can help maintain privacy. One should avoid, for example, leaving a computer logged-on whilst one is away from it. Passwords should be used to protect sensitive material and the password should not be one that can be easily predicted, e.g. a date of birth or name of pet. If one is working on a network one should be aware of who else has access to shared areas.

**FIREWALLS**

Firewall is a generic name for software/hardware that is designed to protect systems from intrusion. While most commercial organisations deploy expensive and sophisticated systems, there are simple and relatively cheap versions available for the individual user. The latest version of Windows has a built-in Internet Connection Firewall that provides some protection for the individual user.

# Encryption

## What is encryption?

Encryption is the practice of disguising a message so that it cannot be read and understood by any unauthorised persons. It is neither a new practice nor one restricted to the world of ICT. The Roman army used encryption techniques to obscure messages between military commanders, and it has been used throughout time by a variety of people, from merchants who wished to keep their business transactions private to lovers who wanted their assignations to remain secret. In ICT terms it refers to the deployment of dedicated programs that convert ordinary text (plaintext) into a disguised form (ciphertext) through the use of algorithms (step-by-step instructions for the encryption and decryption of text). The formula that is applied is referred to as the key.

Simple encryption entails substituting one letter for another or transcribing letters so that their relative positions in the overall message are changed. Computer encryption starts with these basic principles but adds additional levels of sophistication. For example, instead of just transforming the letter A into another letter, an encryption program will assign each typographical character a binary value, e.g. 10101011 and then transform each bit (i.e. each 0 or 1) into another value according to a logical formula. The number of bits used in this process is an indication of the level of security offered by the process. Most encryption keys range in size from 56 bits to over 2000 bits.

There are two basic types of keys: symmetric and asymmetric. These are described below.

## How encryption works

### Symmetric key encryption

The sender inputs a message then applies the encryption program. This uses a key available to the user to transform the plaintext into ciphertext. It is now indecipherable to anybody without the key. The message is now sent.

The recipient also has a copy of the encryption key. When the ciphertext message is received, the encryption key is applied and the message is transformed back to plaintext. Because only the sender and the recipient have a copy of the key, this method is known as 'private key encryption'.

### Asymmetric key encryption

The sender encrypts a message using a key that the recipient has sent to all those people who might need to be in communication. This key is not kept secret and so this mode of encryption is referred to as public key encryption. The message is now in ciphertext and can be sent securely.

As well as making her public key available, the recipient has the only copy of a private key. This key is mathematically related to the public key and so is able to decipher text that has been encrypted using this method. This system is generally considered to be the more secure of the two, although the process does take longer.

# Back-up: 1

### The importance of backing-up data

Regardless of how many security measures an organisation has in place, systems are still vulnerable to a number of threats. Consequently, in addition to standard security procedures, an organisation should have a clear, well-organised back-up and recovery system. A back-up strategy is similar to an insurance policy: it will allow an organisation to recover data even if the loss is disastrously widespread. The back-up policy should be set out in a formal document and all personnel involved should be aware of procedures and responsibilities both for backing-up and recovering data. In developing such a policy a number of different factors will need to be taken into account. These are set out below.

### Factors to be considered when developing a back-up strategy

**Medium**

A decision must be made about which storage medium will be used. The most commonly used options are:

- A DAT drive which runs a magnetic tape cartridge. These cartridges are a relatively cheap method of storing large amounts of data. The process of backing up to them is slower than with other media and they process information sequentially. This means that in order to find a particular piece of data one has to run through the entire tape up to the point where it is stored.
- Zip drives can be used where there is a relatively small amount of data. These devices can store around 250MB of data, are fairly cheap and can facilitate speedy access of individual files. They are, however, only suitable for small organisations or individual users.
- CD ROM may be used when the data need to be backed-up once and then kept, e.g. a piece of applications software. Rewritable optical discs, capable of storing up to 10GB, are increasingly being used.

Which medium is used will depend on factors such as cost, capacity required, speed of recovery, how long the data needs to be kept, etc.

**Schedule**

The back-up procedure will need to be completed at regular intervals and according to a fixed schedule. This schedule may be different for different parts of the system. For example, some transaction data may need to be backed up more or less at the same time it is processed. Other data – i.e. data which changes less often – may only require backing-up once a week. The policy will also need to specify how long backed-up data should be kept for. In some cases, backed-up data will be overwritten as soon as a new back-up file is created, in other cases it may be necessary to keep an archive file for a set period of time. The schedule will need to take these factors into account and establish set times for the backing-up of each part of the system.

**Location**

The policy will need to specify where the data should be kept. Those responsible for back-up procedures should always consider the worst case scenario – e.g. the main site, together with all hardware, software and data, being destroyed. Even small to medium-sized organisations should consider provision of a secure, fireproof safe in a secondary location for storing backed-up data. Larger organisations, especially those that rely on ICT systems for day-to-day operations, should consider backing-up to various locations, including a secondary server based on another site.

**Recovery**

The effectiveness of the back-up system should be regularly tested by undertaking recovery of backed-up data. In its simplest form this might mean accessing specified pieces of data at set intervals. Some large organisations may choose to undertake full-scale rehearsals of disaster recovery scenarios, i.e. where there has been a disastrous loss of data which needs to be recovered.

**Responsibility**

The responsibility for organising, running and monitoring the back-up procedures cannot be left to chance. Various people in the organisation have to be given distinct responsibilities in regard to different aspects of the procedure. Account should also be taken of what happens if personnel are absent. There therefore needs to be a clearly established rota which also includes reference to 'cover for absence'.

# Back-up: 2

## Different back-up strategies

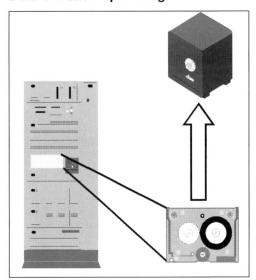

### Standard data back-up procedure

This involves periodically copying data files on to a separate storage device. Typically, this would be performed at scheduled intervals, often overnight when servers are not in use, with data being copied on to a DAT drive. In the morning, the network manager would check a printout to ensure that the back-up had been successfully performed. The resulting tape is then stored off-site in a secure, fireproof safe.

The organisation can choose whether to complete a full back-up where all files are copied. This will make recovery easier but may take a long time if copied on to tape. Alternatively, they may perform an incremental back-up, i.e. all files are copied, for example, once a week. Then, each night, only those files that have been created or updated will be backed up. This is a less time-consuming process but it makes recovery more complex.

One limitation of this strategy is that the back-up is never fully up to date. If, for example, there is a system crash in the late afternoon all the changes made during that day will be lost. This is because the back-up tape will only contain changes made up until the end of the previous day's business. This back-up strategy is therefore suitable only for small- to medium-sized organisations in which day-to-day transactions are not critical.

## RAID system

RAID stands for 'Redundant Array of Inexpensive Discs'. There are various RAID systems but they all involve writing data to a series of magnetic discs. In one system, called 'disc mirroring', whatever data is written on to one hard drive is copied on to another at the same time. This means that if one hard drive is corrupted the user can switch straight to the mirrored version without any loss of data. In order to protect such a system from disaster scenarios (e.g. a fire), one of the disks to which the data is being written may be located in a different site.

**Data is written simultaneously to two discs. If one device fails the other can take over**

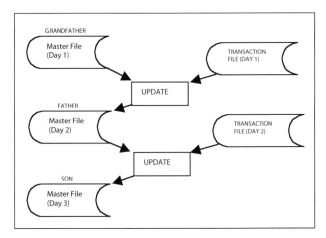

### Grandfather–father–son

This approach involves 'generations' of master files. In the example shown, the 'grandfather' master file is merged with another file, the transaction file, which contains all the changes that need to be made to the master file. This results in a new master file, called the 'father' file. This, in turn, is merged with the next transaction file to create a new master file, the 'son' file. By keeping the master files and transaction files of three generations, the organisation will always be able to recover a lost or missing master file. This strategy is most appropriate for a batch processing system, i.e. where there is a regular updating of a master file using new transactions.

## Backing-up program files

It is sometimes necessary to restore program files. If a system has been bought 'off the shelf' this might be achieved by using the CD ROM(s) on which the original program was stored (or a copy of the same). There are circumstances, however, where this not an appropriate strategy, e.g. where a program will need to be configured in a particular way before it can be installed on a system. If it is critical to restore such a program quickly, it will not be sufficient to rely on an original copy of the (unconfigured) version. Also, programs have changes made to them, e.g. an anti-virus security patch might be added on to the original version. For these reasons, it might be necessary to maintain an up-to-date copy of all program files so that they can quickly be restored. A grandfather–father–son strategy may be suitable for this task.

# Disaster recovery management: 1

Organisations that rely heavily on their information systems to conduct their business need to prepare themselves for the failure of those systems. While they may have a number of procedures and resources in place to protect their systems from expected threats and small-scale system failures, they also have to be prepared for unexpected, large-scale system failures. This is referred to as disaster recovery management and is, as the name implies, a set of resources and procedures to cope with the aftermath of a disastrous breakdown of systems/loss of data. The aim of such a program is to minimise negative consequences.

## Threats and consequences

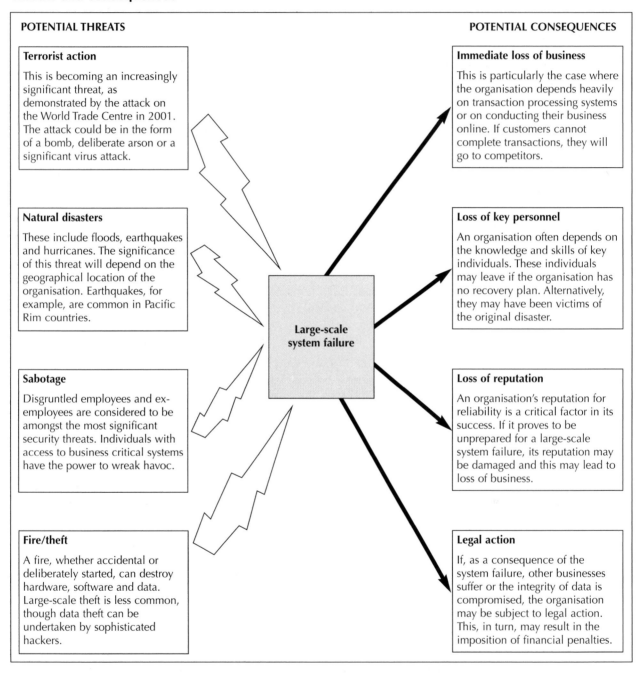

**POTENTIAL THREATS**

**Terrorist action**

This is becoming an increasingly significant threat, as demonstrated by the attack on the World Trade Centre in 2001. The attack could be in the form of a bomb, deliberate arson or a significant virus attack.

**Natural disasters**

These include floods, earthquakes and hurricanes. The significance of this threat will depend on the geographical location of the organisation. Earthquakes, for example, are common in Pacific Rim countries.

**Sabotage**

Disgruntled employees and ex-employees are considered to be amongst the most significant security threats. Individuals with access to business critical systems have the power to wreak havoc.

**Fire/theft**

A fire, whether accidental or deliberately started, can destroy hardware, software and data. Large-scale theft is less common, though data theft can be undertaken by sophisticated hackers.

**Large-scale system failure**

**POTENTIAL CONSEQUENCES**

**Immediate loss of business**

This is particularly the case where the organisation depends heavily on transaction processing systems or on conducting their business online. If customers cannot complete transactions, they will go to competitors.

**Loss of key personnel**

An organisation often depends on the knowledge and skills of key individuals. These individuals may leave if the organisation has no recovery plan. Alternatively, they may have been victims of the original disaster.

**Loss of reputation**

An organisation's reputation for reliability is a critical factor in its success. If it proves to be unprepared for a large-scale system failure, its reputation may be damaged and this may lead to loss of business.

**Legal action**

If, as a consequence of the system failure, other businesses suffer or the integrity of data is compromised, the organisation may be subject to legal action. This, in turn, may result in the imposition of financial penalties.

## Risk analysis

The aim of risk analysis is to identify the following:

- What are the potential risks to the organisation's information systems?
- What is the statistical probability of each threat becoming real?
- What would be the short- and long-term consequences for the organisation of the threat becoming real?
- How well equipped is the organisation to deal with the threat?

Following this analysis, the organisation is in a position to judge how much to spend on developing controls to minimise the risk and establishing contingency plans for recovery from unavoidable disasters.

# Disaster recovery management: 2

## Precautionary measures

- Some of the disasters described on page 124 are preventable. An awareness of potential threats combined with a comprehensive ICT security policy can minimise the risk of a disastrous system failure. For example, the threat of sabotage can be minimised by the implementation of strategies such as: secure password systems, clearly defined dismissal procedures, regular user audits, etc. In some cases the organisation must take precautionary measures that are specific to its geographical location. For example, organisations located in developing countries where power supplies are unreliable, must ensure that they have an uninterrupted power supply (UPS).

- Some disasters – fires, floods, terrorist outrages, etc. – are not preventable and may involve loss of software, hardware, data and even personnel. In order to be prepared for such instances it is necessary for an organisation to have a contingency plan, i.e. a well-established and organised routine that will enable the organisation to continue functioning following a disaster.

## Elements of a contingency plan

### PREMISES/FACILITIES

Some major disasters may involve extensive damage to or even destruction of the organisation's main premises. It may be necessary, therefore, to have a secondary site available for staff to move into. The site would be set up with all the facilities needed for the organisation to resume operations. A cheaper alternative option is to have a 'mutual lease' arrangement with another organisation.

### PERSONNEL

**Training** Employees will need to know what their responsibilities are in the event of a disaster.
**Counselling** A disaster that involves loss of life may be traumatic for some employees and they may require support.
**Role replacement** Some employees may have been injured or even killed in a disaster. The plan will need to plan for all essential roles to be covered.

### COORDINATION
Somebody within the organisation should have responsibility for:
- coordinating all aspects of the plan;
- ensuring all employees are aware of what they have to do;
- keeping the plan updated;
- testing the effectiveness of the plan using simulations or full-scale rehearsals.

### DATA

Recovery of key data that may have been lost or damaged is a critical aspect of disaster recovery. Critical data should be backed-up and stored off site on a regular basis. If this has been managed successfully, restoration of data should be a straightforward matter. Even with back-ups, however, some data – e.g. that day's transactions – may have been lost and their source will need to be traced.

### HARDWARE/SOFTWARE/ COMMUNICATION

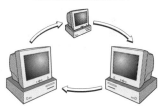

If a secondary site is part of the contingency plan, it must be equipped with sufficient hardware for the organisation to continue functioning. Communication links must be established and software must be available. It will help if an organisation doesn't locate all of its information systems in one place but distributes them across several locations, or outsources some of its processing or data storage.

## Criteria for choosing a contingency plan

The scale and complexity of a contingency plan will depend in part on the results of a risk analysis such as that outlined on page 124. Additionally, the organisation will need to take into account the relative cost (in terms of time, money and personnel) involved in maintaining a contingency plan and the relationship of that cost to the size of the organisation, the critical nature of its ICT systems, the likelihood of disaster, etc. For example, a multinational investment bank with many business critical systems may consider it cost-effective to maintain a secondary site; a small business with only a few systems may not be able to justify such a costly solution. There are organisations that offer a complete Disaster Recovery program to businesses. Such a service may be expensive, but for a business that lacks the requisite expertise, it may be cost-effective.

# The impact of legislation: 1

## How does legislation impact on the organisation?

All organisations have to operate within a legal framework. There is a wide range of laws – local, national and international – that apply to organisations and failure to comply with them can make a company liable to legal action. Because an organisation is responsible for the actions of its employees while they are at work, it must ensure that those employees are fully aware of their rights and responsibilities under the law. In order to achieve this, organisations develop policies that establish a rule-based framework to ensure that employees do not contravene existing legislation. From an ICT perspective, there are some key pieces of legislation that affect organisations based in the UK. Their implications for organisational policy are discussed below.

| IMPLICATIONS FOR ORGANISATION | ENFORCING AND CONTROLLING THE LEGISLATION |
|---|---|
| **The Data Protection Act** | **Policies should be in place to ensure that:** |
| The main aim of this legislation is to protect the rights of individuals who have data held on them by organisations. Under its terms the organisation is held responsible for the security, accuracy and conditions of use of the data it holds. Organisations that do not comply with the terms of the DPA can be prosecuted. It is therefore critical that all data-using organisations have procedures in place to ensure that data is held securely, that its accuracy is maintained and that it is used by the organisation correctly. | • Data held by the organisation is accurate and up-to-date, e.g. through the use of validation and verification procedures. Ensuring that data is up-to-date may involve regular contact with data subjects, asking them to verify currently held details. <br> • Data use is consistent with the requirement that data must only be used for the originally designated purpose. <br> • There are measures in place to protect the integrity and physical security of the data held. This will involve the employment various security measures, including: physical access, system access, firewalls, back-ups, etc. <br> • All staff are aware of data protection issues and of their personal responsibility for ensuring the terms of the act are complied with. <br> • Data subjects are aware of their rights under the terms of the Act. |
| **Computer Misuse Act** | **Policies should be in place to ensure that:** |
| This was designed to prevent computer crimes involving unlawful access to information systems/data. It is unlikely that a legitimate organisation would deliberately breach the terms of this Act, but individual employees may use company resources to hack into other systems. If it were shown that the organisation was negligent in taking steps to prevent this, it could be held partly liable for the actions of its employees. | • Employees are aware of the terms of the Act and the consequence of being in breach of it, i.e. organisational disciplinary procedures. <br> • Computer use by employees is audited and suspect access activity is fully investigated, i.e. by looking at what systems have been accessed by different employees at specified times. <br> • Access to different areas of the system is tightly controlled – i.e. employees should have no more system access than is necessary for the completion of their work. <br> • Controls are in place to prevent employees using the organisation's ICT resources for illegitimate activity, e.g. using communication links to 'hack' into other systems. |
| **Health and Safety at Work Act** | **Policies should be in place to ensure that:** |
| Health and safety legislation is designed to protect employees in the work place. There are some specific concerns relating to the use of ICT and organisations must have measures in place to ensure the welfare of their employees who work in this area. If an organisation is negligent in this area and an employee suffers injury as a consequence, the organisation can be deemed liable and may have to make compensation payments. | • There is a Health and Safety Officer (or team, depending on the size of the organisation) with responsibility for monitoring the organisation's compliance with the terms of the Act. <br> • Regular inspections of equipment and procedures are undertaken and potential problems are followed up. <br> • All employees are trained in the correct use of ICT resources and are made aware of the health risks associated with them. <br> • The procedures followed by employees are in keeping with health and safety requirements. <br> • The design of work spaces and the purchase of resources should take into account health and safety factors. |
| **Copyright Designs and Patents Act** | **Policies should be in place to ensure that:** |
| This legislation is designed to protect the ownership rights of the originators of intellectual property such as design, music and software. The greatest concern in the area of ICT is software piracy, i.e. the illegal copying of software. This may occur on an organisation-wide level (e.g. a small business trying to save money) or an individual level (an employee 'borrowing' software disks and copying them at home). Organisations have to ensure that they do not permit their resources to be used for this purpose. Failure to do so can result in legal action. | • All employees are aware of the terms of the Act and the consequences of being in breach of it. <br> • The organisation audits the software that it owns and monitors who has access to that software. <br> • Licensing agreements are fully adhered to – i.e. if the company has a software licence for 100 users that's how many there should be. <br> • Application files are kept secure and employees are not allowed access to them for personal use. <br> • Employees are only allowed to have authorised programs on their PCs. Unauthorised software, perhaps brought from home or downloaded from the Internet, is not permitted. <br> • There is a centralised mechanism for purchasing software. There should be a senior manager with technology expertise who authorises all software acquisition. |

# The impact of legislation: 2

### Ensuring that an organisation complies with legislation

For an organisation to comply with existing and new legislation, it must have a systematic approach to staying informed about legislative changes, interpreting their impact on the organisation, developing policies to ensure compliance and monitoring the effectiveness of these policies. Legislation is too important to be managed in an *ad hoc* manner; set procedures must be employed.

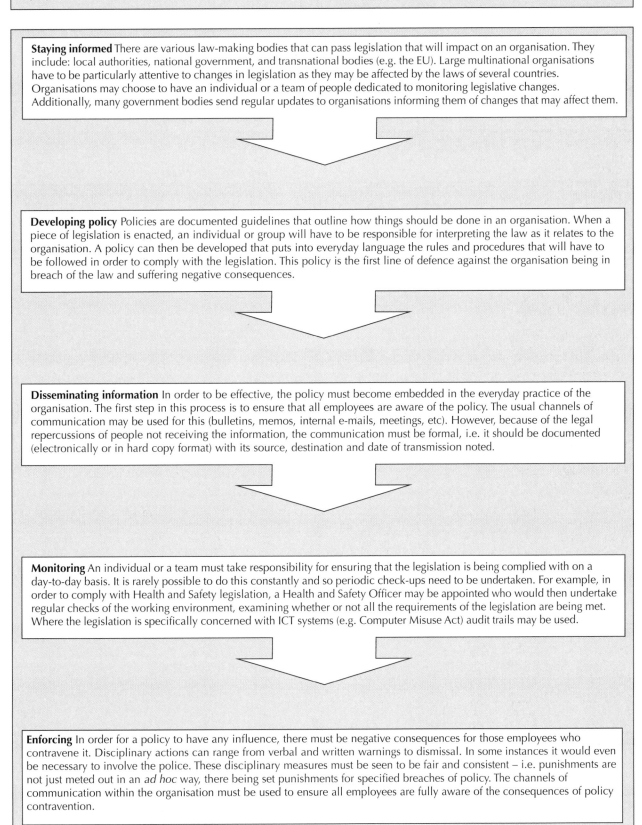

**Staying informed** There are various law-making bodies that can pass legislation that will impact on an organisation. They include: local authorities, national government, and transnational bodies (e.g. the EU). Large multinational organisations have to be particularly attentive to changes in legislation as they may be affected by the laws of several countries. Organisations may choose to have an individual or a team of people dedicated to monitoring legislative changes. Additionally, many government bodies send regular updates to organisations informing them of changes that may affect them.

**Developing policy** Policies are documented guidelines that outline how things should be done in an organisation. When a piece of legislation is enacted, an individual or group will have to be responsible for interpreting the law as it relates to the organisation. A policy can then be developed that puts into everyday language the rules and procedures that will have to be followed in order to comply with the legislation. This policy is the first line of defence against the organisation being in breach of the law and suffering negative consequences.

**Disseminating information** In order to be effective, the policy must become embedded in the everyday practice of the organisation. The first step in this process is to ensure that all employees are aware of the policy. The usual channels of communication may be used for this (bulletins, memos, internal e-mails, meetings, etc). However, because of the legal repercussions of people not receiving the information, the communication must be formal, i.e. it should be documented (electronically or in hard copy format) with its source, destination and date of transmission noted.

**Monitoring** An individual or a team must take responsibility for ensuring that the legislation is being complied with on a day-to-day basis. It is rarely possible to do this constantly and so periodic check-ups need to be undertaken. For example, in order to comply with Health and Safety legislation, a Health and Safety Officer may be appointed who would then undertake regular checks of the working environment, examining whether or not all the requirements of the legislation are being met. Where the legislation is specifically concerned with ICT systems (e.g. Computer Misuse Act) audit trails may be used.

**Enforcing** In order for a policy to have any influence, there must be negative consequences for those employees who contravene it. Disciplinary actions can range from verbal and written warnings to dismissal. In some instances it would even be necessary to involve the police. These disciplinary measures must be seen to be fair and consistent – i.e. punishments are not just meted out in an *ad hoc* way, there being set punishments for specified breaches of policy. The channels of communication within the organisation must be used to ensure all employees are fully aware of the consequences of policy contravention.

# Copyright legislation

The Copyright Designs and Patents Act of 1988 is designed to protect the property rights of those individuals and organisations that create and produce material based on original ideas. Material of this kind, sometimes referred to as 'intellectual property', includes books, articles, music, films, software, etc. In relation to ICT, there are three main areas where legislation may be needed:

- software piracy: the illegal copying or downloading of software;
- the 'theft' by one company of the ideas and methods of other ICT companies;
- the use of ICT to copy or download material such as music/video/text-based files, thus avoiding the price of purchase.

Software piracy is widespread. The US computer industry believes that the extent of illegal copying is impossible to quantify but must be measured in billions of dollars. One estimate that was made – in 1994 by the Software Publishers Association – placed the figure at 8.8 billion world-wide. Piracy takes two main forms:

- individual users borrowing CDs or using the Internet to copy a piece of software to their own computers;
- professional criminals making copies in bulk and selling them through illegal outlets.

The software industry believes that there are two negative effects of this piracy: first, it results in higher prices for those customers who are buying software legally; and, secondly, it discourages software houses from being innovative.

## Licensing

Most organisations run their computers on networks. When they buy a piece of software, they also purchase a licence for a certain number of users. They are then legally permitted to distribute the software for a fixed number of users at any one time. If the organisation wants more users to access the program, then they have to pay for more licences. Some organisations, however, do not do this. They distribute the software over the network with no regard for how many licences they have or, indeed, whether they have a licence at all.

## What can be done?

| Technical solutions | Software companies have experimented with techniques to prevent illegal copying. The main approach is based on giving each instance of the software an electronic signature. It can then be determined whether the version on any one machine originated from a legal version or an illegal copy of the software. |
|---|---|
| Enforcement | Organisations and individuals can be and are taken to court for copyright violations. This might involve the arrest of individuals trading illegally copied CDs from market stalls or car boot sales, or spot checks on organisations where copying or breaches of licensing agreements are suspected. |
| Education | 'Don't copy that floppy' was an advertising slogan run as part of a campaign by the Software Publishers Association. The aim of this campaign was to alert people to the indirect costs that resulted from software piracy. This organisation and others like it have also encouraged organisations to develop codes of practice that will discourage employees from using organisational resources to copy software. |
| Abandon copyright | A more radical solution has been suggested by some individuals and organisations. They believe that software should be seen as a 'public good' and that its distribution should be largely free. Given the commercial forces involved in this issue, and the money at stake, it is unlikely that this argument will become anything other than a minority view. |

## Difficulties in preventing illegal copying

There are three main difficulties in preventing the practice of software piracy:

- Many people do not view small-scale copying as a crime at all, or at least not a serious one. They weigh up their resources against the wealth of the software companies and consider it justified to copy a borrowed edition.
- Privacy laws prevent investigation into the contents of server files or hard drives unless there is reasonable suspicion that a crime has been committed.
- A significant amount of copying takes places in countries that are less regulated in this regard and jurisdiction then becomes a problem.

# The Computer Misuse Act (1990)

## How the Computer Misuse Act came about

As general computer use grew during the 1970s and 1980s, so did the incidence of people using computers for criminal purposes, e.g. accessing and amending data in bank accounts. Additionally, a new crime emerged: 'hacking'. Hacking may be defined as intentionally gaining access to an ICT system without the owner's consent. Hacking might have a 'mischievous' intent, e.g. the hacker proving that they can beat a security system, or a more malicious one, e.g. to damage a system or compromise data integrity.

In the late 1980s individuals were taken to court for such activities and tried using existing legislation relating to theft, criminal damage or the interception of telecommunications. These cases were rarely successful and, in the case of Crown v. Gold, the House of Lords ruled that, in effect, hacking was not a crime. This prompted a Private Member's Bill that became law as the Computer Misuse Act in 1990.

## Offences under the Computer Misuse Act

**1 Gaining unauthorised access to data or programs on a computer**

Individuals can be prosecuted under this section of the Act if:

- *they have caused a computer to perform a function with the intent of allowing the user access to data and/or programs;*
- *they do not have authorisation to access the said program and/or data;*
- *they know and understand that they do not have authorisation.*

This offence would be handled by magistrates and could result in a £2000 fine or up to six months in jail.

**2 Gaining unauthorised access with intent to commit a further serious offence (even if that offence is not committed)**

Individuals can be prosecuted under this section of the Act if:

- *they have gained unauthorised access to a computer system in order to use that system to commit a serious crime. Serious, in this case, is defined as an offence for which the maximum sentence is not less than five years (e.g. theft, blackmail, obtaining property or services by deception).*

This offence is punishable by up to five years' imprisonment.

**3 Intentional unauthorised modification to impair operation**

Individuals can be prosecuted under this section of the Act if:

- *they have modified the content of any computer without authorisation with the intention of impairing the operations of programs or the reliability of data. This would include the deliberate introduction of a virus.*

This offence is punishable by up to five years' imprisonment and a fine.

## Difficulties with the Computer Misuse Act

*The intention behind the Computer Misuse Act was to prevent both the use of ICT systems to commit crimes and deliberate attacks on those systems. The act is not, however, without its critics and some legal experts believe that it is too full of loopholes to function as an effective deterrent. These are some of the difficulties:*

- Organisations are often unwilling to acknowledge publicly that they have a problem with their security. To do so, they believe, will result in a decline in public confidence. The consequence of this is that organisations sometimes choose to manage their security problems internally and without reference to law enforcement agencies.

- The global nature of ICT communication means that offences on the ICT systems of one country are often committed by a citizen of another country. This is particularly the case where viruses are concerned. This leads to problems with jurisdiction: which country's laws should be invoked against the perpetrator?

- The complex nature of ICT systems can mean that it is difficult to prove intent. A defendant could argue that unauthorised access was gained accidentally and that there was no intent to cause damage or commit an offence.

# The Data Protection Act (1984, 1998)

*The Data Protection Act (DPA) first became law in 1984. The Act was the consequence of increasing concern about the number of computer-based systems that stored data. People were concerned about how secure this data was, how accurately it was recorded, and the purposes to which it was being put. The DPA aimed to allay some of these concerns. In 1995 the European Union published its Data Protection Directive. The aim of this was to bring into line the data protection legislation of member states. This required the UK to update its DPA. The consequence of this was the amended DPA of 1998.*

## The eight principles

The Act sets out legal guidelines for the way that personal data should be obtained, processed, stored and maintained. These guidelines are set out as eight key principles:

1. Personal data shall be processed fairly and lawfully. This principle also sets out the criteria that should be met for processing to be lawful, e.g. the data subject has given their consent.
2. Personal data shall be obtained for only one or more specified purposes and shall not be processed any further for purposes incompatible with the original purpose.
3. Personal data shall be adequate, relevant and not excessive in relation to the purpose for which it is being processed.
4. Personal data shall be accurate and up to date.
5. Personal data shall not be kept for longer than is necessary to fulfil the original purpose.
6. Personal data shall be processed in accordance with the rights of the data subject.
7. Personal data shall be held securely and appropriate technical and organisational measures shall be taken to prevent unauthorised access and/or processing.
8. Personal data shall not be transferred outside the EU without appropriate safeguards being put in place.

## Exemptions from the Act

All data users (i.e. any organisation or individual that holds personal data on individuals) have to register with and pay a fee to the office of the Data Protection Registrar unless they covered by one or more of a number of exemptions, including data that is:

- for personal, family or recreational purposes;
- for the processing of information relating to wages, pensions, accounts, etc.;
- being held in the interests of national security or for the prevention of a crime;
- being used for statistical or research purposes;
- being used for the processing of mail-merged documents.

The registration process involves data users registering their name and address, a description of the data that they hold, the purposes to which it is being put, how and where the data is being held, etc.

## The role of the Data Protection Registrar

*The office of the Data Protection Registrar is responsible for:*

- maintaining a register of data users and making that register publicly available;
- ensuring that the terms of the Act are widely known and that detailed information is freely available to the public;
- promoting compliance with the terms of the Act and prosecuting individuals/organisations who breach it;
- encouraging organisations to develop codes of practice that will help them comply with the terms of the Act.

## The rights of the data subject

*The data subject is the individual on whom a data user holds information. Under the terms of the Act the data subject:*

- has the right to access data that is held on them (they may choose to pay a fee to the data user in order to have it made available to them more quickly);
- has the right to be compensated if the data held on them is inaccurate and they can show that the inaccuracy has caused them damage;
- has the right to be compensated if data held on them has been accessed by unauthorised users;
- has the right to insist on the modification of data held on them that is inaccurate.

# Organisation structure

An organisation is a collection of human and non-human resources brought together in order to fulfil a designated purpose. An organisation may be a large, commercial enterprise such as IBM, or a small, informally structured, non-commercial group, e.g. a local charity. All organisations have structures. In some instances these structures are clearly defined and fairly inflexible; in other instances, the structure is looser and less formally defined.

## The hierarchical model

This used to be the standard model for large, commercial organisations. Recently, other models have grown in popularity, but hierarchical models still dominate the business world. Many hierarchical models are based on a division of personnel on the basis of the role that they play within the organisation. This is known as functional specialisation.

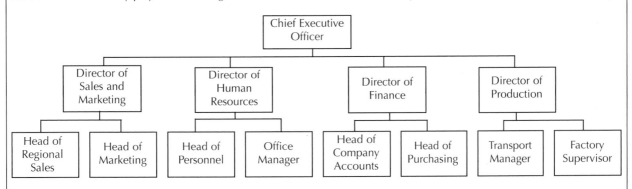

The above diagram represents the basic structure of the hierarchical model. If this were a real organisation, the diagram would be more extensive and would include further levels. For example, the Head of Regional Sales might be responsible for a number of heads of specific regions who, in turn, would have responsibility for sales representatives. Some further points to note about this model:

- **The chain of command** is the path through which instructions are given and decisions are requested. Instructions move from the top downwards, following the line of authority; problems requiring decisions follow similar paths but move from the bottom upwards.
- **The span of control** refers to how many people a manager is responsible for. Too wide a span of control can lead to inadequate control; too narrow a span can lead to unnecessary layers of management.

## Problems associated with a 'tall' hierarchical structure

- The organisation may become inflexible, unable to change quickly because decisions have to travel a long way 'down the line' and so take time to implement.
- Communications which have to travel through a number of levels may become lost or distorted in the process.
- Upper echelons of management can become remote from what is happening 'on the shop floor'. This can lead to opportunities being missed and problems going unnoticed.
- Junior employees can feel that they have no stake in the organisation because they are not required to make any decisions.

## The flat structure

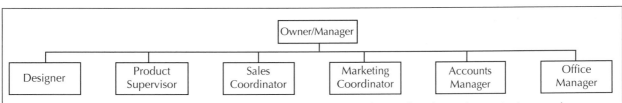

In this structure there are fewer layers of management but the span of control is much wider. Such organisations can be more flexible as the implementation of decisions can happen more quickly. Greater independence is given to different departments and there is more delegation of responsibility. However, specialisation of departments may lead to inadequate communication between departments.

## Factors which determine organisational structure

- The size and complexity of the organisation: the larger and more complex the organisation, the more likely it is to formalise clear lines of authority.
- The nature of the organisational goals: some organisational goals (e.g. a multinational business trying to establish markets in different countries) require the establishment of separate areas of specialisation.
- The beliefs and values of the head(s) of the organisation: some executives prefer looser, more flexible structures, believing that they make better business sense.
- The geographical spread of the organisation: organisations spread across a number of regions often develop structures that reflect this, i.e. regionally based departments.

# Information systems and the successful organisation

Effective information systems – i.e. those which efficiently collect and process data to produce high-quality information – have increasingly become a critical factor in determining organisational success. The ways in which such systems can contribute to success are set out below. The model described refers to business (i.e. profit-oriented) organisations, but many of the points are applicable to non-profit making organisations like schools, charities, etc.

## Tangible savings

Information systems can help organisations make savings in several ways:

- By automating processes that were previously manual, thus reducing labour costs, e.g. an OCR system being used to process invoices.
- By monitoring operations (e.g. deliveries) and analysing the resulting information to determine where there are efficiency savings to be made.
- By providing feedback to optimise operations such as stock control, i.e. 'just-in-time' stocking.

## Legal requirements

All businesses have to operate within a complex legal framework. They may be subject to local bylaws, national laws, and transnational laws. Failure to comply with these laws might result in a legal action that could damage their reputation and cost them money. Information systems help them to manage this process, either directly (e.g. by helping them comply with data protection legislation) or indirectly (e.g. by providing information that external agencies and auditors need to see).

## Competitive edge

Businesses compete with each other to gain market advantage. Good-quality information can assist a business in this process. The organisation can, for example, measure its progress against other organisations by comparing critical data (monthly sales, stock valuation, etc.). It can also use information to analyse, with a high degree of precision, current market conditions. This process will help them make good decisions about what products to develop and how to market them.

## Feedback

The successful organisation needs to create a loyal customer (or client) base. Information systems can assist in this process by enabling the organisation to gauge their customers'/clients' responses to their products/services, i.e. it can provide an answer to the question 'How are we doing?'. The business can thus create a dialogue so that they are more attentive and responsive to customers' needs and the customers are kept better informed of what the organisation can offer them.

## Responsiveness to environmental changes

Organisations have to exist within an environment, i.e. a theoretical space consisting of all those factors that might affect them. The more sensitive an organisation is to subtle changes in this environment, the more likely it is that they will be able to adapt their practice to exploit new opportunities (or avoid new dangers) that are consequent upon these changes. Some commentators have likened this to evolutionary theory: those organisations that can best adapt to changes in their environmental niche are most likely to thrive.

## Decision-making

Decision–making is a critical factor in the success or failure of a business. Even a seemingly small, everyday decision can be business-critical. There is a direct correlation between good quality decision-making and successful organisations. The quality of a decision is reliant upon two factors: the quality of information the decision is based on and the wisdom and insight of the person/group making the decision. In short, good-quality information contributes significantly to decision-making, the quality of which plays a large part in determining the success/failure of an organisation.

# Information management policy

## Centralised versus decentralised model

Organisations regularly have to make decisions about how their ICT systems should develop. These decisions may cover many different aspects of ICT, including hardware, software, networking capabilities, communication systems, etc. In many organisations these decisions are business-critical, i.e. they impact directly on the ability of the business to function effectively. It is therefore inadvisable for organisations to make such decisions in an *ad hoc* manner. Rather, they should develop a strategic ICT policy. Such a policy would place ICT-oriented decisions in the overall context of organisational needs and goals.

There are, broadly speaking, two models for developing an ICT policy: the centralised and decentralised models.

**Centralised**  In this model an Information Systems Department takes responsibility for the development of all ICT systems in the organisation, regardless of which functional area is being served. All decisions about purchasing, development, training, etc. go through this centralised department. It therefore determines the overall ICT policy of the organisation.

**Decentralised**  In a decentralised model, each functional area makes it own decisions about what systems to develop and/or acquire. If accounting, for example, needed a new application it would evaluate what was on the market and make a decision based on its own criteria.

The decentralised model is rarely found these days. The need for interconnectedness between systems based in different functional areas makes the centralised model much more desirable. The decentralised model had one main advantage: it allowed individual departments/functional areas the autonomy to make ICT-based decisions using criteria that related primarily to their own functional needs. This one advantage is, however, outweighed by the advantages of a centralised approach. These include:

- increased ability to maintain compatibility between the different elements of an organisation's ICT infrastructure;
- improved discounts as a consequence of high volume purchasing;
- better deals on service level contracts;
- easier for employees to move from department to department if systems are similar;
- greater control over security issues.

## Factors in ICT policy development

**Developing an integrated system** An organisation's ICT systems must be able to communicate with each other. Users must be able to integrate data held in different systems and transfer files without encountering problems. Systems must also communicate with external systems, especially if such systems are integral to its operations, e.g. the Internet. Each ICT development must therefore be consistent with this overall aim.

**Budget** Organisations often have to dedicate large proportions of their budget to ICT systems. It is therefore important that all ICT-based decisions are cost-effective. If a development is going to take place it must be costed thoroughly, taking into account both open and hidden costs, e.g. the cost of retraining users. The cost must then be justified in terms of what value will be added to the organisation by the new development.

**ICT POLICY**

**User impact** Decisions regarding ICT developments often have significant impact on an organisation's employees. This impact might be minor, e.g. the need for retraining, or more dramatic, e.g. loss of job or relocation. An organisation's workforce is often its single most valuable asset. An ICT policy must therefore ensure that policy decisions do not have an unnecessarily detrimental effect on the day-to-day lives of employees.

**Consistency with organisational goals** ICT policy decisions must be justified in terms of the overall strategic goals of the organisation. If, for example, an organisation has, as a key strategic goal, the development of new markets for existing products, new ICT developments and acquisitions should be able to contribute to that process. If this factor is not taken into consideration, new technologies might be developed/acquired unnecessarily.

## Future-proofing

Ideally an ICT policy will 'future proof' its systems. That is, it will predict future needs and build in functionality and system capacity to deal with these needs. In practice, future proofing is all but impossible. There are too many unknowns, including events in the business environment of the organisation, changes in key personnel, developments in technology, unexpected budget constraints, etc. None the less, ICT policy decisions will have to <u>try</u> to take into account possible future developments that might impact on the organisation and its ICT systems.

# ICT and the organisation: 1

### The position of ICT in the organisation

When ICT was first introduced into organisations its main function was to improve efficiency, i.e. by performing repetitive data processing more quickly and more accurately than humans were able to. Information systems serviced the needs of the different functional divisions of the organisation, e.g. processing invoices for the accounts department. Different divisions ran different systems and there was only a partial attempt to coordinate these systems. As information systems grew in complexity, a greater degree of coordination was required. Systems had to be able to 'talk' both to each other and to other systems beyond the organisation. Additionally, the functionality offered by advanced information systems meant that it was no longer appropriate to position ICT as a mere service. Increasingly ICT came to be at the heart of the organisational structure, not only fulfilling the requirements of different functional divisions but determining the strategic decisions of the organisation.

### Service Model versus Integrated Model

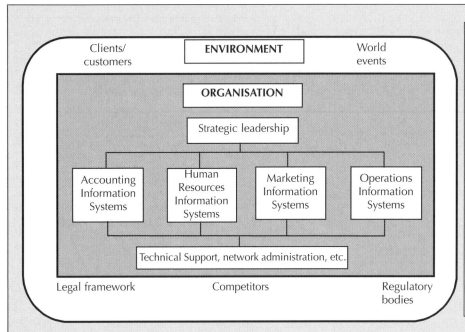

**The Service Model**

In this model, different divisions or departments take responsibility for their own information systems. They buy applications and/or services as they need them and make their own resourcing decisions. The ICT department exists to provide technical support (e.g. hardware maintenance) and to administer any network requirements (e.g. setting passwords, maintaining Internet links, etc.). This model, in which ICT is there only to service the needs of others, is increasingly rare. It tends to occur in small- to medium-sized organisations that do not rely on ICT for their core activity.

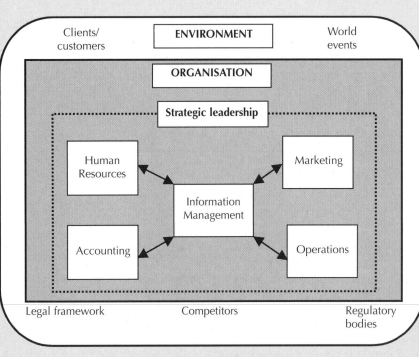

**The Integrated Model**

In this model there is an ICT department that coordinates all ICT activities. Its function is to ensure that all systems within the organisation are integrated and compatible. It develops and/or purchases systems for the different functional divisions, but it also defines the overall strategy for information management. The ICT division is represented at the highest level of the organisation (e.g. an ICT Director) and contributes to the definition of organisational goals. This model is increasingly the norm in business. This change has come about because ICT systems have grown in complexity and often act as the main facilitator of core business activities.

# ICT and the organisation: 2

## Outsourcing

Sometimes it makes sense for an organisation to pay another company to take responsibility for providing one of its services or taking care of some of its day-to-day maintenance requirements. For example, many organisations do not employ their own security guards; instead, they pay a specialist security firm to provide that service. This is called 'outsourcing'. Some organisations choose to outsource some or all of their ICT provision. Such organisations argue that their core business is not ICT and they do not, therefore, possess sufficient expertise in this field. It therefore makes sound business sense to outsource the maintenance of a large, expensive and (possibly) troublesome ICT infrastructure to a specialist ICT company. The degree of outsourcing will vary from company to company: some may choose to outsource all of their ICT needs, from specialist application provision to basic maintenance; other companies may outsource only one aspect of their ICT provision, e.g. network security. When a significant amount of outsourcing is undertaken, the function of an ICT manager changes: instead of being primarily responsible for maintaining and developing systems within the organisation, their main function becomes one of liaison, i.e. finding and communicating with various third party providers. This is shown in the diagram below.

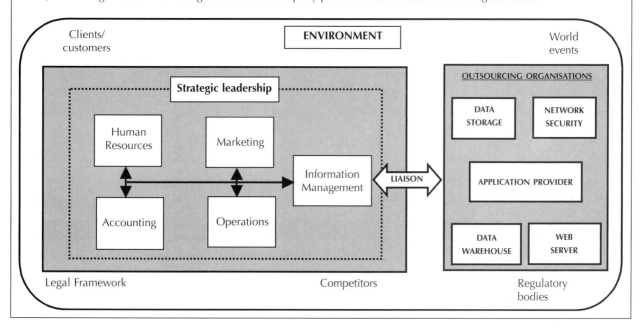

## Application Service Providers

Application Service Providers (ASPs) are companies that deliver software via a networked connection (usually the Internet). There are various types of ASP: some simply sell downloadable software via the net, others allow users to 'lease' the applications, paying a fee according to how much use they make of the ASP. It has been argued that such an arrangement offers a model for distributing software to consumers. Businesses would only need to use those applications that suited them for as long as they needed them and they wouldn't have to worry about upgrades, as the applications would be kept up-to-date by the ASP. Some of the disadvantages of such a system are similar to the general disadvantages of outsourcing (see below) but, additionally, companies have to have robust broadband capabilities if they are going to run their business-critical applications online. The ASP's main concern is that their software might be 'stolen', i.e. downloaded on to the hard drive of the user during the time when it is being leased.

## Advantages and disadvantages of outsourcing

| ADVANTAGES | DISADVANTAGES |
|---|---|
| • The company can focus on its core business and not have to worry about acquiring and developing expertise in an area (i.e. ICT) that is not its main concern. This is particularly true of those companies whose core activities are not intrinsically wrapped up with ICT, e.g. manufacturing. <br> • Space, and therefore, money can be saved by locating servers and mainframes off site. <br> • If a company does not have sufficient in-house expertise, there is a strong possibility that they will make errors in the development of systems and the acquisition of ICT resources. These problems can be avoided if all ICT services are outsourced. | • There may be a concern about lack of control. The organisation has to rely on the expertise of the provider. This can be limiting if the provider doesn't understand the specific needs of the core business. <br> • Security can be an issue. Although providers will promise robust security procedures they are still out of the hands of the organisation. This may make some organisations feel vulnerable. <br> • The provision has to be reliable. Some businesses can fold if they lose their ICT capability, even temporarily. Providers will offer Service Level Agreements to guarantee service but these cannot always be counted on. |

# Corporate information systems strategy

### Why is a corporate information systems strategy necessary?

A corporate information systems strategy is a coordinated approach to the planning, resourcing, development and implementation of ICT systems in an organisation. The aim of such a strategy is to ensure that ICT systems add value to the organisation by contributing to organisational goals (e.g. maximising profit, reducing hospital waiting lists, etc.) in an efficient, reliable and cost-effective manner. It is important to have a strategy to achieve this aim, i.e. as opposed to an *ad hoc* approach, for several reasons, including:

- Information systems may be found in the different functional divisions of an organisation. They fulfil different functions in these divisions but there is still a necessity for the divisions, and therefore the systems, to be able to 'talk' to each other. Systems must therefore be compatible and allow for the free exchange of data.
- ICT is fast-changing and influenced by external events. There needs to be a planned and coordinated response to these changes and events or the organisation will suffer by being unprepared.
- ICT incurs cost and often this cost is a significant proportion of the organisation's budget. An unplanned, unstructured approach to ICT resourcing is likely to lead to poor decision-making and financial loss.
- ICT systems are increasingly likely to be 'business-critical' – i.e. without them the business cannot operate successfully (in some cases it can't operate at all).

### What factors will influence the development of an ICT systems strategy?

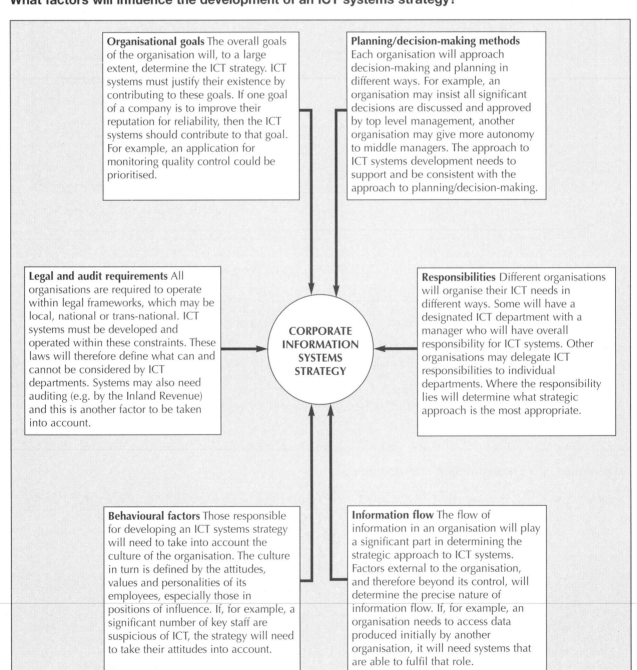

**Organisational goals** The overall goals of the organisation will, to a large extent, determine the ICT strategy. ICT systems must justify their existence by contributing to these goals. If one goal of a company is to improve their reputation for reliability, then the ICT systems should contribute to that goal. For example, an application for monitoring quality control could be prioritised.

**Planning/decision-making methods** Each organisation will approach decision-making and planning in different ways. For example, an organisation may insist all significant decisions are discussed and approved by top level management, another organisation may give more autonomy to middle managers. The approach to ICT systems development needs to support and be consistent with the approach to planning/decision-making.

**Legal and audit requirements** All organisations are required to operate within legal frameworks, which may be local, national or trans-national. ICT systems must be developed and operated within these constraints. These laws will therefore define what can and cannot be considered by ICT departments. Systems may also need auditing (e.g. by the Inland Revenue) and this is another factor to be taken into account.

**CORPORATE INFORMATION SYSTEMS STRATEGY**

**Responsibilities** Different organisations will organise their ICT needs in different ways. Some will have a designated ICT department with a manager who will have overall responsibility for ICT systems. Other organisations may delegate ICT responsibilities to individual departments. Where the responsibility lies will determine what strategic approach is the most appropriate.

**Behavioural factors** Those responsible for developing an ICT systems strategy will need to take into account the culture of the organisation. The culture in turn is defined by the attitudes, values and personalities of its employees, especially those in positions of influence. If, for example, a significant number of key staff are suspicious of ICT, the strategy will need to take their attitudes into account.

**Information flow** The flow of information in an organisation will play a significant part in determining the strategic approach to ICT systems. Factors external to the organisation, and therefore beyond its control, will determine the precise nature of information flow. If, for example, an organisation needs to access data produced initially by another organisation, it will need systems that are able to fulfil that role.

# Approaches to organisational computing: 1

### Mainframe computers

Mainframes are powerful computers that are able to deal with large-scale processing demands. The first large-scale organisational computing involved mainframe computers. The early models were huge – some of them took up the entire floor of an office block – but their physical bulk has gradually been scaled down. In many businesses, especially small- to medium-sized businesses, mainframes have been replaced with client–server systems. There is still, however, sustained demand for mainframes from larger organisations, especially those that have to manage a significant volume of transaction processing, e.g. banks, insurance companies, large-scale retailers, etc.

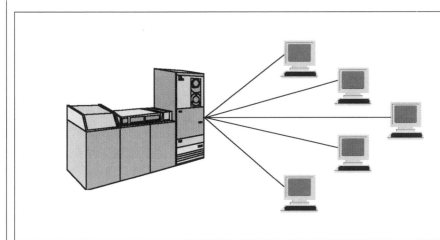

Users connect to mainframes using workstations which may or may not have stand-alone capacity. Those that do not are usually referred to as 'dumb terminals'. These are simple, low cost devices consisting only of a keyboard and monitor. These devices do not have any processing capacity and are, in effect, input devices. They tend to be restricted to text-based inputting and are not provided with user-friendly Graphical Users Interfaces (GUIs).

| Advantages | Disadvantages |
|---|---|
| • They can handle large volumes of transaction processing, e.g. the financial transactions of banks.<br>• Their centralised access systems increase security.<br>• They have the capacity to complete fast repetitive processing on large volumes of data, e.g. meteorological computations. | • They are restricted to command-line applications and this limits their use.<br>• They are costly to purchase and this restricts their use to 'capital-rich' organisations.<br>• Over-reliance on them can lead to major problems if they 'go down'. |

### Personal computers

Mainframes were the dominant mode of organisational computing throughout the 1950s and 1960s. The capital investment and maintenance costs that such systems incurred meant that they were only cost-effective for large organisations whose core business involved large-scale processing. With the development of the personal computer in the late 1980s, computerised information processing became available to smaller organisations. With the growth in demand, PCs became both more powerful and cheaper. By the 1990s the majority of homes in developed countries owned a PC with computing power comparable to some of the early mainframe devices. The low cost and user-friendliness of PCs helped them to revolutionise the work place to the extent that it would now be highly unusual to find a business – regardless of size – that did not use computer technology for information processing.

In many organisations PCs are linked together in a Local Area Network. This facilitates the sharing of resources – such as printers – and the exchange of data.

A PC typically consists of:

• a boxed unit that contains a central processing unit, a hard drive, various drives for secondary storage devices, expansion cards for enhancing the processing of sound, graphics, etc.;
• output devices, usually a monitor, a printer and speakers;
• input devices, usually a keyboard, mouse, scanner and joystick for games.

| Advantages | Disadvantages |
|---|---|
| • *De facto* standards of hardware and software, i.e. the Intel processor and Windows operating system.<br>• The development of the Graphical User Interface made PCs user-friendly.<br>• Low initial capital investment required.<br>• Distributes processing power to desktops. | • Although initial costs are low, maintenance costs tend to be high.<br>• There is pressure to update regularly both software and hardware – this incurs cost.<br>• The lack of centralised control increases security risks. |

# Approaches to organisational computing: 2

### Client–server computing

PCs connected in a network allowed small- to medium-sized business to access the type of processing power they needed to support their core business activities. There were, however, problems with such an approach, mainly associated with the absence of centralised control. A system was needed that combined the centralised control of a mainframe system with the usability and distributed processing of a PC-based network. This led to the development of client–server systems.

A client–server system consists of a combination of computer devices that act as either clients or servers. A server will act as a host device, providing a centralised resource that other devices – clients – can make requests to. A typical client–server system consists of one powerful computer that acts as a server and is connected, via a network, to a number of workstations that act as clients. When a user makes a request for a service via a workstation – e.g. access to a software application, a query to a database, a printer request – the server provides the service required. In addition to providing the functionality necessary for the storage and processing of data, servers manage background functions such as file management, user permissions and access rights, back-up facilities, etc.

Although 'clients' and 'servers' are often used to refer to devices, in fact it is the 'client software' and 'server software' that handle the necessary processing. It is therefore possible to run different types of client/server software on one machine.

### How a client–server system works

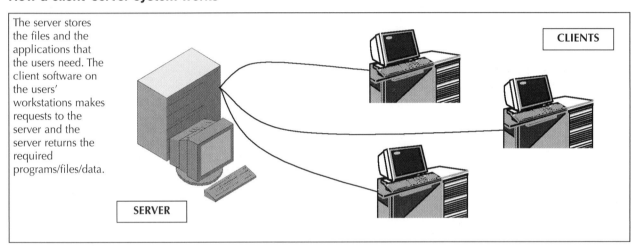

The server stores the files and the applications that the users need. The client software on the users' workstations makes requests to the server and the server returns the required programs/files/data.

SERVER

CLIENTS

### Different types of client

Workstations used in client–server systems fall into two broad categories, usually referred to as fat clients and thin clients.

**Thin clients**  The workstation consists of a network computer that is designed to work only as part of a network, i.e. it does not have any stand-alone capacity. It does not have a built-in hard drive or expansion slots and only has such processing capacity as would be needed to run applications and output to a monitor.

**Fat clients**  The workstation is a PC with stand-alone capacity. It has its own secondary storage components and central processing unit. This means that it is less economical than a 'thin client' because there is an unnecessary duplication of storage and processing facilities – i.e. the PC has the capacity to do work that is in fact performed by the server.

### Different types of server

Servers fall into different categories. These categories are related to the service they provide and include:

| | |
|---|---|
| **File server** | provides clients with access to data files and software |
| **Database server** | provides access to databases and handles queries |
| **Web server** | stores and handles requests for individual web pages |
| **Application serve** | handles high speed processing for applications |
| **E-mail server** | manages the sending, receipt and temporary storage of e-mails |
| **Print server** | manages requests to the printer, controlling job queues, print quotas, etc. |

Different types of server software may be located in one machine.

# Approaches to organisational computing: 3

### Three-tiered client–server architecture

One popular set-up involving different servers comprises a network of clients, an application server and a database server. In this arrangement the user – working through client software installed on a networked PC or network computer – makes a request for data to the application server. The application server determines what data is needed and queries the database accordingly. The database server returns the required data to the application server which, in turn, processes the data into a suitably user-friendly format before returning it to the client. This is referred to as three-tiered architecture.

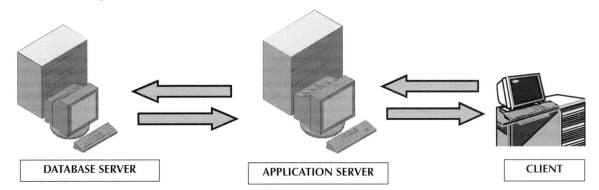

| DATABASE SERVER | APPLICATION SERVER | CLIENT |

### Peer-to-peer systems

An alternative to client–server set-ups that may be employed by small organisations is a peer-to-peer system. A peer-to-peer system comprises a group of workstations that are joined together in a network. Each workstation acts as both client and server, sharing resources and communicating data to each other. One computer can both request data held on another file and provide data for another user.

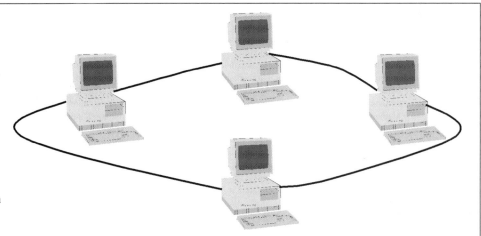

### Peer-to-peer system versus client–server

| Peer-to-peer system | Client–server |
|---|---|
| ✓ Initial start up costs are lower because an expensive server isn't required. The network operating system is also less sophisticated and therefore cheaper. | ✓ There is efficient centralised management of security, back-up and file management systems. |
| ✓ There is less reliance on one central computer and therefore less vulnerability to crashes. | ✓ It offers users easy access to a central pool of data. |
| ✓ It is simpler to set up and maintain than a client–server system. | ✓ The system will perform processing tasks more quickly than a peer-to-peer system. |
| ✗ The system only works well when the number of nodes (network connections) is small, i.e. below 15. | ✓ Users do not have to worry about performing network management tasks as the server does this work. |
| ✗ Security and back-up are not centralised and so are more difficult to manage. | ✗ The initial start-up cost can be high: dedicated servers are more expensive than PCs and the network software required also costs more. |
| ✗ Data can be more difficult to find because it is not centrally stored and organised. | ✗ Client–server systems often require specialist personnel – network managers – to run them. This incurs cost. |
| ✗ Users need more technical knowledge because they are required to perform jobs that would otherwise be taken care of by a server. | ✗ Reliance on one central server can cause problems – i.e. if the server crashes the whole system is out of commission. |

# Management information needs

Managers in organisations have a variety of functions depending on their position in the hierarchy and the nature of the organisation. There are, however, some generic functions that all managers have as part of their work. The ability of managers to perform these functions effectively may be enhanced by their use of information systems. Managers therefore have 'information needs'. The nature of these needs can be directly related to the management function being performed.

| Function | Example | Information needs |
|---|---|---|
| **Planning**<br>Managers need to plan for the future. This entails analysing current situations and forecasting future scenarios. They need to establish goals that are consistent with the organisation's overall strategic aims. They then need to define courses of action that will ensure that the goal is attained. This will involve planning how resources – human and non-human – will be allocated for optimum efficiency. | The area manager of a computer retail business has been asked to plan an expansion of the business, i.e. by opening two more stores. The manager will need to ensure that necessary resources are available to those who need them, e.g. shop-fitters have been engaged, publicity for the opening has been organised, staff have been trained, etc. | • Schedules and costings from tradespeople who will be required to fit out the shop.<br>• Information about the local area: what shops do local people visit, what type of jobs do they have, etc.<br>• Information about local bylaws relating to planning applications, permitted opening hours, etc. |
| **Decision-making**<br>Some decisions are structured, i.e. predictable and planned for. Managers are able to deal with structured decisions by applying a set of generic rules (e.g. 'if this is the case, do this'). Some decisions are semi-structured: there is an element of predictability about them but they are not susceptible to the rigid application of formulaic rules. Managers have to apply a degree of judgement and initiative. Unstructured decisions cannot be predicted or planned for. They arise as the result of unforeseen events and require managers to rely on their understanding of the situation and their judgement about the optimum course of action. | The area manager has to decide on a location for one of the stores. There are two possible locations. Both have advantages and disadvantages. The decision will be critical: if the incorrect location is chosen, the business may fail to thrive and so lose money. The manager needs a grasp of all the factors that might affect her decision and then needs to model the possible outcomes of each choice. Finally the manager needs to decide upon the optimum location and implement the choice. | • The overheads – rates, rents, local taxes, etc. – that each location would incur.<br>• The likely customer base that each location would attract, their relative affluence, their likely interests, where they currently shop, etc.<br>• The proximity of competitors and the relative success of their businesses.<br>• Transport and delivery implications: would distance from suppliers affect costs?<br>• The success/failure rate of other similar sized businesses in each area.<br>• Availability of labour: who will work there? |
| **Control and monitoring**<br>Managers must ensure that the area that they are responsible for functions efficiently, i.e. with maximum productivity and minimum waste. They need to be aware of what is working well and what is not. This involves monitoring processes and outcomes so judgements can be reached about relative success and failure. Where there is a lack of efficiency, remedial action must be taken. | The two new branches have opened. The area manager must now monitor their effectiveness and needs to know if they are offering a good service, if they are operating in a cost-effective manner, and if their sales figures are comparable with other similar branches. | • Weekly sales figures of all branches in the area, presented so as to make comparisons easy. The figures should also show the week-on-week performance of each branch.<br>• Market research, showing customers' attitudes to and satisfaction with the stores.<br>• Wage sheets showing number of employees, hours worked, etc. |
| **Coordination/liaison**<br>Managers must act as a point of contact between different parts of the organisation. They have to liaise with the managers of other functional areas (e.g. accounts, marketing, etc.), with managers above them in the hierarchy and with subordinates. They have a responsibility to ensure that information flow is effective: that people receive the information that they need when they need to receive it and in an appropriate format. | The area manager must report on the relative success of the two new branches to her line managers. The manager must also ensure that other managers in the organisation receive information they need, e.g. the company website is updated. There will also be a need to communicate information to branch managers, e.g. changes in pricing and marketing strategies. | • Summaries of sales figures, labour costs, rental costs, etc. Comparisons with similar stores in other areas.<br>• Communications from senior management of relevance to branch management, e.g. guidelines on appearance and dress.<br>• Personal information on employees, to be communicated to Human Resources Department. |

### Management information needs: other factors

| | |
|---|---|
| **Quality of information** | Having information is not enough. The information must be of good quality, i.e. accurate, complete, relevant, up to date, etc. |
| **Interpretation** | The information is not enough on its own. Managers must interpret the information – i.e. they must apply their knowledge and understanding of the context in order to make sense of what the information is telling them. Information is only a means to an end. Managers still require intelligence and good judgement to use the information effectively. |
| **Management functions** | There are some management functions, e.g. leadership, which are not significantly aided by information provision. |

# Management Information Systems

### What are Management Information Systems?

- Management Information Systems (MIS) are organised collections of people, procedures and resources designed to support the decisions made by managers. In order to make good decisions managers need access to timely, relevant and accurate information. An MIS is designed to produce this.
- The information usually comes in the form of reports. Some of these reports will be produced regularly (e.g. weekly sales figures) others will be produced on demand (e.g. sales figures for a specific branch). For the information in these reports to have value it must have been processed into an appropriate format. These reports are usually in 'hard copy' format but may also be available online.
- The information contained in these reports will be generated from various sources, both internal and external. External data may include stock market reports, market research, supply costing, etc. Internal data may include processed transaction data and data drawn from centrally held databases, e.g. personnel files.
- An MIS typically supports the functions of planning, controlling, monitoring and decision-making at all management levels, i.e. strategic, tactical and operational.
- Older MIS were relatively simple systems, designed to summarise and report on day-to-day operations at scheduled intervals. They did not have analytical/modelling capabilities and were designed to operate in an environment where information needs were known. Newer MIS are more flexible and may include software that allows managers to create their own customised reports. More complex MIS are perhaps better defined as Decision Support Systems (DSS) (see page 145).

### Some qualities of an effective MIS

- It should be accessible to a wide range of users, including those with a relatively poor level of computer literacy.
- It should provide useful information by summarising data in an effective way and by presenting it in the most appropriate format, e.g. by using graphs or tabulated formats.
- It should connect multiple levels of detail so that a user can start out looking at a high-level issue, then easily drill down to more detail where necessary.
- It should be flexible, allowing the user to extract specific sub-sets of data which have been ordered in the most useful way.
- It must be accurate. There should be no question about the credibility of the information being produced by the system.

### MIS in action

Below is an example of how an MIS would produce a scheduled report to a Head of Sales and Marketing, showing weekly sales figures and a comparison of those figures with the sales figures of a leading competitor.

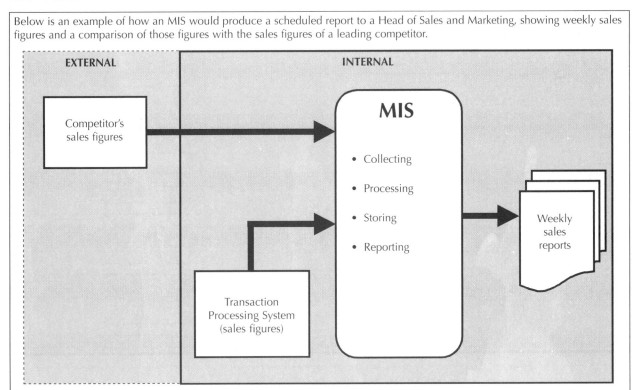

# Data-processing systems

### Data-processing systems

- Data-processing systems – also known as transaction processing systems – are designed to deal with the day-to-day processing needs of an organisation, e.g. the sales of goods in a supermarket via Electronic Point of Sale terminals.
- Typically these processing needs will include: payrolls, invoices, stock control, order entry, etc. Data processing involves carrying out routine and repetitive tasks, accurately and at speed. Computers have the ability to complete tasks of this kind much more efficiently than humans do and many of the early computer systems were designed to perform these labour-intensive business tasks.
- Although routine, this type of processing is critical for a large number of businesses, firstly because without automated procedures these necessary tasks would take up many person-hours and, secondly because the data produced forms the basis of higher-level information systems (MIS, DSS, etc.).
- Data-processing systems tend to be 'simple', inflexible systems with little room for manipulation by the end user. They require the data to be inputted in a designated format and will only produce a limited range of specified reports.

### Example

The example below is based on a car parts firm. They receive orders during the day. Orders can be placed by fax, by telephone or via the firm's website. Fax orders are keyed by data entry clerks, telephone orders are entered using an on-screen form and website customers have their own on-screen form that can be used to enter order details. The transaction processing system validates the inputted data and creates a new order record in the order file, drawing on data held in the customer file and the stock file.

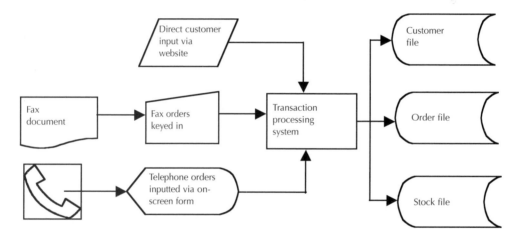

This system can then produce simple operational reports. This will aid the distribution process by providing stock requirements, address labels, customer invoices and, by linking up with a Transport Details file, delivery lists for each of the van drivers.

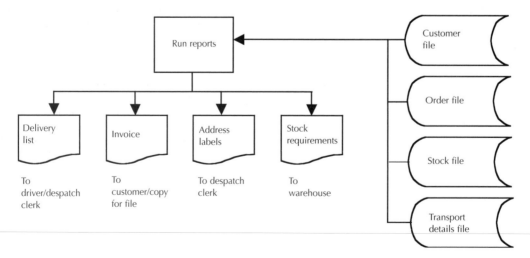

The data held in the various files can now be used by higher-level information systems to produce information for analysis and to aid decision-making.

# Different modes of transaction processing

Many systems are designed to process transactions. The term 'transaction' covers a broad spectrum of events from the borrowing of a library book to the purchase of a house. In general, however, it refers to an event where there is an exchange of goods/services/money between different parties. There are, broadly speaking, two distinct approaches to transaction processing: batch processing and interactive processing.

| | BATCH PROCESSING | INTERACTIVE PROCESSING |
|---|---|---|
| **DEFINITION** | • Batch processing involves collecting groups of transactions over a set period of time and processing them all at the same time. The information associated with the transactions may be collected on paper (e.g. invoices) or inputted directly into a computer (e.g. ATM cash withdrawals). <br>• The process that then follows will depend on whether the information is held on paper copy or as computer files. If the 'batch' to be processed is a set of computerised transactions, an automated process will run. This process will use the data held in the transaction file to update information held in various master files. For example, a business may complete a number of computerised transactions during any one day. These transactions are held in a transaction file. During an overnight process, the master files (e.g. clients' accounts) are updated to take into account the day's transactions. <br>• A paper-based version involves some additional stages. For example, a set of invoices would be sorted into batches of 50, control totals calculated for validation purposes and all information relating to the batch written on a batch header form. The information on the sheets would then be keyed in and then validated and corrected where necessary. The inputted information would then be held in a transaction file. This would then be used to update master files. | • This approach is sometimes referred to as 'online transaction processing'. The basic principle behind this approach is that as transactions take place, all associated files are updated. <br>• For example, when a customer makes a booking with an airline the details are entered via a computer screen by an agent. The bookings file is then updated so that double bookings cannot be made. It would clearly be inappropriate to use a batch process for this form of transaction. <br>• Other businesses use the phone to take orders. The agent taking the order speaks to the customer on the phone and takes the details of his order. She has a computer screen in front of her and fills the details in as the customer speaks. The appropriate files are updated immediately. An invoice, delivery order or any similar report can be produced immediately and will be based on up-to-date data. <br>• A distinction may be drawn between systems that are 'real-time' and 'pseudo real-time'. Real-time systems react immediately to changes – an example would be the fly-by-wire system of an aeroplane – whereas pseudo real-time systems seem to react instantly, but there may be a slight delay between the transaction taking place and the updating of files. |
| **ADVANTAGES** | • Batch processing is still used in a number of different contexts, e.g. processing wage slips, customer order forms, etc. <br>• It is especially useful for situations where there are predictable blocks of information that need inputting but where there is not an urgent need to update files immediately. <br>• It can make economical use of computer resources by running at a time when other usage is minimal, e.g. overnight, at weekends. | • Online processing is increasingly used for a variety of transaction processing. This has been made possible by the increased processing power of computers and the growing sophistication of communication technology. <br>• Online processing means that files are always up to date and paperwork is kept to a minimum. <br>• These systems are more flexible and responsive to users' needs than are batch-processing systems. |
| **DISADVANTAGES** | • The system is not particularly flexible nor responsive to *ad hoc* needs. <br>• Data is not always up to date and, though batch processing is usually completed on data that does not need to be kept absolutely up to date, errors can still occur. | • Online systems require a more complex infrastructure. This means increased capital investment and maintenance costs, as well as reliance on a system that might fail. <br>• Audit trail, and other security checks, are more difficult to perform because updating is happening constantly rather than at set intervals. |

# Data warehouses and data mining

### What is a data warehouse?

Some businesses generate huge quantities of data as a consequence of everyday transactions. A credit card company, for example, will process tens of thousands of transactions every day. The resulting data will be valuable to the organisation if analysed in an intelligent way. This is not, however, a straightforward process as the data may reside in a number of different systems, some of which may be incompatible. This is where the concept of a data warehouse comes in.

William Inmon, the man usually credited with inventing the concept of the data warehouse, first outlined the defining features of a data warehouse in 1992:

- a data warehouse comprises a quantity of data stored on a mainframe-sized application or database server;
- the data may be drawn from many other systems (mainly transaction processing systems) but is stored in a consistent format to make interrogation more productive;
- the data is nonvolatile, i.e. once it has been stored it is not amended;
- the data is 'time-invariant', i.e. it offers a snapshot of organisational operations at a particular moment in time;
- the data is used to support organisational decision-making.

### What is involved in creating a data warehouse?

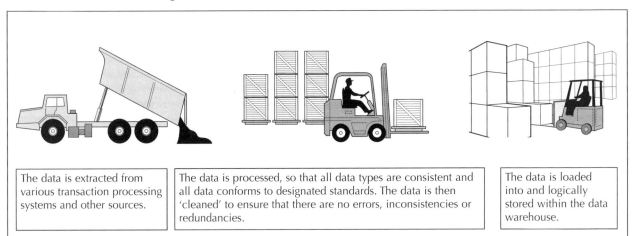

| The data is extracted from various transaction processing systems and other sources. | The data is processed, so that all data types are consistent and all data conforms to designated standards. The data is then 'cleaned' to ensure that there are no errors, inconsistencies or redundancies. | The data is loaded into and logically stored within the data warehouse. |

### What is data mining?

Data mining starts from the principle that the data held in a data warehouse can be the source of valuable information if correctly interrogated. Unlike the standard interrogation of a relational database, where the user defines the criteria and knows (more or less) what they are searching for, data mining is an essentially *speculative* process. The presumption is that that dormant within the data are undiscovered patterns, groupings, sequences and associations. The data-mining software uses complex algorithms to search through the data looking for these unseen relationships. The returned information can then be tested for plausibility and logical consistency. If the process has yielded information that can add value to the organisation, it is processed into a report that can help to inform strategic decision-making.

For example, a supermarket 'warehouses' its stock and transaction data. The data-mining process uncovers a previously unseen relationship between different regions in the country and food preferences. This information is presented to the marketing department who can then design targeted promotions for different regions.

*The following approaches to data mining may be used:*

| Approach | Aim | Example |
|---|---|---|
| Associations | To find a correlation between two different events. | Discovering that customers who buy a certain type of car tend to have holidays in certain places. |
| Sequences | To discover where one event tends to lead to another event. | Finding that people who buy one type of kitchen appliance tend to upgrade one of their other appliances within six months. |
| Clustering | To find new ways to group and classify data into groups. | Defining social groups of consumers in non-traditional ways, e.g. rather than using age, social class, gender, etc., using patterns of purchases to define consumer types, e.g. 'trendsetters'. |

# Information systems: other examples

In addition to Data-processing Systems and Management Information Systems, there are a number of other information systems that can be identified. As software becomes more sophisticated and system capacity grows, the distinction between these systems is becoming blurred.

## Some other types of information systems

| Name | Characteristics | Role in organisation |
|---|---|---|
| Decision Support Systems | <ul><li>Decision Support Systems (DSS) go beyond the reporting and summarising of data. They enable managers to perform analyses on the data and model 'what-if' scenarios.</li><li>They draw mainly on internal data but can also incorporate external data to aid the modelling process.</li><li>They are flexible and allow the end user to determine the analysis/modelling that will be undertaken and the format of the output.</li><li>Outputs are often in the form of interactive on-screen displays rather than printed reports.</li></ul> | <ul><li>Like MIS, the primary function of a DSS is to help managers at different levels in the organisation make effective decisions.</li><li>They are particularly useful during the phase of decision-making when different options are being considered. DSS can be used to provide information about the likely impact of each of the options, thus making it easier to select the optimum solution.</li><li>DSS are best suited to semi-structured decisions, i.e. where part of the problem can be specified but there is still a degree of judgement and insight required of the manager.</li></ul> |
| Executive Information Systems | <ul><li>EIS are user-friendly systems designed to suit the needs of specific strategy-level executives.</li><li>They have 'drill-down' capabilities, i.e. the ability to take a piece of aggregated data and focus down to the individual pieces of data that it is built on.</li><li>They support the need for external data. Many strategic level decisions require analyses of factors such as population trends, government level finances, etc. EIS can incorporate such data into its analysis of internal data.</li><li>They are flexible systems that allow the user a degree of choice in regard to what data is displayed, what analysis is performed on it, etc.</li></ul> | <ul><li>EIS are designed to support the work of executives working at the highest level of an organisation. They support the process of strategic decision-making, i.e. long-term planning which will impact on the whole organisation.</li><li>They are future-oriented, enabling managers to monitor trends and model the effects of proposed changes.</li><li>They are most appropriate for supporting unstructured decision-making, i.e. where there are no predictable patterns to develop set procedures from. In such cases the need is for managers to bring their insight and judgement to bear on the problem.</li></ul> |
| Expert Systems | <ul><li>Expert systems are rule-based, domain-specific systems that are designed to reproduce the role of (human) expert advisers.</li><li>The terms of a problem are inputted into the system. The system then draws upon a database of facts and knowledge and gives a response to the enquiry.</li><li>They have a user-friendly interface that allows the user to make enquiries and determine output formats.</li><li>Many expert systems are able to explain the reasoning behind their response, i.e. how they came to a particular conclusion.</li><li>They are structured in a manner appropriate to the field that they are serving, i.e. medical, legal, business, etc.</li></ul> | <ul><li>Expert systems are used in a wide range of fields, including: medicine, engineering, construction, financial services, etc.</li><li>They may be used in various areas within a commercial organisation. They can assist in decision-making by offering 'expert advice'.</li><li>They can be useful in situations where an expert in a field is required but not available.</li><li>They can act as a stimulus for discussion, providing solutions that may not be accepted in their entirety but which may act as a springboard for further ideas.</li><li>There are, however, limitations associated with expert systems: they lack the flexible, intuitive response of the human mind; they need to be constantly updated with new knowledge/rules; they can lead to a decline in skill level in personnel who overuse them.</li></ul> |

# Levels of management and information needs

| Roles and functions | Information needs | Decision authority | Planning orientation | Nature of information |
|---|---|---|---|---|
| **Chief executives, directors, leadership teams, etc.**<br><br>• To define objectives and policies for the whole organisation.<br>• To establish long-term goals.<br>• To make decisions on resourcing and large-scale investment.<br>• To decide upon plans for expansion/contraction/changes in direction.<br>• To respond to significant external events which may impact upon the organisation (e.g. new legislation). | • Reports showing overall performance of the organisation, relative to past performance and to that of competitors.<br>• Modelled information showing the possible effects of different decisions.<br>• Accounting information showing overall financial performance.<br>• Information about external developments that might impact upon the organisation.<br>• Summary reports on the performance of different departments. | HIGH ↑ | LONG-TERM ↑ | SUMMARY ↑ |
| **Heads of large departments, functional supervisors, project coordinators, etc.**<br><br>• Managing budgets and allocating resources.<br>• Monitoring progress and ensuring quality of outcome.<br>• Appointing, supervising and assessing staff.<br>• Developing operational policies and ensuring their implementation.<br>• Providing information to line managers. | • Reports showing available resources and budget allocations.<br>• Summary reports on departmental performance.<br>• Information and performance data on subordinate staff.<br>• Reports on availability of products and services.<br>• Information on requirements of senior management. | | | |
| **Heads of small departments, individuals with specific areas of responsibility**<br><br>• To ensure efficient practice on a day-to-day basis.<br>• Making effective use of existing resources.<br>• Ensuring effective contribution to the overall objectives of the organisation. | • Instructions from supervisors regarding operational requirements.<br>• Information that can be used to monitor the effectiveness of operations.<br>• Day-to-day task information, e.g. what needs to be done by when? | LOW ↓ | DAY-TO-DAY ↓ | DETAILED ↓ |

STRATEGIC

TACTICAL

OPERATIONAL

MARKETING   ACCOUNTING   PRODUCTION   OTHER FUNCTIONAL AREAS

# Decision-making

## Different levels of decision-making

Decision-making is one of the key functions of managers at all levels. The nature of the process will vary according to the level of management involved:

- **Strategic decision-making** involves making decisions that will determine the overall direction of the organisation and the establishment of organisation-wide policies and goals.
- **Management control** involves making decisions that will ensure the optimum utilisation of human and non-human resources. It is the interface between strategically established goals ('what we want to achieve') and how, operationally, those goals will be achieved ('how we will achieve it').
- **Knowledge level decision-making** deals with the management of information within the organisation and the evaluation of new ideas and products.
- **Operational control** determines how exactly the decisions made at a strategic and tactical level are put into practice in day-to-day operations.

## Structured versus unstructured decision-making

**Structured decisions** are routine decisions that are made on a regular basis. When a decision of this kind is to be made there is a defined procedure to follow. These are decisions that organisations expect to have to make and so they establish 'rules' for dealing with them. For example, a decision may be needed about when to re-stock a certain product. The organisation will decide that once stock falls below a certain level then re-stocking will take place. Once the manager has information about current stock levels, the decision can be made quickly and without having to consider other possibilities.

**Unstructured decisions** are not routine and therefore contain unexpected elements. They require managers to consider the existing situation and evaluate possible courses of action. Decisions of this kind are not predictable and so procedures cannot be laid down for dealing with them. Rather, managers have to use the available information and apply their knowledge and insight in order to come to a decision.

## The process of decision-making – how information helps

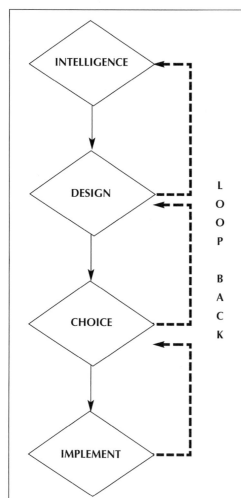

**Intelligence** This involves identifying a problem/opportunity that requires a decision and gathering together all the information that may be needed to make that decision. Management Information Systems are designed to support this process.

**Design** Different possible solutions are developed and formulated. Each different scenario is researched and the possible costs and benefits established. This then provides a fixed number of options for the decision-maker(s) to select from.

**Choice** The designs are evaluated and the consequences for the organisation of implementing any one of them are considered. Modelling software can be used to support this process. One designed solution is selected as being the optimum one.

**Implementation** The chosen solution is put in place and its effect is monitored and evaluated. Regular reports will be needed in order to establish whether the solution was indeed the best one.

**Loop back** Decision-making rarely follows a simple, linear pattern. It is often necessary, having reached one stage, to loop back to a previous stage, either to gather more information or to reconsider a choice.

# Group decision support systems

Decision Support Systems (DSS) are designed to support the decision-making requirements of individual managers. Sometimes, however, decisions are not made by isolated individuals but by teams of people. Indeed, in most organisations, collaborative group decision-making is the norm. Effective group decision-making is characterised by the following attributes:

| | |
|---|---|
| **Collaborative style** | Colleagues should work with each other for a common purpose, rather than using the process to advance personal agendas. |
| **Open idea generation** | All ideas should be considered equally and without prejudice and not dismissed without consideration. |
| **Clear focus** | All members of the group should focus their ideas on the topic under consideration and not become caught up in irrelevant side issues. |
| **Plan of action** | The meeting should result in a decision – or set of decisions – being made and a clear plan of action to implement those decisions. |

Just as DSS supported the needs of individual managers, Group Decision Support Systems (GDDS) were designed to provide ICT support for group-based decision-making.

## A typical arrangement for a GDSS

It is difficult to characterise a typical GDDS as different organisations may approach the procedure in different ways. However, the following elements are generally present:

- For each member of the group there should be an individual workstation that is connected to a central control and can both read from and write to a common application.
- There should be a means of projecting the desktop image on to a large screen that can be seen by everybody.
- There will be applications that facilitate group participation (e.g. Lotus Notes, MS NetMeeting, Collabra Share). Such applications will allow group members to demonstrate ideas to others, suggest amendments to documents, vote on ideas, etc.
- There will need to be a means of storing information and producing documentary evidence of decisions taken.

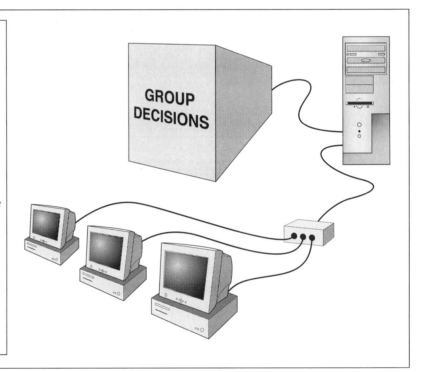

## Advantages and disadvantages of a GDSS

| Advantages | Disadvantages |
|---|---|
| • This approach may allow for a more collaborative atmosphere. The discussion, being mediated through the ICT facilities, is less vulnerable to domination by aggressive/charismatic speakers. This is especially the case where the system allows for anonymous voting on decisions.<br>• If linked with other systems, relevant information can be made accessible to all the participants at the touch of a button.<br>• If used in conjunction with videoconferencing/Internet facilities, members of the group making the decision can be based in several remote locations. This can improve the quality of decision-making as it incorporates a wider variety of perspectives. | • Although GDSSs are designed to be user-friendly, some group members may feel less relaxed using ICT than others. They may thus feel marginalised from the decision-making process.<br>• Such systems are costly to set up. In addition to the development of a suitable information infrastructure, expensive hardware needs to be purchased and maintained. This is even more the case if videoconferencing/Internet facilities are being used.<br>• Because such a system is expensive to create and maintain, an organisation may feel obliged to use it as the basis for all group decision-making situations. In fact, there may be times when a different approach to group decision-making would be more effective. |

# Information flow

## What is information flow?

Information flow refers to the procedures whereby information is communicated to various parties both within an organisation and between the organisation and the outside world. Effective information flow is essential for an organisation as it enables the efficient maintenance of key processes. These processes include:

- informing employees of organisational changes;
- issuing management instructions to subordinates;
- receiving communication from clients, customers, suppliers, etc.;
- maintaining awareness of 'environmental' changes that might impact upon the organisation.

## Formal methods

| FORMAL METHODS | COMMENT |
| --- | --- |
| Meetings | Formal meetings may be scheduled or called as a response to a particular issue/incident. A formal meeting will be chaired, have an agenda and have minutes taken. A meeting may be between two people or many hundreds (e.g. a shareholders' meeting). It may be held 'live' or using videoconferencing technology. The participants may be based entirely within the organisation or be a mixture of organisational members and outside agencies. Meetings allow for a two-way flow of information, with ideas being exchanged and different opinions being aired. |
| Memos | Memos convey information from one individual to another individual or group of individuals. Traditionally they were printed or handwritten on paper and distributed by hand. It is now more often the case that e-mail or intranet links are used to distribute the message electronically. Memos generally convey information within the organisation. It is usually (though not inevitably) the case that memos convey 'top-down' information, i.e. where a manager wishes to convey information to subordinates. |
| Documents/manuals | Organisations often maintain policy documents both in hard copy and electronic format. These are used as a repository of organisation-specific information (e.g. staff lists), policy statements that everybody in the organisation needs to be aware of (e.g. an Equal Opportunities Policy), and instructions for Standard Operating Procedures (e.g. what to do if an accident happens at work). The document is then made available to everybody that needs access to the information. |

## The restraints of organisational structures

Many formal communication methods use the layers and connections of the organisational structure to guide the flow of information. For example, an executive-level manager will send a memo to Heads of Department instructing them to advise their subordinates of changes that will affect the organisation. This relationship between channels of communication and organisational structure can lead to problems, for example:

- If an organisation has many levels of communication, the information can become lost or distorted during its 'journey'.
- There may not be clear, well-established lines of communication between different functional areas. This can lead to business-critical information not finding its way to the right person at the right time.
- A wide, geographical distribution of organisational elements can lead to problems with maintaining information flow. This has been made easier with the advent of electronic communications.
- The flow of information can become too unidirectional. The information flows down from managers to subordinates, but there is no equivalent mechanism for managers at higher levels to receive information from below. This can lead to them becoming remote from shop-floor operations.

## Informal flow of information

The above procedures are formal, i.e. they involve planned, officially sanctioned events with an agreed format. Formal modes of communication also tend to be documented, i.e. there is a stored record of whatever communication took place. This may be important if, at some future date, the content of the communication is disputed.

Information also flows in an organisation via informal mechanisms such as casual conversations, personal e-mails, telephone conversations, etc.

Informal methods have their value. For example, a casual conversation between a senior manager and a production worker can enable a flow of information that a rigid hierarchical structure might otherwise inhibit. However, informal methods are, by their very nature, unreliable. They cannot be counted on to deliver critical information to the right person at the right time.

# Benefits and drawbacks of ICT systems

## Benefits

### Storage

Computer-based systems reduce all data to a digital format (i.e. a series of 0s and 1s). Large amounts of data can therefore be held on compact storage devices. This capability allows organisations to cut down on office space and thus on rent and/or building purchase costs. It also leads to a cleaner, tidier working environment.

### Efficiency

Increased processing speed results in tasks being completed more quickly by fewer people. For example, sending a form letter to a number of specified clients can be completed using a mail merge program. Previously this would have been a laborious, time-consuming job. Computers therefore save time and allow the organisation to respond more quickly to client needs.

### Quality of information

Data held in digital form can be interrogated quickly and flexibly. For example, a search for clients who live in a certain area can be completed more or less instantly. This leads to better quality information which, in turn, improves the standard of decision-making by the organisation. Data can also be combined with that held in other databases to enhance the information provision still further.

### Presentation

Computers offer a range of facilities that allow an organisation to present information about itself economically and in a professional and visually impressive manner. It could, for example, use DTP facilities to produce a regular newsletter with facts, figure and images of company activities. Presentation software could be used to create slide shows for meetings.

### New services

In some cases the processing power of computers enables an organisation to provide services for clients that were previously beyond its capabilities. For example, an organisation may be able to provide online processing of transactions which, previously, would have involved the client visiting its premises.

## Drawbacks

### Capital investment

Setting up a computer-based system costs money. The establishment of a networked system with reliable hardware will involve considerable capital investment. The requirement to update software and hardware periodically and the necessary maintenance of systems will also incur regular costs.

### Over-dependence

An organisation can come to depend for its very existence on computer-based systems. These systems, however well-maintained, inevitably malfunction from time to time. In some instances the system that breaks down is a critical one and this leads to a loss of business. There are a number of examples of organisations going bankrupt following a temporary collapse of their ICT systems.

### Hardware/software/communications limitations

Computer-based systems are limited by the capacity of hardware, the quality of software, and the speed of communications links. These, in turn, require significant and ongoing capital investment by the organisation. Failure to keep up with technological development can lead to a weakness in one of the above areas, thus restricting the efficiency of the whole system.

### Loss of flexibility

In some areas of business, external circumstances can change quickly. Organisations, therefore, need to be swift and flexible in their response. This can be impeded by a reliance on systems that take time to change. For example, a change in a tax rate may require the rewriting of software. In a complex, interdependent system, this can be time-consuming.

### Staffing difficulties

The introduction of ICT systems often requires the retraining of staff. This can be time-consuming and costly. In some instances specialist ICT staff – who may be both costly and in short supply – will need to be employed. Finally, although it may be beneficial for the organisation to shed jobs, it is less desirable for the individuals who lose their jobs.

**THE ORGANISATION**

# The success or failure of an information system

## Characteristics of a successful system

A successful information system:

- will be implemented on schedule and within the original cost constraints;
- will, through regular use, 'add value' to the organisation, thus justifying the time/money invested in its development;
- will be viewed favourably by users – they should consider the system to be supportive of their work;
- will have fulfilled the original objectives as specified at the start of the project;
- will be 'low maintenance', requiring only minimal post-implementation support and 'bug-fixing';
- will be fully integrated into the organisation's overall information strategy.

## Factors contributing to the failure of an information system

### Lack of formal methods

It is important that the approach taken to the development of systems is a formalised and systematic one. Systems development involves significant capital investment. There is, therefore, too much at stake for an *ad hoc* approach to be adopted. Formal methodologies allow managers to monitor the various stages of development and only authorise further progress if they are satisfied that the system is developing along expected lines. A haphazard approach to systems development is almost bound to lead to systems that fail to fulfil the above criteria for success.

### Inadequate analysis

The aim of the analysis stage is to collect and organise *all* information that pertains to the new system. This involves a precise mapping of the existing information systems in the organisation. Existing hardware, software and procedures will also need to be fully described. If this information is not fully or correctly compiled, the developers will gain an inaccurate view of the system requirements. They will therefore design and produce a system based on this inaccurate view. The final system will inevitably be inadequate in regard to the original requirements.

### Lack of management involvement in design

In large organisations the development of information systems is undertaken by ICT specialists. These specialists may not have a comprehensive understanding of the business area that they are designing the system for. In developing a new system, the developers should maintain a constant dialogue with managers of the area that the system is being developed for. Only in this way can the developers fully take into account the needs of the users and the specific information issues of the relevant business area.

SYSTEM FAILURE

### Over-emphasis on computer systems

Information systems consist of a wide variety of elements, of which computer technology forms only one part. There is a danger that developers will focus all their attention on the development of software and the acquisition of hardware. If this occurs, the personnel involved in the system and the procedures that they follow will receive insufficient attention. Since any system relies on the successful interaction of all elements, this limited focus can lead to problems at the implementation stage.

### Lack of management knowledge of ICT

Managers of specialist business areas are not always aware of all of the latest developments in ICT. This can mean that they can miscalculate what ICT systems are capable of. This in turn can lead to them making excessive or inappropriate demands. They can, for example, set out requirements that cannot possibly be met by developers working within the constraints of existing technology. Additionally, managers who do not understand the procedures of systems development can have false expectations about what can be achieved within a specified time/budget.

### Lack of teamwork/inadequate standards of work

Systems are generally developed by teams of people, with each member of the team taking responsibility for different aspects of the development. In order for a system to be successful, all those professionals involved need to be adequately skilled in their areas, and professional and conscientious in their approach. It is also important that the team as a whole demonstrates a high level of co-operation, mutual support and effective communication. Failure to do so will almost certainly lead to system inadequacies.

# Managing change

## The consequences of change

The development of ICT systems in organisations often results in significant change. In fact, it has been argued that the introduction of ICT systems has, over the last twenty years, been the key change agent for many organisations. The speed of technological advancement in the field of ICT has meant that both the rate and extent of change has increased markedly over the last couple of decades. Change can take many different forms:

| | |
|---|---|
| **Skills required** | New systems often require new skills. This is especially true of ICT systems, where employees may have to learn to navigate new on-screen forms, new keyed instructions, etc. This requires a continuous commitment to skills updating. |
| **Organisational structure** | New systems can create opportunities to change the structure of an organisation. For example, a more efficient method of communication may enable the dismantling of an unnecessary layer of management, thus making the organisation less top-heavy. |
| **Work patterns** | The introduction of new ICT systems can have an effect both on the hours that employees have to work and their work conditions. For example, a new system may require the monitoring of operations that take place 24 hours a day. Some work conditions may change for the better, e.g. by creating the possibility of teleworking. More dramatically, new systems can create a change both in the number and type of employees that are needed. |
| **Internal procedures** | A new system will involve changing the way that operations are carried out in an organisation. This will inevitably impact on employees: some may find that their work has been made easier (e.g. by being automated) whereas some may feel it has become more difficult (e.g. because they now have to perform tasks more quickly). |

## Fear of change

For many members of an organisation these changes can be a source of fear. They may fear that:

- they will lose their job because the new system will make their present role redundant;
- they will be relocated to another role, department or geographical location, thus causing upheaval and possible separation from friends and family;
- they will not be able to learn the skills required by the new system and they will be replaced by somebody that can;
- they will have to change their work patterns (their hours of work, for example) and this will have a negative impact on other aspects of their life;
- they will lose their current status and (possibly) the salary that goes with it as a consequence of organisational restructuring.

As a consequence of these fears some members of an organisation may be resistant to change. This resistance, if not taken seriously, can have a negative impact on an organisation's ability to change. Specifically in relation to ICT systems, it can determine the success/failure of the implementation process.

## A model of successful change management

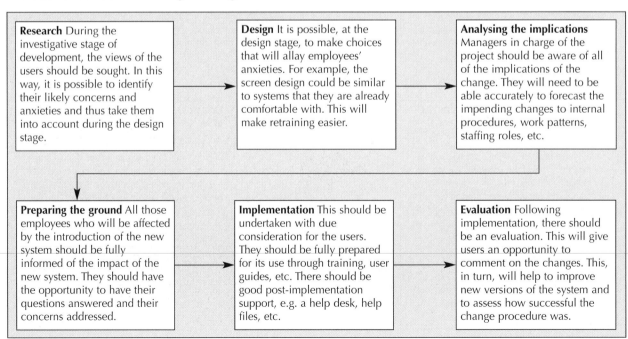

**Research** During the investigative stage of development, the views of the users should be sought. In this way, it is possible to identify their likely concerns and anxieties and thus take them into account during the design stage.

**Design** It is possible, at the design stage, to make choices that will allay employees' anxieties. For example, the screen design could be similar to systems that they are already comfortable with. This will make retraining easier.

**Analysing the implications** Managers in charge of the project should be aware of all of the implications of the change. They will need to be able accurately to forecast the impending changes to internal procedures, work patterns, staffing roles, etc.

**Preparing the ground** All those employees who will be affected by the introduction of the new system should be fully informed of the impact of the new system. They should have the opportunity to have their questions answered and their concerns addressed.

**Implementation** This should be undertaken with due consideration for the users. They should be fully prepared for its use through training, user guides, etc. There should be good post-implementation support, e.g. a help desk, help files, etc.

**Evaluation** Following implementation, there should be an evaluation. This will give users an opportunity to comment on the changes. This, in turn, will help to improve new versions of the system and to assess how successful the change procedure was.

# Audit requirements

## The process of auditing

- The purpose of an audit is to ensure that all procedures are being carried out effectively, accurately and lawfully. Traditionally, auditors would look through a company's account books and compare them to documentary evidence of transactions, e.g. invoices.
- If irregularities come to light, they are investigated. If it is discovered that they came about as a result of error, the auditor recommends changes to the system to improve accuracy. If they are the result of fraudulent activity, the auditor may pass evidence on to the police and recommend changes to the ICT security policy.
- Auditing may be an internal or external process. An internal audit may be commissioned by an organisation's management to ensure that their systems are working well and their resources are being well used. An external audit may be more concerned with whether or not the organisation's systems are operating within legal frameworks, e.g. the Data Protection Act. In some cases there are regulatory bodies that undertake this work. For example, some financial organisations have their systems audited by the Investment Management Regulatory Organisation (IMRO).

## Auditing ICT systems

There are specific difficulties associated with auditing ICT-based systems:

- The auditor will not only need to be ICT literate but will have to understand the particularities of the organisation's ICT systems.
- ICT systems are designed to hide a lot of their processes and data is not always visible.
- Some systems do not, as a matter of course, maintain historical data.
- Transactions that are conducted electronically do not always produce a hard copy equivalent.
- Real-time and pseudo real-time systems pose particular problems: transactions are more difficult to trace and their accuracy more difficult to check.

## Audit trails

In order to audit ICT systems it is usually necessary to utilise specifically designed software to run an audit trail. An audit trail is designed to track a particular aspect of the system in order to identify irregularities. There are different approaches to conducting audit trails, some or all of which may be used. These include:

- tracking a particular transaction from source to output;
- tracking changes to data, especially when applied to centralised data repositories;
- tracking when a system has been accessed and by whom;
- creating exception reports, i.e. looking for unusual instances of access to the system;
- using sampling techniques, e.g. randomly selecting transactions on a particular date.

Audit trail software is designed with the functionality to facilitate these and other auditing techniques.

## Auditing a database

The diagram below illustrates one approach to auditing changes to a database:

| Name | DOB | Position | Wage Rate |
|------|-----|----------|-----------|
| J Smith | 12/03/74 | Sales Man | 10.75 |
| K Brown | 15/01/80 | Sales Ast | 5.60 |
| M Tyler | 23/08/78 | Sales Ast | 5.60 |

| User Login | Date | Time | Field change | Old value | New value |
|------------|------|------|--------------|-----------|-----------|
| BroK04 | 22/09/01 | 13.46 | Wage Rate | 5.60 | 6.70 |
| | | | | | |
| | | | | | |

The original database table, in this case a personnel file, contains some code that runs every time an action is performed on it. In this case a wage rate is updated.

The code updates another table with the time and date of the change, who made the change, and what change was made. The legitimacy of this change can then be checked.

# Upgrading hardware and software: 1

Upgrading a piece of computer hardware/software entails acquiring a newer, enhanced version of the existing component. There are a number of reasons why an individual or organisation may wish to upgrade components. These can be categorised as 'push' and 'pull' factors.

- The current component is functioning inadequately and needs replacing.
- There is a new business requirement that cannot be met by current resources.
- The acquisition of another resource requires associated components to be upgraded, e.g. a new software package requires enhanced memory resources.

**PUSH**  **UPGRADE**  **PULL**

- New products come on to the market that offer functionality that will be beneficial to the individual/organisation.
- There is a financial incentive associated with upgrading, e.g. a company offers free upgrades if other items are purchased.
- A resource, available on the market, offers the facilities needed to undertake a new venture, e.g. creating a website.

## Different types of upgrading

**HARDWARE**

The processing speed and memory capacity of computers has increased steadily over the past few years. At the same time their cost in real terms has declined. This has encouraged users to upgrade regularly, purchasing new machines with faster processors and increased memory capacity. This trend is driven by the 'need for speed', i.e. impatience with the time taken by an existing computer to perform simple actions. This works in tandem with the development of new software: new programs become available with enhanced functionality, users acquire these programs and then realise that they need higher specification machines for the programs to run properly.

In some cases the individual/organisation may choose to replace old computers with new ones. Equally, they may install additional resources (e.g. adding more RAM) or replace one particular element of a system, e.g. network cabling.

Some types of hardware, e.g. printers, will wear with age and use and need replacing.

**SOFTWARE**

Software manufacturers are constantly upgrading their merchandise and offering it to consumers. In their drive to increase their market share, they improve the functionality of existing software and try to tie the consumer in to their products.

The Microsoft products are a good example of this. A new version of a generic package, e.g. MS Word, is released every few years. It offers enhanced facilities and the consumer is encouraged to accept it as the new standard.

Other software may need upgrading because changes in the organisation's requirements mean that it can no longer perform adequately. For example, business users may have to upgrade their software in order to process transactions involving the euro.

## Some issues associated with upgrading

| | |
|---|---|
| **Compatibility** | The upgraded component will need to be compatible with existing systems. In the case of software this will mean that files created in an earlier version can still be opened and edited. This is referred to as backward compatibility. |
| **Scale** | There is often an issue about the extent to which an organisation should upgrade at any one time. For example, if part of an organisation upgrades their software, should the rest of the organisation do likewise? If they do not, there is the risk of compatibility problems when files are transferred from one user to another. Likewise, upgrading one element of a system (e.g. software) often creates a demand for upgrading in other parts of the system (e.g. memory resources). |
| **Need** | It is easy for organisations and individuals to be drawn into a constant cycle of upgrading, but this might not be in their best interests. A question must be asked of an upgraded component: how will it justify the cost and disruption associated with its implementation? |
| **Training** | Upgraded software, with new functionality and a changed user interface, may mean that users have to be trained in its use. There may also be a need for additional user support resources. |

# Upgrading hardware and software: 2

## Reasons and process

| Organisational ethos | New developments | New requirements | Maintenance issues |
|---|---|---|---|
| The image an organisation presents to potential clients/ customers is very important. One aspect of this image is the extent to which the organisation appears technologically advanced. Both in regard to the hardware/software on show and the material that is produced as a consequence, a successful organisation will want to present itself as current with the latest ICT developments. | New software and hardware technologies are emerging constantly and an organisation will be regularly presented with new products. Some of these products will not add anything of significance to the organisation but some will. Such products may help to perform existing procedures in a new way (perhaps a more cost-effective way) and are therefore attractive because they have the potential to 'add value'. | Organisations – and the environment they operate in – are constantly changing. Consequently, new needs and requirements regularly emerge. This may occur as the result of:<br>• a change in legislation – e.g. new data protection laws;<br>• a change in business practice – e.g. the development of a new product;<br>• a change in scale – e.g. a growth in the volume of business. | A piece of hardware or software can become a liability by constantly breaking down or failing to perform as it should. This might occur as the result of an inherent weakness – i.e. a badly designed product – or as the consequence of wear and tear. Organisations often have (sometimes costly) maintenance contracts in order to manage such eventualities, but sometimes the answer will be to acquire a new piece of software/hardware. |

**Make the decision to upgrade** Whatever the reason for the upgrade, someone must make a decision to go ahead. This decision will usually be based on a cost-benefit analysis, i.e. what will the upgrade cost (in terms of time, money, disruption, etc.) and what will be gained from it (in terms of increased efficiency, greater reliability, an improved product, etc.). Clearly the benefits will need to outweigh the costs.

**Evaluation and choice** An individual or team must now take responsibility for choosing the product. First, they must find out what products are available; secondly, they must establish criteria for making a judgement; and thirdly, they must measure possible acquisitions against the criteria they have established. This last part of the process may involve using benchmark tests or running trials with demonstration copies in their own environment.

**Analysis of consequences** Due to the interconnectedness of ICT systems, even a minor change is likely to have consequences for other aspects of the system. For example, if a new version of software is to be introduced there will be consequences for any user who still has to run an earlier version, i.e. they may not be able to transfer data. A decision will then be needed as to whether the whole organisation should upgrade at the same time or whether it should be done in phases.

**Preparing the ground** Once the choice has been made and the consequences analysed, the systems must be prepared for the upgrade. Depending on the likely impact of the product, it may be necessary to perform a 'dry run' in a test environment to discover any problems that might emerge. If the change is a significant one, users will need to be prepared for its implementation. This may involve dissemination of documents, training, etc.

**Implementation and monitoring** The implementation itself may be a complex process: some upgrades require the server to be 'downed' for a period of time. If this is the case, the down-time will need to be planned for, especially if it involves business-critical systems. One the upgrade has been completed it will require close monitoring. If compatibility problems do occur, they are likely to emerge in the period immediately after implementation.

# Standardisation

Organisations need to consider whether or not – or rather to what degree – they should impose defined standards on the ICT systems that are used. These standards can apply to platforms, versions, user interfaces, reports, file types, etc.

Typically an organisation will be divided into different functional areas. These areas will fulfil different functions in relation to the organisation's core activity. For example, a school will have a teaching staff, an administrative team, a catering staff, an examinations officer, a site supervision team, etc. A commercial organisation will be similarly divided, some of the typical functional specialisations being: Accounts, Marketing, Sales, Administration, Production, Human Resources, Legal, etc.

Each of these areas may use three different types of applications:

**Shared**
Some applications need to be shared because they are required for access to the organisation's resources. These might include front-end programs for a Database Management System or browsing software for the organisation's intranet. Such applications are therefore standardised across the organisation.

**Common**
Examples of common applications are generic off-the-shelf solutions such as the 'office suites' that give the user access to word-processing, spreadsheet and simple database facilities. Such applications are not necessarily standardised. For example, two departments may be running different versions of the same software.

**Functionally specific**
There are a number of applications that are designed to perform a specific task. Such applications may have been produced according to a user specification by a software provider or may have been bought 'off the shelf' and customised. The Marketing Department, for example, may have an application that analyses customer responses. This application will be unique to this department and may even be incompatible with systems running elsewhere in the organisation.

## To standardise or not to standardise?

Actually, the question should really be: to what degree should an organisation standardise its ICT systems? Some degree of standardisation is inevitable: most large organisations need access to commonly held data and this requires a common 'front-end' access application. Should an organisation extend this standardisation to all its applications, enforcing the requirement that all users operate on the same platforms and run the same applications where possible and compatible ones where not?

| The need for standardisation | The problems with standardisation |
|---|---|
| • The most obvious need for standardisation is where it enables the straightforward transfer of data. People within organisations need to share data and if this process is made more difficult by the use of different proprietary systems, there will be a corresponding loss of efficiency. That said, the problem can be overcome through the use of common file formats, e.g. .txt files. | • Depending on the nature of the organisation, different functional areas will have more or less autonomy. An autonomous department may wish to make its own choices about the applications it runs and the way it configures and customises them. Enforcing standardisation can create resentment at what will be seen as a challenge to autonomy. |
| • Standardisation can prevent compatibility problems when two applications have to interact with each other. In fact, the applications don't even have to interact with each other to cause problems. Sometimes, just the fact that they are open on the desktop at the same time can cause problems. | • Standardisation may force an organisation to sacrifice quality for conformity. For example, they may acquire an application not because it is the best for the task, but because it provides the best fit with the rest of the organisation's resources. |
| • Users sometimes have to transfer between departments and use different systems. Standardisation of user interfaces assists the familiarisation process, thus aiding efficiency. | • There can be all manner of logistical problems caused by enforcing widespread standardisation. For example, an organisation may be running an early version of an application on some of its machines and a later version on others. It wants to update all machines so that they are running the later version. But it is not just a matter of upgrading the software. The later version may require more memory resources and this may entail upgrading hardware as well as software. |
| • Standardisation of report formats can help to create a corporate identity and make the presentation of information more accessible, i.e. because it is in a format that the reader is used to. | |

# The system development life cycle (SDLC)

## What is the development life cycle?

- New information systems are developed as responses to problems in an organisation, i.e. when existing systems cannot provide an appropriate solution to a specified problem. This process is cyclical because as one system is completed, new requirements become apparent and the process begins again.
- In large organisations the development of new systems can be an enormous undertaking, involving significant human and non-human resources, a time frame measurable in years, and a considerable amount of capital investment.
- For this reason it is a process that must be approached in a systematic and methodical way. Formal methodologies have been developed which break down the process into a series of distinct activities, with measurable outcomes at the end of every stage.
- **Formal methods** are necessary because managers need to be able to identify what stage of development a particular project has reached. Also, people involved in the project need to be accountable for completing specified tasks. This is easier to monitor and control if a set procedure – one that is known to all parties involved – is rigorously followed.
- The breakdown of distinct activities helps to create **clear time scales** for task completion. Without this, the project can easily over-run. If a project significantly over-runs, the finished system may no longer be of use to the organisation.
- At the end of every stage of the life cycle there will be a '**deliverable**', i.e. a specified element of the development (a feasibility study, a finished program, etc.) will be completed. This allows managers to judge whether or not the system is developing along expected lines. If it is, an '**approval to proceed**' can be given; if not, the process can 'loop back' a stage in order to correct the problem.
- The traditional approach, which is summarised in the diagram below, allows for considerable management control but is not without drawbacks. The end-users are consulted in the early stages of the process but may not be consulted in the latter stages. This absence of a feedback loop through all the stages of development can lead to user dissatisfaction with the final product.

## A summary of the system development life cycle

Each stage of the process outlined below is described in more detail on pages 158–62.

**If the system fails to get approval to proceed, it loops back to an earlier stage.**

**SYSTEMS INVESTIGATION** The stage at which the problem is initially identified. The question is asked: how will a new system provide a solution to this particular problem? Consideration is given to the resources that will be required and a feasibility study is undertaken to determine the potential costs and benefits of the proposed development.

**SYSTEMS ANALYSIS** The stage at which the existing system is described and evaluated; the user requirements for the new system are determined; an analysis of the data which will be used in the system is undertaken; and the way in which the new system will solve the problem is outlined.

**SYSTEMS DESIGN** At this stage all of the different elements of the solution are designed in line with the requirements set out in the systems analysis. This will involve creating design specifications for hardware, software, databases, telecommunication/network links, personnel and procedures.

**SYSTEMS IMPLEMENTATION** This involves several, clearly defined substages: acquiring hardware, acquiring software, preparing users, training personnel, preparing data, installing the system, testing the system, running the start-up, and overseeing user acceptance.

**SYSTEM MAINTENANCE/EVALUATION** An installed system needs to be checked periodically to ensure that it is working as it should. Any errors in the program will need to be fixed and users will need access to support. The whole system will need to be evaluated in order to determine to what extent it has fulfilled its original aims.

# The SDLC: investigation phase

## System request

The investigation phase comprises the first stage of the System Development Life Cycle (SDLC). It entails the identification of a possible project, an initial consideration of its feasibility and a preliminary investigation into the implications of undertaking the project.

The SDLC begins with a Systems Request. Systems Requests may be instigated by teams and/or individuals within the organisation and engendered by a combination of internal and external factors, as shown in the diagram below.

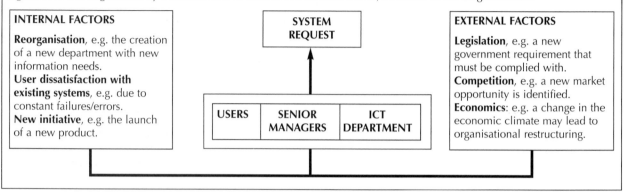

**INTERNAL FACTORS**

**Reorganisation**, e.g. the creation of a new department with new information needs.
**User dissatisfaction with existing systems**, e.g. due to constant failures/errors.
**New initiative**, e.g. the launch of a new product.

**SYSTEM REQUEST**

| USERS | SENIOR MANAGERS | ICT DEPARTMENT |

**EXTERNAL FACTORS**

**Legislation**, e.g. a new government requirement that must be complied with.
**Competition**, e.g. a new market opportunity is identified.
**Economics**: e.g. a change in the economic climate may lead to organisational restructuring.

## Feasibility study

The next stage of the investigation phase is the production of a Feasibility Report. A feasibility study considers the system request from different perspectives (usually defined as Economic, Operational and Technological) to determine whether it is advisable for the organisation to undertake the project.

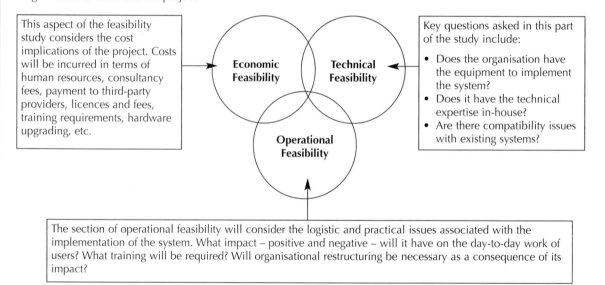

This aspect of the feasibility study considers the cost implications of the project. Costs will be incurred in terms of human resources, consultancy fees, payment to third-party providers, licences and fees, training requirements, hardware upgrading, etc.

**Economic Feasibility**

**Technical Feasibility**

**Operational Feasibility**

Key questions asked in this part of the study include:

- Does the organisation have the equipment to implement the system?
- Does it have the technical expertise in-house?
- Are there compatibility issues with existing systems?

The section of operational feasibility will consider the logistic and practical issues associated with the implementation of the system. What impact – positive and negative – will it have on the day-to-day work of users? What training will be required? Will organisational restructuring be necessary as a consequence of its impact?

## Preliminary investigation

If the Feasibility Report advises that the project is worth pursuing, the next stage is to undertake a preliminary investigation. This results in a report to management, the components of which are shown in the diagram below.

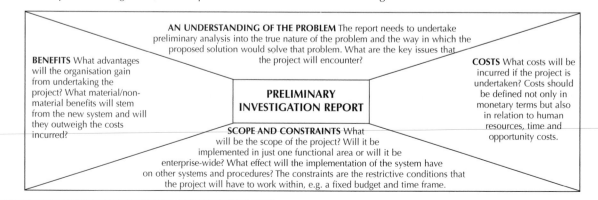

**AN UNDERSTANDING OF THE PROBLEM** The report needs to undertake preliminary analysis into the true nature of the problem and the way in which the proposed solution would solve that problem. What are the key issues that the project will encounter?

**BENEFITS** What advantages will the organisation gain from undertaking the project? What material/non-material benefits will stem from the new system and will they outweigh the costs incurred?

**PRELIMINARY INVESTIGATION REPORT**

**COSTS** What costs will be incurred if the project is undertaken? Costs should be defined not only in monetary terms but also in relation to human resources, time and opportunity costs.

**SCOPE AND CONSTRAINTS** What will be the scope of the project? Will it be implemented in just one functional area or will it be enterprise-wide? What effect will the implementation of the system have on other systems and procedures? The constraints are the restrictive conditions that the project will have to work within, e.g. a fixed budget and time frame.

# The SDLC: analysis phase

The analysis phase, which is designed to investigate the requirements of a new system in detail, can be divided into three distinct sections: determining requirements; analysing requirements; report production.

## Determining requirements

During this stage the individual(s) responsible for systems analysis must gather information about the status of the existing system and the requirements of the new one. This entails defining a set of questions, deciding on which sources of information to use and determining the most appropriate information-gathering technique to use.

**What questions need to be asked?**

- What function does the current system perform?
- What are the shortcomings in the current system that the new system will eradicate?
- What data will be required for the new system?
- What are the sources of the data?
- How will the data be collected and inputted?
- What outputs will be required by the new system?
- How will the new system interact with existing systems?

**What sources of information can be used?**

**External sources, including:**
- customers/clients
- suppliers
- government agencies
- consultants
- competitors.

**Internal sources, including:**
- direct users
- indirect users
- senior managers
- technical support staff
- existing policies, reports, organisational documents
- existing systems and procedures.

**What information gathering techniques can be used?**

- Structured interviews with individuals, i.e. questions determined in advance.
- Unstructured interviews with individuals, i.e. open-ended discussion.
- Observation of existing practice.
- Reading of documentation, policies, journals, manuals, etc.
- Questionnaires to users.
- Examination of documentation/outputs related to current system.
- Visits to other similar organisations.

## Analysing requirements

The collected data will be used to gain a clear understanding of the status of the present system and the requirements of the new system. In order for this process to be effective the raw data needs to be presented in an appropriate format. There are several analytical techniques that can be applied to achieve this.

**Data Flow Diagram (DFD)**

DFDs represent diagrammatically the relationship between different systems in the organisation and how data moves around those systems. They contain four main components: Entities (e.g. customers); Processes (e.g. computing total sales); Data Flow (i.e. the origin, destination and direction of any transference of data); Data Store (any location where data is held, e.g. a customer data file)

**Structured English**

Structured English is a method for describing the logical processes that will be undertaken in the new system. It is similar in style to coding language, and focuses on the key building blocks of sequence, selection and iteration:

**For each RECORD in ORDERS**
  **If TOTAL VALUE => £500.00**
**Then**
    **Print RECORD.**

**Decision table**

A decision table is a graphical representation of the way in which a process may be determined by different conditions.

| CONFIRM ORDER | | | | |
|---|---|---|---|---|
| CONDITION | 1 | 2 | 3 | 4 |
| Credit available | Y | Y | N | N |
| Item in stock | Y | N | Y | N |
| Confirm | X | | | |
| Don't confirm | | X | X | X |

## The systems analysis report

When the analysis has been undertaken a report is presented to the manager(s) responsible for approving the next stage of development. The report will cover the following areas:

- An evaluation of the current system, i.e. its strengths and weaknesses from the users' point of view.
- A detailed description of the user requirements that will be met by the new system.
- A description of the organisation's needs that the new system will meet.
- A description of how the new system will work, i.e. how it will meet the above requirements.

# The SDLC: design phase

There are two aspects to the design phase: logical design and physical design. The logical design specifies how the new system will fulfil the requirements identified in the analysis phase. The physical design specifies the hardware, software, data files, etc. that will be required to put the logical design into action.

## Elements of the logical design

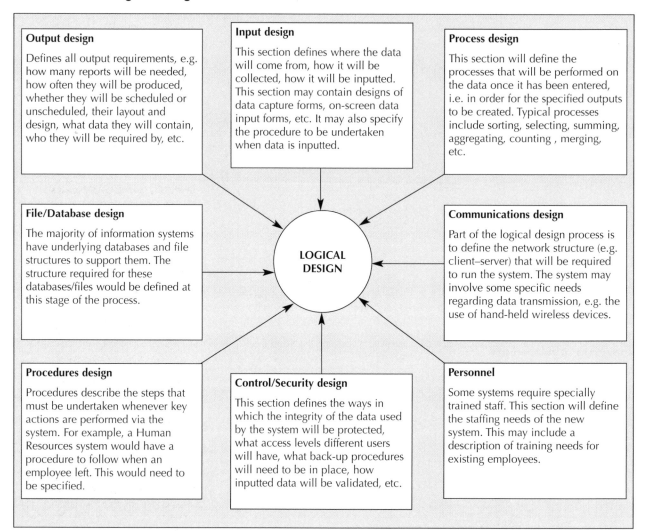

**Output design**

Defines all output requirements, e.g. how many reports will be needed, how often they will be produced, whether they will be scheduled or unscheduled, their layout and design, what data they will contain, who they will be required by, etc.

**Input design**

This section defines where the data will come from, how it will be collected, how it will be inputted. This section may contain designs of data capture forms, on-screen data input forms, etc. It may also specify the procedure to be undertaken when data is inputted.

**Process design**

This section will define the processes that will be performed on the data once it has been entered, i.e. in order for the specified outputs to be created. Typical processes include sorting, selecting, summing, aggregating, counting , merging, etc.

**File/Database design**

The majority of information systems have underlying databases and file structures to support them. The structure required for these databases/files would be defined at this stage of the process.

**LOGICAL DESIGN**

**Communications design**

Part of the logical design process is to define the network structure (e.g. client–server) that will be required to run the system. The system may involve some specific needs regarding data transmission, e.g. the use of hand-held wireless devices.

**Procedures design**

Procedures describe the steps that must be undertaken whenever key actions are performed via the system. For example, a Human Resources system would have a procedure to follow when an employee left. This would need to be specified.

**Control/Security design**

This section defines the ways in which the integrity of the data used by the system will be protected, what access levels different users will have, what back-up procedures will need to be in place, how inputted data will be validated, etc.

**Personnel**

Some systems require specially trained staff. This section will define the staffing needs of the new system. This may include a description of training needs for existing employees.

## Elements of the physical design

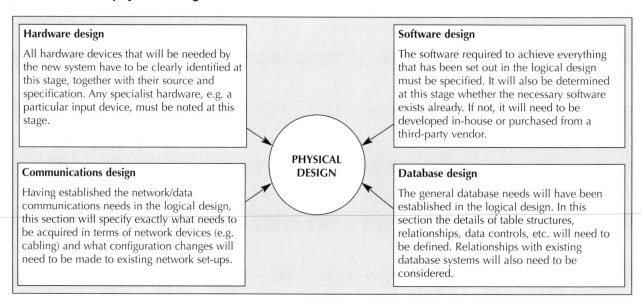

**Hardware design**

All hardware devices that will be needed by the new system have to be clearly identified at this stage, together with their source and specification. Any specialist hardware, e.g. a particular input device, must be noted at this stage.

**Software design**

The software required to achieve everything that has been set out in the logical design must be specified. It will also be determined at this stage whether the necessary software exists already. If not, it will need to be developed in-house or purchased from a third-party vendor.

**PHYSICAL DESIGN**

**Communications design**

Having established the network/data communications needs in the logical design, this section will specify exactly what needs to be acquired in terms of network devices (e.g. cabling) and what configuration changes will need to be made to existing network set-ups.

**Database design**

The general database needs will have been established in the logical design. In this section the details of table structures, relationships, data controls, etc. will need to be defined. Relationships with existing database systems will also need to be considered.

# The SDLC: implementation phase

The implementation phase is when the system specified by the design stage is constructed, tested and put in place. There are three distinct stages:

**Building** The designs created during the previous stage of the SDLC are used to create the system. This may be undertaken by in-house teams or it may be devolved to third-party providers. The main focus during this stage will be the creation of programs using standard programming languages, although some database design and document production will also be involved.

**Testing** The completed system must be tested thoroughly. A rigorous testing programme will be undertaken, with the system being tested both in the programming environment (alpha testing) and in an environment more akin to the live environment it will actually operate in (beta testing). There will be a final testing phase after the system has been installed (user acceptance).

**Installation** The completed, tested program will need to be installed in the environment where it will operate. This involves more than just installing it on a server. The installation process entails preparing users (i.e. ensuring they will be in a position to work with it efficiently), preparing the site (e.g. ensuring the hardware that will be running it is of a sufficiently high specification) and preparing the data (i.e. ensuring that the data that will be needed for the program to run is accessible).

## Installation strategies

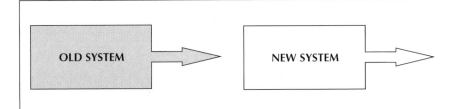

**DIRECT CONVERSION** entails disengaging the old system and starting up the new system on a specified date. It is the least time-consuming strategy but the highest risk. If there is a problem with the new system it is difficult to re-engage the old system.

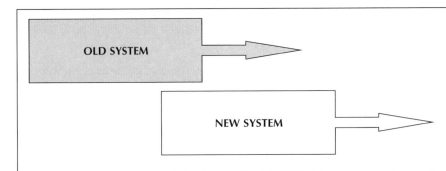

**PHASED CONVERSION** is less high risk than direct conversion since it allows for a 'grace period' when the old system can still be used if the new system has problems. It can be time-consuming and involve more staff if the system needs to be installed at several locations. It is considered to be a moderate risk strategy.

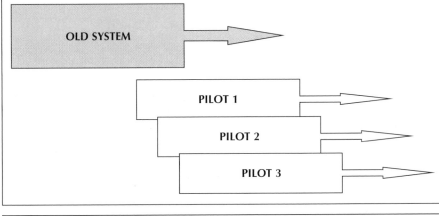

**PILOT CONVERSION** is again considered to be a moderate risk strategy. It entails installing the new system in one area of the organisation and looking for problems before installing it in another area. Depending on the number of pilots involved, this process can be time-consuming but it does aid the 'bug-fixing' process.

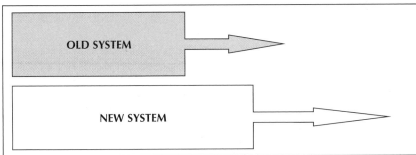

**PARALLEL CONVERSION** is considered to be the lowest risk strategy. The new system is run alongside the old system. The outputs of both the old and new systems are compared and reconciled. When the new system seems to be running well the old system is disengaged. This approach can be expensive in terms of system resources.

# The SDLC: maintenance and evaluation phase

The final phase in the SDLC is the post-implementation maintenance and evaluation. Maintenance entails ensuring that the system is running well, that users' enquiries are dealt with and any 'bugs' are fixed. This is dealt with in more detail on page 163. It is also important that the new system should be evaluated. The outcome of the evaluation will help those responsible for its implementation to judge whether the expenditure on the new system has been justified. A thorough evaluation also helps to improve the quality of future developments by highlighting what worked well and what caused problems.

## Areas to be covered in a post-implementation evaluation

### ACCURACY

A critical test for any system is the accuracy of its output. Erroneous information, produced as a result of processing errors, can have disastrous consequences. Of course, this will have been covered during the test procedure but it is important to ensure that accuracy is maintained during day-to-day operations.

### QUALITY OF OUTPUT

One of the main functions of any information system is to produce high-quality information. The outputs must be judged against the criteria that are used to determine quality of information, i.e. is the information complete, accurate, reliable and available to the right person at the right time in a suitable format?

### USER SATISFACTION

If users don't like using a system they will try to avoid doing so. If they have no choice, they will become disgruntled and therefore less effective. The users should feel comfortable using the system and confident that any problems they do encounter will be resolved quickly.

### CONTROLS AND SECURITY

The system should be fully protected from unauthorised access and the integrity of the data it uses should be comprehensively protected. It should comply fully with legislation (such as the Data Protection Act) that stipulates the level of security required to protect personal data.

**Evaluation report**

### ORIGINAL OBJECTIVES

During the early stages of system development, a set of objectives should have been established. The system should fulfil these original objectives. For example, if one of the objectives was to improve customer service, a judgement must be made as to whether or not this has been achieved.

### RELIABILITY

The reliability of a system can be judged on the basis of how often it breaks down. A reliable system should be robust enough to survive in a busy, working environment, where users may subject it to 'rough treatment'.

### COMPATIBILITY

The system should fit seamlessly into the general working environment. It should be able to 'communicate' when necessary with existing systems. There should be no deleterious effects on existing systems as a consequence of its implementation.

### PERFORMANCE

The system should run at an appropriate speed. Advances in technology have resulted in users having high expectations of computer performance – i.e. they become impatient if the response is not instantaneous. Speed of performance in the operational environment therefore needs to be evaluated.

## Approaches to gathering information for the evaluation report

| Quantitative tests | Performance monitoring software can be used to determine speed of processing and accuracy of output. |
| --- | --- |
| Interviews | Users can be interviewed individually about the system. How do they feel about using it? What problems have they encountered? What has been the quality of support? |
| Error logging | One way of evaluating the reliability of a system is to analyse the errors that occur. This can be done through a help desk log or network based error-logging software. |
| Questionnaire | A questionnaire can be given to all those who use the system, including managers who receive reports. The questionnaire can contain structured questions that will allow the development team to 'score' different aspects of the system. |

# Maintenance issues

## Why do maintenance issues occur?

Even if a piece of software has been tested extensively, it may still be necessary to provide post-implementation maintenance. There may be a number of reasons for this, including:

- 'Bugs', which may not have been identified during the testing process, become apparent when the system is operating in a live environment.
- Users may, after a period of time, find a particular aspect of the software unsatisfactory.
- Changes in the business environment, e.g. a change in legislation, may mean that the software is required to perform tasks it wasn't originally designed for.
- A security issue, e.g. a virus threat, may emerge which means that the system requires an extra level of protection.
- The software provider may discover a way to make the application run more efficiently.
- New software or hardware may be purchased, the integration of which requires changes to existing systems.

When a maintenance issue emerges, the ICT manager will contact the software provider (or in-house team) and outline the nature of the problem. If the problem is a critical one, an immediate solution may be provided. If the change is non-critical, the software manufacturer may add it to a number of other changes and prepare a second release version of the original software. These new versions are numbered according to the sequence of release. For example, a change from version 1.3 to version 1.4 indicates that minor changes have been made, whereas a change to the whole number, from 2.3 to 3.0 indicates a significant upgrade.

## Three types of maintenance

### Corrective

This involves the identification of 'bugs' and errors that haven't been picked up during the testing process. For example, an application may crash every time it tries to connect to another application. This may not have been tested for and so may only emerge after a period of time in a live environment. The problem will be analysed and an appropriate solution will be designed, tested and implemented.

### Adaptive

This occurs when the user or the vendor perceives a new need that could – or must – be catered for. These are referred to as enhancements, i.e. improvements to the system. For example, an accounting package may need to adapt in order to accommodate changes to tax legislation. As with corrective maintenance, the functionality required by the new need is defined and a solution is created.

### Perfective

If a software provider has created an application that is generally popular and successful, it will want organisations to keep using it. It is therefore in its best interests to keep working on the software, seeking ways to make it perform more efficiently. In this respect software manufacturers are no different to soap powder manufacturers, i.e. in seeking to maintain their market share by regularly introducing 'new' or 'improved' versions of their product.

## The pattern of maintenance types

This diagram shows the degree to which each type of maintenance is likely to take place in relation to the age of a system.

| | Straight after implementation | Early operational period | Middle operational period | Late operational period |
|---|---|---|---|---|
| Corrective maintenance | HIGH | LOW | LOW | HIGH |
| Adaptive maintenance (minor amendments) | NONE | MEDIUM | MEDIUM | MEDIUM |
| Adaptive maintenance (major amendments) | NONE | NONE | MEDIUM TO HIGH | MEDIUM TO HIGH |
| Perfective maintenance | LOW | LOW TO MEDIUM | MEDIUM | LOW |

# Testing

### Why is testing necessary?

Testing is a critical phase in software development. Most programs are written by teams of people, with each team member working on a different aspect of the application. These different aspects all have to be brought together in order to create a system ready for implementation. Before the system can be fully implemented it must be subject to a rigorous test procedure. If an application is not tested properly and, as a consequence, there are problems when the user operates it, the software provider's reputation will be damaged and they may lose business.

### What is involved in testing?

- Testing will involve the construction of a comprehensive plan that covers every aspect of the system, specifies the types of tests that will be performed on it, defines what the outcome of these tests should be, and notes what remedial action might be required.
- Testing should be conducted using three types of data: typical (the type of data that might normally be entered); erroneous (data that might feasibly be entered but is none the less incorrect); extreme (data that is highly unlikely to be entered). The aim of this process is to take into account all the possible mistakes that a user might make.
- Testing is an iterative process – i.e. if a problem is found at any stage in the process, the process reverts to an earlier stage, corrects the problem and picks up the testing procedure from that point.

### The different stages of testing

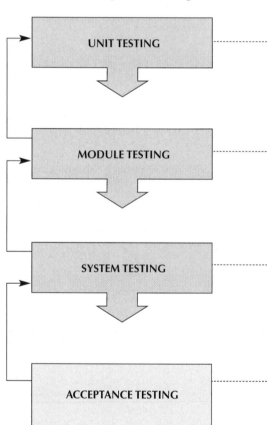

**UNIT TESTING**

A unit is a self-contained section of programming designed to perform a specific action. For example a unit might consist of a subprocedure that makes visible a previously invisible command button, or a function that calculates the average of a set of inputted values. Each of these units must be tested to ensure they perform the action correctly, using both correct and erroneous user actions.

**MODULE TESTING**

A module is a linked collection of units that make up a clearly delineated aspect of the overall system. For example, an accounting system may contain a module that manages the procedure for the end of a tax year. Such a module would consist of subprocedures and functions that would update calculations, create a new week structure, etc. Each unit will have been tested during the previous stage. What must now be investigated is whether these units all work together, i.e. whether actions performed in one unit can affect the performance of another.

**SYSTEM TESTING**

A system is the sum total of all the elements required by an application. System testing ensure that all the modules work together and they connect effectively with any data sources that will be required. System testing should also recall the original functional specifications of the system and ensure that the system meets these specifications.

**ACCEPTANCE TESTING**

Acceptance testing is where the system is tested in something approximating the 'live' operational environment in which it will have to function. This is often performed in a specially designed 'test environment'. A test environment creates a copy of all the programs, data files, stored procedures, etc. that the organisation currently uses. The data in this test environment will be exactly the same as that in the 'live' environment but won't be affected by any changes made to it during the testing procedure. The system can now be tested to see if it will function under normal operational conditions.

### Alpha and beta testing

**Alpha testing** takes place in the development environment. It is usually undertaken by those responsible for creating the program, though final users may also have an input. The process is essentially that outlined above, i.e. proceeding through a series of stages, using typical, erroneous and extreme data to see where the program falls down. This first stage is necessary because fundamental problems may come to light and this will mean reverting to an earlier stage of development.

**Beta testing** involves releasing the fully tested application to real users who will then use it in a live environment for a test period. During this time the users may notice problems with the system which they can then report to the software producer. This approach allows software vendors to put their application though a 'dry run' in a variety of live environments over a period of time. They can thus identify and correct shortcomings before fully releasing the product on the market.

# Training: 1

## The need for training

It is in an organisation's best interests to ensure that all of its employees are appropriately skilled for the jobs they have to do. This is partly achieved by employing people with the right skill set in the first place. However, job profiles change and new technologies are introduced, so these skill sets will need to be updated. Training in ICT is especially important because new technologies are emerging with increasing rapidity and an organisation cannot afford to be left behind. An organisation therefore needs to provide training for a number of reasons, including:

**New staff**
The organisation will need to ensure that all new staff are proficient in the hardware and software they will be using. No matter how experienced new staff are, there will be specific features of an organisation's systems that they will need to be trained for.

**New systems**
When a new system is implemented all users will need to be trained to use it and to understand its specific features. Inadequate training on a new system can lead to implementation failure.

**Motivating staff**
Many employees see good training provision as characteristic of a good employer. Training develops an individual's skill set and this, in turn, enables them to seek promotion, either within the organisation or beyond it.

**Improving efficiency**
A motivated, well-trained staff is an organisation's greatest asset. Effective, coordinated training provision will lead to improvements in efficiency as staff become more proficient in the tasks they perform and thus make fewer costly errors.

## Different training for different levels

ICT training provision has to be effectively targeted. Employees operating at different levels within the organisation will have different training needs.

**Senior managers**
Their contact is not likely to be at a user level. They are, however, required to understand how ICT contributes to the organisation's goals. They will also be making decisions about corporate information policy and allocation of resources to ICT. They are more likely to make effective decisions if they understand the latest developments in technology and so their training should be in this area.

**Middle managers**
Middle managers, such as Heads of Department, will play a significant role in the development of systems. They will have to define information needs, make tactical level decisions about resource allocation, plan the implementation of new systems, develop security policies, etc. They will therefore need to take an overview of how and why new systems are developed and how they impact on their specific area.

**Users**
The form of training that end users need can be divided into two categories: skill-based and task-based. Skill-based training develops skills that can be applied in a variety of situations. For example, an employee may be trained in analysing figures using spreadsheets. This skill can then be employed in different contexts. Task-based training focuses on developing proficiency in an organisation-specific task. For example, a data entry clerk may require training in an organisation's procedures for batch processing.

## Developing a corporate training policy

Many organisations view employee training as a key factor in their success. They therefore develop a corporate strategy for training, the elements of which are shown below.

**Needs analysis** The needs of users at different levels have to be identified. Account must be taken of users' current skills, their training history, their current job profile and their professional development (i.e. where their career is going).

**Cost** There are two main costs involved in training provision: the financial cost that may arise, e.g. from paying a training provider; and the time cost incurred when employees are not available for work because they are being trained.

**Coordination**

**Availability** Information related to training providers needs to be collated and the providers evaluated for cost and effectiveness. It may also be necessary to develop and/or evaluate in-house training provision.

**Cost-benefit** Training provision should be a good investment. For example, if the organisation pays for an employee to be trained, they want to be sure that the person's enhanced skill set will benefit the organisation and not just the employee.

# Training: 2

## Different approaches to training

| Approach | Advantages | Weaknesses |
|---|---|---|
| **Computer-based training**<br><br>This can take several forms. Some software packages provide step-through tutorials, showing the user how to work with the application. Some, more complex, online providers allow for some user interaction – e.g. the user can e-mail specific questions that will then be answered. | • There are some cost implications, but provision of computer-based training is significantly cheaper than sending employees on training courses.<br>• It can be undertaken at the employee's own pace; modules that are not understood can be re-visited when necessary.<br>• It is flexible – i.e. it can be undertaken whenever the employee has spare time and without them having to leave the office. It can even be made available on a home PC.<br>• The provision is standardised, so all the employees will learn the same material. This is not necessarily the case where training providers are used. | • Some online training requires reliable Internet connections and other facilities that organisations may have to provide, thus incurring additional cost.<br>• Some people do not respond well to this method of learning. They need the human presence, peer support, and teacher–student interaction of a classroom environment.<br>• There may not be a computer-based training program available for an organisation-specific application. If the organisation then has to develop its own software, this will incur additional costs.<br>• It is more difficult to monitor how effectively employees are learning using this method. |
| **Instructor-led courses**<br><br>These may be based in house or with a training provider. They involve a trainer or trainers leading the class and providing computer and text-based materials. | • Many people learn best in a communal, interactive environment such as this. They have the chance to ask questions, to talk to fellow students and to ask for individual support.<br>• The collaborative atmosphere of a classroom can enhance employees' team-working skills.<br>• The focus of the sessions is wholly on the topic being studied. Being off-site (or at least in a dedicated space) means that there is less chance of being distracted or interrupted by work-based demands.<br>• An effective teacher can respond flexibly to the needs of individual students. So, if one approach to explaining a topic is ineffective, the teacher can try another. A computer cannot do this. | • The main disadvantage of this approach is cost. Training courses run by providers are expensive and less prosperous organisations may not be able to afford them. An alternative approach is to develop an in-house facility, but this too can incur costs.<br>• The quality of the training providers can vary considerably. Some have effective teachers as leaders, others are run by trainers who have the requisite technical knowledge, but do not know how to teach effectively.<br>• Training courses are not flexible. They are run at fixed times and at fixed locations. This may not suit an organisation that needs its staff to be available at short notice. |
| **Self-taught using books, videos, etc.**<br><br>Some organisations do not have the resources and/or inclination to provide effective training for their employees. In such instances, employees may decide they want to develop their skill set by teaching themselves. There are books, CDs and videos on the market that can support this process. | • This approach is infinitely flexible. The individual can fit their learning time into their own schedule and can learn in the appropriate environment (at work in a lunch break, in a library, at home, etc.).<br>• They are not reliant on or answerable to their employers in relation to what they learn. They can develop the skill set that will be of most use to them in terms of furthering their career. | • The individual can feel isolated. They are learning on their own, and though this may suit some people, many prefer to have interaction with other learners and people with more experience of the specific area.<br>• They must bear the cost of resources themselves. Though these need not be excessive, some of the books can be expensive. |

## In-house versus training provider

- Although training providers can be expensive, maintaining an in-house facility can be even more so. Trainers need to be employed, dedicated space has to be found and resources provided.
- The organisation can keep more control of the training process. They can ensure the quality of the trainers they use, can organise schedules to suit their own needs, provide standardised resources so that all employees receive the same information and develop courses that are tailored to their specific needs.
- Which approach an organisation takes will depend on what financial resources they have available for training and the extent and specific nature of their training needs. In-house provision is most appealing to organisations that have constant, year-round training needs that may not be provided for by commercial providers.

# User support: 1

### The need for user support

One of the key factors in the success or failure of information systems is the post-implementation user support. Users want to feel confident about using the system, but if they run into problems they want to be able to solve them quickly. User support can be provided in a number of ways. Large organisations may have their own help desk or they may buy in a help desk service from an outside provider. The way in which help desks work is discussed in more detail on page 168. However, help desks are not always an appropriate form of user support and smaller, less resourced firms may need to depend on alternative methods.

### Different methods of user support

**Existing user base**

Experienced users can be a valuable source of information and advice. This can be accessed informally or through more formal training sessions. The support is free and based within the organisation. Some users, however, will be unable (or unwilling) to explain something clearly to a less experienced user. Also, this process may be impractical in a busy working environment.

**Help files**

Almost all applications, whether off the shelf or bespoke, provide help files that are accessible to the user. These provide a search engine or index so that pages covering different topics can be accessed. Some provide step-by-step multi-media tutorials. The quality of help files will vary from application to application and some fail to address the needs of the less experienced user.

**Internet**

There are a number of resources on the Internet that provide advice for the user. There are official websites run by software manufacturers with e-mail access for users to send in their queries. Unofficial sites created by users can also provide the answers to FAQs (Frequently Asked Questions). There are also sites which store archived articles on different applications.

**Support articles**

There are many magazines that are aimed at users. Articles in these magazines will vary in their level of complexity. Some are aimed at very experienced users who may be considering customising generic applications. Other articles are aimed at the novice user and demonstrate simple procedures in a step-by-step format.

**Documentation**

Various user guides are available for most applications. These might be provided by the manufacturer or they may be produced by a commercial publisher. In the case of popular applications, there are many publications available. Users need to select the publication that is suited to their level of need: some documentation is aimed at developers, some at novice users.

### Criteria for selecting user support

When an organisation is making decisions about what form of support is required, the following criteria should be taken into account.

**COST**  Some of the approaches cited above will cost little or nothing (e.g. help files), others will incur considerable cost to the organisation (e.g. a help desk).

**USER EXPERIENCE**  Users will require different types of support. The more experienced user will need access to material pitched at a sufficiently complex level; novice users will need to have things explained simply and clearly.

**RESOURCES**  Some of the approaches to user support will require resources. For example, dedicated websites will require good Internet access.

**URGENCY**  Users working on business-critical systems will need to have their problems answered more quickly than those working on less critical systems.

**ENVIRONMENT**  Some working environments lend themselves to the exchange of ideas between users. In other environments users may be isolated from one another.

# User support: 2

## What is a help desk?

In many large organisations user support is provided by a help desk. This can take two forms:

**In-house** The help desk is run by employees of the organisation, usually members of the technology department. This is especially the case where an organisation develops its own software. In this instance the team that developed the system is also likely to be responsible for post-implementation support.

**Outsourced** The organisation buys in the services of an organisation that specialises in supporting users. Alternatively, many organisations that develop software solutions also offer a user support service.

A help desk is a service that supports users by answering their questions and advising them on how to solve the problems they face with software, hardware, networks, etc. Users can phone or e-mail the help desk with their enquiries and an operator will provide them with answers, solutions, advice, etc. When help desks work well, they provide an invaluable service. There are, however, some difficulties associated with running help desks. These include:

- Providing advice that is appropriate for different user levels. An experienced user may require some in-depth technical advice whereas a novice user will need a response at a more basic level.
- Ensuring the help desk has the expertise to answer the majority of questions they are asked. A help desk that is incapable of providing useful advice will soon lose the confidence of the users.
- Dealing with the anger and frustration of users whose work is being held up by inadequate or non-user-friendly applications.
- Managing the flow of requests. A telephone-based service, if swamped with requests, may be obliged to put users on hold, thus increasing their frustration.

There are software applications that are dedicated to supporting help desks. These applications typically contain a database with descriptions of problems and appropriate solutions. These can be queried by the help desk operator and relayed to the user. New problems, and solutions, can be added to the database as they occur. The system also allows the help-desk to log details of the user so they can analyse problem 'histories'. Some help desk software allows the operator to view and even take control of a particular user's desktop in order to solve the problem.

## Logging calls

Calls to help desks should be logged. A computerised system is used to log specified details about the call, including:

- a user identification code – this can be used to identify user, department, terminal, organisation, etc. and can also be used to establish the legitimacy of the call.
- the date and time of call.
- the software/hardware involved.
- the nature of the enquiry.
- the response of the help desk (i.e. whether the problem was sorted out immediately or dealt with in some other way).

This logged information can be stored in a database. It can then be used to analyse the frequency of particular problems, which, in turn, can help to improve the quality of service. The information can also be used by the help desk team to demonstrate its efficiency in solving problems or, conversely, its need for greater resources.

## Evaluating help-desk service

An organisation will need to evaluate the effectiveness of a help desk, whether it is one they are providing themselves or one they are paying for. The following criteria may be used:

**Speed** How quickly the users' phone calls are answered or their e-mails responded to.
**Helpfulness** How clearly the operator explains the solution, their general level of politeness, etc.
**Frequency of requests** The number of requests for help received and the proportion of them where successful assistance was given.
**User satisfaction** How happy the users are with the service, whether or not they would be willing to recommend the service to others, etc.

# Project management: 1

## What is project management?

Information systems are almost always developed as projects. Projects comprise a set of associated activities that bring together human and non-human resources in order to achieve a specified goal. Projects are finite (i.e. they are scheduled to be completed within a designated time) and limited in scope (i.e. their objectives are defined). This makes them easier to manage. The advantages of a project-based approach include:

| | |
|---|---|
| **Division into sub-tasks** | Project management involves breaking down the overall task (i.e. the development of the system) into a series of sub-tasks (e.g. analysis of hardware requirements). This makes it easier for managers to monitor the progress of these sub-tasks, especially if they are associated with scheduled deliverables. |
| **Team allocation** | Information system development requires a range of skills and the most cost-effective way of undertaking the work is to have people working in teams. The use of teams means that the expertise of individuals can be applied where it is most needed, ideas can be shared and developed dynamically, and there is not an over-reliance on one person. |
| **Centralised coordination** | Projects are always led by a Project Manager or Project Leader. The Project Manager takes responsibility for planning, organising, leading and controlling the project. She is then in a position to report on the progress of the project to her superiors. |

## Aspects of project management

| | |
|---|---|
| **Project planning** | A project plan starts with a list of the activities that will have to be undertaken in order to complete the task. The activities (or sub-tasks) should be small in scope and manageable within a fixed schedule. Additionally, there will be a series of events or milestones. These act as reference points, i.e. indicators of when one task ends and another begins. The diagram below shows the relationship between activities and events, using the example of the acquisition of a piece of hardware (activities/sub-tasks are defined by arrows; events/milestones by circles): |

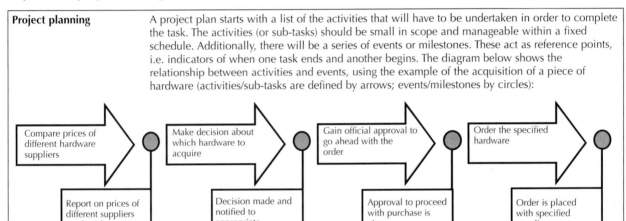

| | |
|---|---|
| **Project estimating** | In estimating the time required to complete the project, the Project Manager must take into account a number of factors, including: the size of the project (i.e. in terms of what needs to be achieved), the size of the team (generally, teams become less efficient as they grow in size), the capabilities of individual team members, the cohesiveness of the team (how well a team works together will affect the rate of progress). |
| **Project scheduling** | Once the overall time estimates have been made, the individual activities need to be fitted into a schedule. This will define the dates by which different milestones should be reached, times when activities will overlap and where there are dependencies (i.e. where one task needs to be completed before another can be started). |
| **Project monitoring** | This involves the Project Manager checking that the progress of the project is consistent with the original planned objectives and schedules. Late-running projects can cause problems for the organisation, especially where there is a requirement to meet an externally set deadline (e.g. to comply with legislation). By monitoring the project closely, the Project Manager can quickly see where the project is falling behind and arrange for remedial action to be taken. |
| **Project reporting** | The Project Manager is responsible for informing senior managers of the progress of the project. They will need to know if the project will be completed on schedule and without exceeding the original cost. |

# Project management: 2

## Success factors in project management

A successfully managed project will result in a system that fulfils the original user requirements, delivered on schedule and within the original cost constraints. Factors that are likely to produce a successful project include:

**Leadership** The project manager will be an effective leader, coordinating the efforts of the team, motivating individuals within the team to produce their best work, taking responsibility for the quality of the outcome, etc.

**Planning** The original planning, costing and scheduling will have taken into account all the factors that might affect the progress of the project. The time/cost constraints are therefore realistic and achievable.

**Resources** The project is adequately resourced, both in terms of human and non-human resources. The team should have everything they need (i.e. skills, hardware, software, access to users, etc.) to complete the task. A lack of availability will lead to delays in project completion.

**Standards** The work must be undertaken with due regard for established procedures and formal methods. Established conventions for documenting code, naming objects, user interfaces, etc. must be adhered to.

**Teamwork** This is discussed in more detail below.

## Effective teamwork

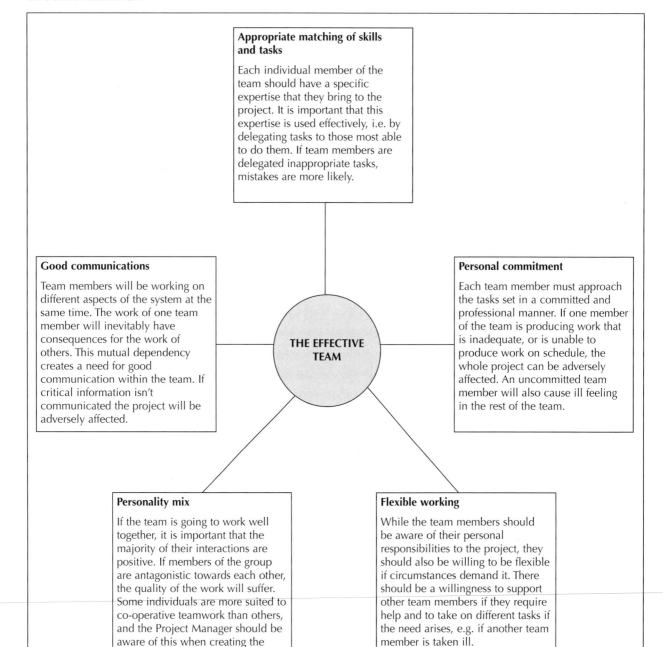

**Appropriate matching of skills and tasks**

Each individual member of the team should have a specific expertise that they bring to the project. It is important that this expertise is used effectively, i.e. by delegating tasks to those most able to do them. If team members are delegated inappropriate tasks, mistakes are more likely.

**Good communications**

Team members will be working on different aspects of the system at the same time. The work of one team member will inevitably have consequences for the work of others. This mutual dependency creates a need for good communication within the team. If critical information isn't communicated the project will be adversely affected.

**THE EFFECTIVE TEAM**

**Personal commitment**

Each team member must approach the tasks set in a committed and professional manner. If one member of the team is producing work that is inadequate, or is unable to produce work on schedule, the whole project can be adversely affected. An uncommitted team member will also cause ill feeling in the rest of the team.

**Personality mix**

If the team is going to work well together, it is important that the majority of their interactions are positive. If members of the group are antagonistic towards each other, the quality of the work will suffer. Some individuals are more suited to co-operative teamwork than others, and the Project Manager should be aware of this when creating the team.

**Flexible working**

While the team members should be aware of their personal responsibilities to the project, they should also be willing to be flexible if circumstances demand it. There should be a willingness to support other team members if they require help and to take on different tasks if the need arises, e.g. if another team member is taken ill.

# Practice questions

## Capabilities and limitations of information systems

1 Using an example, explain what is meant by each of the following elements of an information technology system:
   - Input
   - Output
   - Process
   - Feedback

2 Identify three capabilities that computer-based systems have, that give them an advantage over non computer-based systems.

3 "Computer technology promises much, but we would be ill-advised to ignore the potential dangers inherent in our dependency on such technology." Discuss some of the problems that are associated with the introduction of computer-based systems.

4 There are regular reports in the papers of critical, computer-based systems failing spectacularly. Describe how a combination of factors might lead to such a failure.

5 The fast response time of ICT systems facilitates an organisation's use of feedback. Identify one way in which a commercial company could make use of this facility.

6 Identify three distinct ways in which medical health providers might benefit from deploying ICT systems.

7 Identify some of the concerns that have been expressed about the use of ICT systems in education.

8 ICT systems have transformed the way in which business is done, both at a national and a global level. Describe some of the means by which this transformation has taken place.

9 How might CAD and CAM systems be used to improve efficiency in the manufacturing sector?

10 Identify some of the different ways in which computer-based systems have found their way into people's homes.

## The nature of information

11 Using appropriate examples, explain clearly the difference between data, knowledge and information.

12 "Information adds value but incurs cost." Using appropriate examples, identify three ways in which information can add value to an organisation and three ways in which the production of that information incurs costs.

13 "Good-quality information is a prerequisite of good-quality decision-making." Identify five characteristics of good quality information.

14 Identify some of the negative consequences for an organisation of using poor quality information.

15 Using an appropriate example, explain the difference between:
- internal and external information;
- quantitative and qualitative information;
- disaggregated and aggregated information.

16 The senior managers of a company receive a weekly report showing their company's sales figures. Describe some of the ways in which such a report could be designed effectively.

17 What factors influence the method by which information is presented to an end user? Illustrate your answer with appropriate examples.

## Data: collection and processing

18 Using an appropriate example, explain the difference between the direct and indirect collection of data.

19 Identify three different methods that may be used for inputting data into a computer system and describe one advantage and one disadvantage of each method.

20 "The quality of information is dependent on the data it is derived from." Describe some of the problems that can occur at the data capture stage that might have a negative effect on the information produced.

21 Using an appropriate example, describe the stages involved in capturing and inputting data so that it is ready for processing.

22 Identify some of the reasons why it may be necessary and/or desirable to encode information before it is inputted.

23 What are some of the specific issues associated with the encoding of value judgements?

24 Validation routines are used to improve the quality of data input. Identify three distinct types of validation routines that might be used and explain what type of errors they are designed to trap.

25 Describe one way in which errors that occur during data transmission might be trapped.

26 Using an appropriate example, explain the difference between validation and verification.

27 "Just because a piece of data has been accepted as valid does not mean that it is accurate." Explain, using an appropriate example, what is meant by this statement.

28 Computer systems operate on binary principles. Explain briefly what is meant by this.

29 Explain clearly the difference between the way that text-based data and numerical data is stored in computer systems.

30 Identify the difference between vector-based and bit-mapped images and explain the advantages and disadvantages of each format.

31 Explain fully two different methods that might be used to import an image into a document.

32 What role does a sound card play in the processing of audio files?

33 A user has created a file on their home PC but when they try to open their file on their office workstation it won't load. Explain (a) what the problem might be and (b) what might be done to solve the problem.

34 Identify two advantages and two disadvantages of using an integrated package.

35 Explain, using an example, the difference between linking and embedding an object in a document.

36 Explain why there is an increasing need to develop effective file compression techniques. Describe one compression technique that can be used.

37 Explain the difference between digital and analogue transmission of data, and describe a method that might be used

to effect a conversion from one mode to the other.

## Computer hardware

38 For each of the following input devices: (*a*) describe how it works; (*b*) identify one advantage and one disadvantage of using it; (*c*) identify an appropriate context for its use.
- Bar code reader
- Magnetic strip
- Optical mark reader
- Touch screen

39 What factors should an organisation/individual take into account when making a decision about acquiring a printer?

40 Describe two different types of printer that are currently available and explain the advantages and limitations of each.

41 Explain how a printer communicates with a computer's CPU.

42 Describe two different monitor types that are currently available and explain the advantages and limitations of each.

43 For each of the following secondary storage devices (*a*) describe how it works; (*b*) evaluate it in terms of strengths and weaknesses; (*c*) identify an appropriate context for its use:
- Re-writable compact disc
- Digital tape
- Hard drive

44 Explain briefly the role of the CPU in a computer-based system.

45 Explain clearly the difference between Read Only Memory (ROM), Random Access Memory (RAM) and cache memory.

## Computer software

46 Explain clearly the difference between generic software, specific task software and bespoke software.

47 Identify five features that are desirable in any software package.

48 When an organisation wants to acquire a new software package it has a number of approaches it can take. Describe what is involved in any two of these approaches, identifying the strengths and weaknesses of each.

49 Describe the step-by-step process an organisation would undertake when choosing a software solution.

50 Identify four criteria that would be used to make a decision about which software solution to choose and explain the importance of each of these criteria.

51 Identify four features that you would expect to find in a standard word-processing package.

52 Word-processing packages often have a function known as mail merge. Explain how this function works and in what context it might be used.

53 Identify some of the advantages of using a spreadsheet package over a 'paper and pen' system for processing accounts.

54 Identify some of the advantages of using presentation software over non-computer-based methods for giving presentations.

55 Identify three functions you would expect to find in a presentation software program.

56 Identify and explain three typical features of most graphics packages.

57 What are the advantages of using a CAD system over a non-computerised design system?

58 What additional resource demands do graphic programs make?

59 What is meant by computer modelling?

60 Explain the processes involved in modelling (*a*) climatic patterns, (*b*) crash tests of prototype vehicles, (*c*) design prototypes.

61 Explain how Global Positioning Systems work.

62 Describe the main function of web-browsing software in helping the user access the World Wide Web.

63 What functionality would you expect to find in a program that helped users create their own websites?

64 Explain the difference between systems software and application software.

65 Identify – and explain the importance of – three key functions of a computer's operating system.

66 Apart from the operating system, identify three other types of *systems* software that might be found on a standard computer.

## Databases

67 What capabilities do computers have that make them ideal for database systems?

68 Identify two different types of organisation that might use databases, explaining how these might help to make those organisations more efficient.

69 What problems, relating to data redundancy and data integrity, tend to occur with flat-file databases?

70 Identify the key features of a relational database.

71 Identify three different data types that might be used in a database and, in each case, give an example of the type of data it might be used for.

72 Explain the difference between sequential and direct organisation of data.

73 Describe the step-by-step process involved in creating database reports based on queries.

74 The development of databases often involves two processes: entity relationship modelling and normalisation. Explain what is meant by each of these two processes and what important function they serve.

75 Explain what is meant by a database management system.

76 What are the relative advantages and disadvantages of a database management system for an organisation?

77 What are the advantages to the user of working with a client–server database?

78 Identify four key functions of a database administrator.

79 In addition to the usual security issues, what security concerns are particular to database management systems?

80 Explain what is meant by a distributed database system.

## Networks and communication systems

81 The users in a company move from working in a stand-alone environment to a networked one. Identify three changes they would notice when they worked on their computers.

82 Identify two key differences between a Local Area Network and a Wide Area Network.

83 Identify four decisions that will have to be taken into account when setting up a network from scratch.

84 In relation to computer networks, describe the function of the following components:
   • Network interface card
   • Firewall
   • Network operating system
   • Hub
   • Bridge
   • Gateway

85 Explain the difference between a client–server and a peer-to-peer network strategy, stating the advantages of one system over the other.

86 Explain the difference between a Star and a Bus network.

87 Explain the difference between Ethernet and Token Ring systems in relation to the transmission of data around a network.

**88** Identify four functions that a network administrator would be expected to undertake.

**89** Describe some of the security issues that affect networks and the protective measures that can be implemented by a network administrator.

**90** Explain what is meant by a protocol and, by using examples, explain why they have been so important in the development of ICT.

**91** Explain, with reference to examples, the difference between *de facto* and *de jure* standards.

**92** Some organisations have moved to a wireless network communication system. Identify two advantages and two disadvantages of this approach.

**93** The use of mobile wireless devices is on the increase. What are some of the issues associated with the introduction of such devices?

## The Internet

**94** The Internet has had a revolutionary impact in many areas of human life. Describe four ways in which the Internet has affected the way people live and work.

**95** Outline the arguments surrounding the issue of censorship as it applies to the Internet.

**96** Describe step-by-step the process involved when a computer accesses a website via the World Wide Web.

**97** Identify three ways in which business has been able to utilise the facilities offered by the Internet.

**98** What are the relative advantages and disadvantages of using e-mail over other forms of communication, i.e. letters, fax, telephone, etc?

**99** Explain how search engines can help the user access information on the World Wide Web.

**100** Identify three different ways that users can connect to the Internet. For each method, state the advantages to the user and the possible drawbacks.

**101** Explain what is meant by the following terms:
- Hypertext
- IP address
- HTML
- Router
- Cookies

**102** Explain how TCP/IP provides a framework for data transmission across the Internet.

## Human–computer interfaces

**103** Identify four elements you would expect to find in a well-designed HCI.

**104** Describe some of the psychological factors that designers should take into account when designing an HCI.

**105** Describe the step-by-step process involved in a user employing a speech recognition system to enter data.

**106** What is meant by a Graphical User Interface and what are the resource implications of employing one in an application?

**107** What are the advantages and disadvantages of a speech recognition system over other methods of data input?

**108** Identify four ways in which a user might customise the user interface of an application.

## ICT in the workplace

**109** Describe two different roles that an ICT professional might take on and identify the particular skill set required for each role.

**110** Apart from their computer skills, what personal qualities is it advantageous for an ICT professional to possess? For each quality you describe, explain why it is useful.

111 What is the function of an employee code of conduct?

112 Not all types of employment are suitable for teleworking. Describe some of the conditions that are necessary for this method of working to take place.

113 Identify one advantage and one disadvantage of teleworking for (a) the organisation and (b) the individual worker.

114 Explain what is involved in videoconferencing and what resources an organisation needs to facilitate it.

115 Identify one advantage and one disadvantage of using videoconferencing as a way of facilitating meetings between members of an organisation.

116 Describe three health hazards that employees working with computers need to be aware of.

117 Describe four steps that an organisation can take to ensure that it complies with Health and Safety legislation.

118 Describe two moral/ethical problems that an ICT professional might face.

119 Faced with an ethical problem, what approach might an ICT professional take to deal with it?

**Security, privacy and the law**

120 "Computers have provided criminals with new tools to commit old crimes." Describe two forms of computer crime that support this statement.

121 Describe two ways in which law enforcement agencies have used ICT to combat various forms of criminal activity.

122 Explain how the following can be used to improve the security of ICT systems:

- Encryption
- Firewalls
- Virus checkers
- Staff training
- System access restrictions

123 Describe two different types of viruses and for each outline the measures that might be taken to prevent them from 'infecting' a system.

124 From an organisational point-of-view, identify some of the negative consequences of breaches in security.

125 Describe one threat to the security of ICT systems that might come from within an organisation and one that might come from outside it.

126 Describe four different aspects of security you would expect to find in a corporate information security policy.

127 Identify three measures an organisation can employ to ensure that its staff remain aware of security issues that might affect them.

128 Describe two issues relating to the privacy of the individual user that have arisen as a result of developments in ICT.

129 Identify three measures that an individual user can take to ensure the privacy of their communications.

130 Describe the step-by-step process involved in public key encryption.

131 Describe in detail four factors that should be taken into account when an organisation is developing a back-up policy.

132 What are the particular issues associated with backing up program files?

133 Describe an appropriate back-up strategy for a medium-sized business that processes a large number of on-line transactions every day.

134 What processes are involved when an organisation undertakes 'risk analysis' in relation to its ICT systems?

**135** Describe four elements you would expect to find in a large organisation's disaster recovery plan.

**136** What steps should an organisation undertake to ensure that its employees comply with the Copyright Designs and Patents Act (1988), especially in regard to 'software piracy'?

**137** The Computer Misuse Act identifies different categories of 'computer crime'. What difficulties have been encountered in enforcing the terms of this Act?

**138** Give an example of each of the three offences defined by the Computer Misuse Act.

**139** In relation to the Data Protection Act (1998), identify:
- four responsibilities of a data user
- two exemptions from the Act
- two functions of the Data Protection Registrar
- two rights of a data subject.

**140** What general procedures should an organisation put in place to ensure that its employees comply with all legislation relevant to the use of ICT systems?

## Management of information in an organisation

**141** Many large organisations have 'tall' hierarchical structures. Identify some of the defining features of structures such as this.

**142** Identify some of the ways in which efficient information systems will help an organisation succeed and give it a competitive edge.

**143** Organisations have two choices regarding the management of information systems: a centralised model whereby all decisions have to pass through the ICT department and a decentralised model whereby different departments make ICT decisions more or less autonomously. What are the advantages of the centralised approach over the decentralised approach?

**144** What are the advantages and disadvantages for an organisation of outsourcing some or all of its ICT functions?

**145** Describe four factors that would need to be taken into consideration in the development of a corporate information systems strategy.

**146** Describe a context where an organisation might wish to use a mainframe system to manage a significant proportion of its information needs.

**147** Explain fully how a client–server system works and how it can benefit the user and the organisation.

**148** Peer-to-peer systems provide an alternative to a client–server strategy. Describe an organisation context where a peer-to-peer strategy might be preferred over a client–server strategy.

**149** Describe what is meant by a Management Information System and explain how they are used by organisations to aid efficiency.

**150** Explain what a Data Processing System is and outline the importance of such systems to the efficient operation of some organisations.

**151** Explain the difference between batch processing and interactive processing. For each approach, describe an appropriate context for its use.

**152** Explain what is meant by data warehousing and data mining and describe how an organisation might employ such facilities.

**153** Explain how an expert system might help an organisation or individual in a work context.

**154** Describe the different information needs of each of the following levels of management:
- Strategic
- Tactical
- Operational

**155** Explain exactly how the availability of good quality information can enhance the decision-making process.

**156** Explain what is meant by a Group Decision Support System and outline how an organisation might use one to improve its efficiency.

**157** Explain the difference between formal and informal information flows within an organisation. Illustrate your answer with an example.

**158** Identify and explain four features of a successful organisation information system.

**159** Sometimes a great deal of time and resources are put into the development of an information system which, none the less, fails. Explain, using examples where appropriate, some of the factors that are likely to lead to such a failure.

**160** The introduction of new systems into organisations, especially those that entail a significant amount of change to working patterns, can create fear and anxiety amongst organisation members. Using appropriate examples, outline some of these fears/anxieties.

**161** What steps can an organisation take to manage successfully the change involved in the introduction of a new system?

**162** Outline three reasons why an organisation might undertake an audit of its ICT systems.

**163** When auditing takes place, a special type of software is used to aid the process. Explain the purpose of this software.

**164** Identify four reasons why an organisation may choose to upgrade a particular piece of hardware/software.

**165** Describe a process step-by-step that might be undertaken when an organisation wishes to upgrade a significant element of its ICT system.

**System development**

**166** In the context of the development of a new system, explain what is meant by the following:
- deliverable,
- formal methods,
- approval to proceed.

**167** The first stage of the System Development Life Cycle is the system request. Identify four reasons why a system request may be made, illustrating your answer with appropriate examples.

**168** Outline what you would expect to find discussed in a system feasibility report.

**169** During the analysis phase, developers have to gather a great deal of information from parties both within and beyond the organisation. Outline three methods that might be used to gather this information.

**170** Identify four items you would expect to find in a systems analysis report.

**171** Describe fully three tasks that would be undertaken during the design phase of the System Development Life Cycle.

**172** In relation to the implementation of a new system, explain the difference between direct conversion, phased conversion and parallel conversion. Explain the advantages of each system.

**173** Outline three methods that might be used to evaluate a new system after it has been implemented.

**174** Despite rigorous testing, it is sometimes necessary for software developers to undertake maintenance on systems. Explain why this might happen and outline some of the different types of maintenance that might be undertaken.

175 An organisation wishes to develop a policy to cover the training of all its employees in the use of ICT systems. Outline what would be contained in such a policy.

176 Identify two different methods of training employees in the use of ICT systems. Describe what is involved in each approach and what its relative advantages and disadvantages are.

177 Why might an organisation choose to develop an in-house training facility rather than rely on external providers?

178 Identify three means by which post-implementation support might be provided for users.

179 Explain, and illustrate with appropriate examples, three problems associated with running an in-house help desk.

180 Outline two different ways in which the effectiveness of a help desk can be evaluated.

181 Describe three tasks that would be undertaken by a project manager. Explain the importance of each task in relation to the successful development of the system.

182 Identify three attributes of an effective team. Explain, in the context of the development of ICT systems, the importance of each of these attributes.

183 Describe some of the different stages involved in testing a new system. Include in your answer a reference to Alpha and Beta testing.

# Index